ABOUT THE ROBERT K. GREENLEAF CENTER
FOR SERVANT-LEADERSHIP

THE ROBERT K. GREENLEAF Center for Servant-Leadership was organized as the Center for Applied Ethics in 1964. The name changed to the Center for Applied Studies before becoming the Greenleaf Center in 1985. The Robert K. Greenleaf Center for Servant-Leadership is an international, not-for-profit, educational organization that seeks to encourage the understanding and practice of servant-leadership. The Center's mission is to fundamentally improve the caring and quality of all institutions through a new approach to leadership, structure, and decision making.

The Greenleaf Center's programs include the worldwide sale of books, essays, and videotapes on servant-leadership, a membership program, presentation of workshops, seminars, institutes, an international conference, and the archives project, which provided the foundation for the production of this volume of Greenleaf essays. Because of the dissemination of the servant-leadership idea, individual and collective lives have been affected in several areas. Servant-leadership is now used as an institutional model, as the basis for educating and training not-for-profit trustees, as the foundation for educating and training community leadership organizations, as an aspect of experiential education, as leadership education in college and university courses and corporate training programs, and as a vehicle for personal growth and transformation.

For further information about the resources for study and programming available from the Center, please contact the Robert K. Greenleaf Center for Servant-Leadership, 921 E. 86th St., Suite 200, Indianapolis, IN 46240; telephone (317) 259-1241; fax (317) 259-0560.

SEEKER AND SERVANT

Robert K. Greenleaf

SEEKER AND SERVANT

Reflections on Religious Leadership

Anne T. Fraker   Larry C. Spears

editors

o

foreword by
Parker J. Palmer

Jossey-Bass Publishers
San Francisco

Substantial discounts on bulk quantities of Jossey-Bass books are available to corporations, professional associations, and other organizations. For details and discount information, contact the special sales department at Jossey-Bass Inc., Publishers (415) 433–1740; Fax (800) 605–2665.

For sales outside the United States, please contact your local Simon & Schuster International Office.

T☉F Manufactured in the United States of America on Lyons Falls Pathfinder Tradebook. This paper is acid-free and 100 percent totally chlorine-free.

Credits are on page 360.

Book design by Claudia Smelser.

Library of Congress Cataloging-in-Publication Data

Greenleaf, Robert K.
    Seeker and servant : reflections on religious leadership : the private writings of Robert K. Greenleaf / editors, Anne T. Fraker, Larry C. Spears.—1st ed.
        p.   cm.
    Includes bibliographical references and index.
    ISBN 0–7879–0229–2
    1. Christian leadership. 2. Leadership—Religious aspects—Christianity. I. Fraker, Anne T., date. II. Spears, Larry C., date. III. Title.
    BV652.1.G73   1996
    262'.1—dc20   95-48145

FIRST EDITION

HB Printing 10 9 8 7 6 5 4 3 2 1

CONTENTS

PART THREE
Seminaries, Churches, and Foundations: Partners in Spirit

PART FOUR
Toward the Caring Community:
Reflections on Seeking, Giving, and Receiving

FOREWORD

THE WORK OF Robert Greenleaf grows more important every day, for at the heart of his work is a spirit of hope for the wide range of institutions about which many people feel increasingly hopeless as the twentieth century comes to its close.

Whether we think of Congress or the courts, business or industry, the news media or mass entertainment, the church or other voluntary associations, many of us feel deepening despair about the capacity of our dominant institutions to harbor a human agenda, to foster human purposes. Some analysts have sunk into cynicism, urging us to watch out for "number one" without care for the common good. Others have sunk into opportunism, pitching cheap fixes of the "one-minute manager" ilk. But Robert Greenleaf steadfastly points us toward a path of institutional renewal that is demanding and yet possible, visionary and yet real.

I remember a time when the word "institution" implied high praise, as in the phrase "Baseball is an American institution." But today, the word carries meanings of a very different sort (and baseball is an excellent case in point!). *Institution* is often used to connote bureaucracy, hierarchy, rigidity, and gridlock—images that depict the inertia and lack of responsiveness far too frequently found in the institutions our lives depend on.

Sadly, the word *institution* today also suggests something far more sinister than rigidity and gridlock. Is *sinister* an overly dramatic word? Well, if you are a loyal fifty-something employee who has been permanently "downsized" by a large corporation—while the CEO receives a hefty increase in his or her seven-figure salary; if you live in a struggling inner-city neighborhood that has been slated for gentrification by local banks—

leaving you nowhere to go but a neighborhood even more dangerous and depressed; if you are a Brazilian who watches rain forests being destroyed so that Americans can have their fill of fast food—while native people and indigenous medicinal plants and global weather patterns suffer; then you might think that *sinister* is too mild a term, that *evil* would do the job better.

There is a widely shared perception that large-scale institutions in our time are more death-dealing than life-giving to the people who inhabit and rely on them. Small wonder, then, that we see a growing spirit of anarchy in the land. Those of us who care about institutions and the commonweal may regard anarchy as folly and madness, for we know that no complex modern society can survive without institutions to give it direction and form. But if we wish to be part of the solution rather than part of the problem, we must stop blaming victims: institutions themselves must become more humane if they expect to regain people's confidence.

The hope inherent in the work of Robert Greenleaf is not cheap hope, for it focuses on one of the most demanding aspects of institutional life: leadership. Greenleaf calls for a transformation in how leaders understand and execute their responsibilities, a transformation that he obviously knew would not be easily achieved. To prepare the groundwork for this transformation, he takes us beyond cynicism and cheap tricks and simplistic techniques into the heart of the matter, into the spiritual lives of those who lead.

In 1841, in an essay called "Self Reliance," Ralph Waldo Emerson wrote a famous sentence that is as insightful today as it was a century and a half ago—but insightful in a way that is exactly the inverse of Emerson's intentions: "An institution is the lengthened shadow of one man." With his image of the "shadow," Emerson meant to praise great leaders—or at least the male of the species—but many modern readers will immediately see the irony: many of our institutions are clouded and confounded by the unexamined shadow lives of the people who lead them.

Who are those leaders willing to deprive others of a living wage while indecently increasing their own? Who are those leaders willing to destroy neighborhoods for the sake of short-term profits? Who are those leaders willing to crucify the ecology so that more junk can come to market? Without naming names, it seems safe to say that they are people bereft of what was once called heart, or spirit, or soul, leaders in whom the shadow has overcome the light with which every person is born.

Since all the "restructuring" we can muster will fail to bring leaders out of the shadows into the light, Robert Greenleaf issues a summons far more daring than that of "reinventing the corporation." He calls upon leaders to take an inner journey that can illumine their own souls—and thus illumine the lives of the institutions they lead, of the folks who work in them, and of the people they serve.

This book is a series of reflections on "religious leadership," and it would be a great shame if that phrase were narrowly understood. Alfred North Whitehead claimed that all true education is religious education. In the same spirit, all true leadership is religious leadership—for religion has to do with cleansing the human self of the toxins that make our leadership more death-dealing than life-giving.

The toxins that Robert Greenleaf is concerned with have nothing to do with creedal orthodoxy or theological turf—after all, he was a Quaker! The toxins Greenleaf cares about are ancient ones: ego, greed, spiritual blindness, lack of compassion, lust for power, and all the other shadow forces that, left unexamined in leaders, will spread the long night that is already settling upon our land.

I had the privilege of knowing Bob Greenleaf and of spending time with him in conversation. He was a realist about institutions and leadership, and his discourse was always tinged with the sadness that comes when one is too experienced to expect miracles. But at the same time, his discourse was laced with the liveliness that comes when one knows that the human heart has the potential to transcend the most demanding of circumstances—and even to find in those very circumstances the energy of transcendence itself.

The ultimate test of Robert Greenleaf's hope for institutions is not to be found in a critical analysis of the words he left behind. It is to be found in the willingness of those of us who read these words to incarnate them in the living of our lives.

Madison, Wisconsin   PARKER J. PALMER
February 1996

PREFACE

IN THIS LAST DECADE of the twentieth century, various writers have turned their attention to the deeper values which should and perhaps can be reflected in our lives: a sense of community and meaning, commitment to human growth, empowerment that relies on both education and trust, service, and organizational structures that reflect order without the traditional hierarchical lines of authority. Robert K. Greenleaf's writings have provided the foundation upon which many of these contemporary ideas are based. The essays in this book presage today's searching by offering some of his answers to those who are now seeking more meaningful professional and personal lives.

In these writings, the reader finds inspiration for beginning or continuing a personal quest for a more fulfilling life. Those who know some of Robert Greenleaf's work and wish to read more of his wisdom, and to know a bit more about him as a person, will receive fulfillment in these pages. Here they find more references to Robert K. Greenleaf the spiritual seeker, and to his conviction that our society can be made more serving through individuals' efforts within institutions. This volume also serves as an introduction to his thought for students of organizations. Even though these essays are spiritual in focus and emphasize religious institutions, the ideas they raise are applicable to people in all types of institutions: religious, educational, business, nonprofit, voluntary.

Because Greenleaf did not present "bulleted" lists of how-to's, some readers might be disappointed by what they see in this volume. On the other hand, these very readers might find themselves "stretched" in their thinking and challenged to exercise creativity in their institutional leadership roles. For those who are already converted to his ideas, these essays provide inspiration for the continuing quest to live out the servant-leadership concepts.

The essays in this volume, all previously unpublished or seen only by readers of specialty publications, reflect Greenleaf's ongoing interest in and concern for our society, its religious institutions, and ways to guide society and those institutions into serving people in a more caring way through servant-leadership. Many of these themes and the stories used to illustrate them have appeared in Greenleaf's published writings and are repeated in various essays herein. But each use of a story is integral to the essay in which it appears. Even though there are repetitive themes and stories, the patient reader discovers new slants and reiterations of old ideas, along with fresh insights that jump off the page. By presenting many of the unpublished essays on their own as well as in combination with one another or with some published essays on the same topics, we hope to provide the reader of this volume with a more complete picture of Greenleaf's thoughts on our society, its institutions, and the individual's place in helping them serve each of us in a more caring manner.

The essays in this book are gleaned from the personal papers and related materials Greenleaf gave to the Andover Newton Theological School archives in Newton Centre, Massachusetts, in 1987. This collection documents his personal and professional life between 1929 and 1987. (He died in 1990.) Amid correspondence and fragmented records are copies of approximately ninety unpublished essays which Greenleaf wrote over a period of more than fifty years. The archival materials chosen for use in this particular volume present ideas that occupied Mr. Greenleaf's thinking for many years, but especially the last fifteen years of his life.

These papers seem to fall naturally into four thematic categories. Part One, "Nurturing the Spirit: The Challenges of Religious Leadership," presents essays Greenleaf wrote reflecting his concerns about leadership in religious institutions and the challenges he issued to those leaders. These pieces stress the importance he placed on restoring and nurturing the spiritual aspects of human existence for the long-term health of society. In these essays, he ranged from optimism to pessimism as he contemplated the roles religious leaders and their institutions could and should play in making ours a more caring society.

Part Two, "Leaders as Inspirited Persons," includes essays that take the reader from thinking about religious institutions and their leadership in abstract terms to learning about those whom Greenleaf called inspirited leaders. In this section, the reader discovers the importance he placed on the development of spirit in leaders as they try to be servant-leaders in the organizations of which they are a part.

The essays in Part Three, "Seminaries, Churches, and Foundations: Partners in Spirit," bring the reader to the point of examining the key institutions Greenleaf viewed as integral to fostering change in our society. Throughout, he emphasized that churches should be the most useful change agents in society and that seminaries have vital roles in energizing the churches to fulfill their callings. Readers may be puzzled by his including foundations as important partners in transforming ours into a more caring, serving society. But Greenleaf believed that foundations could serve as catalysts in this whole process by inviting the involvement of religious institutions in this transformation.

Part Four, "Toward the Caring Community: Reflections on Seeking, Giving, and Receiving," offers the reader the opportunity to reflect on his or her own life through Greenleaf's examination of the process, as he saw it, involved in an individual's search for meaning in life, internally and in community, and how that might be manifested in concrete terms. That concreteness is illustrated with his discussion of the issue of giving and receiving gifts of money, and the larger questions that as an individual or as part of a community one should ask before becoming involved in the transaction. Three of the unpublished essays are coupled with short, related articles he wrote for the

Quaker magazine *Friends Journal*. In an Afterword, three people who worked closely with Greenleaf for several years share their recollections of him in a conversation originally published (1991) in *In Trust*. They paint a portrait of Robert K. Greenleaf the person, and Robert K. Greenleaf the institution-watcher, which adds to the reader's understanding of the essays contained in this volume.

Throughout his writing, Greenleaf emphasized his belief in gradual, rather than cataclysmic, change to make a more caring society through servant-leadership. This was important to him as he believed that true change comes about only when people are persuaded in their own hearts of the value of that change. Studying these essays is in itself a practice in gradualism, as the reader needs to meditate on what he or she reads, relate it to his or her own life and the role of institutions, and then begin to formulate how one person can begin the "gentle revolution" leading us toward a more caring society.

Acknowledgments

This book was made possible through the support of two grants from the Lilly Endowment, Inc. We are particularly indebted to Craig Dykstra and Ed Queen for their belief in the Greenleaf archives project.

During the first two years of this project, a special panel carefully reviewed nearly one hundred unpublished writings by Robert K. Greenleaf, which he had produced over a period of fifty years. We are most grateful to the other members of that panel and wish to acknowledge their major contribution to this project: Dwight Burlingame, Joseph DiStefano, Don Frick, Newcomb Greenleaf, and Larry Lad.

We are particularly indebted to Don as a colleague at the Greenleaf Center and a member of the review panel, and for his significant editorial contributions to this book and to its companion work, *On Becoming a Servant-Leader* (Jossey-Bass, 1996). We also wish to express our appreciation to our other colleagues at the Greenleaf Center who have shared in a journey in servant-leadership: Michele Lawrence, Geneva Loudd, Jim Robinson, Richard Smith, Kelly Tobe. This journey also has been enriched through our relationships with past and present Greenleaf Center trustees: Bill Bottum, Linda Chezem, Diane Cory, Joyce DeShano S.J., Joseph DiStefano, Harley Flack, Newcomb Greenleaf, Carole Hamm, Jack Lowe Jr., Jeff McCollum, Andy Morikawa, Jim Morris, Paul Olson, Bob Payton, Sister Joel Read, Sister Sharon Richardt, and Jim Tatum. Additional thanks go to Richard Broholm, Peter Drucker, Karen Farmer, Robert Wood Lynn, Marcia Newman, and Parker Palmer.

Special thanks are extended to the Franklin Trask Library at Andover Newton Theological School, where the Greenleaf archives are housed. We are highly appreciative of the efforts of the library's associate director and special collections librarian, Diana Yount, who organized the archival materials and provided valuable advice throughout this endeavor.

We also wish to thank our editors at Jossey-Bass Publishers, Alan Shrader, Susan Williams, and Jeff Wyneken, for their own work, belief, and support of these two books.

Anne Fraker especially thanks her husband, Rupert A. D. Wentworth, for his encouragement, technical assistance, and, most of all, his love not only through this process but through each day.

Larry Spears offers special thanks to his family and friends for their love and encouragement along the way: his wife, Beth Lafferty; his sons, James and Matthew; and his mother and father, Bertha and L. C. Spears.

Finally, we wish to express our deep appreciation to the many women and men everywhere who are striving to be servant-leaders. Your efforts at nurturing spirit in the workplace, the church, the community, and elsewhere truly inspire others.

Indianapolis, Indiana
February 1996

ANNE T. FRAKER
LARRY C. SPEARS

THE AUTHOR

ROBERT K. GREENLEAF spent most of his organizational life in the field of management research, development, and education at AT&T. Just before his retirement from being director of management research there, he held a joint appointment as visiting lecturer at the Massachusetts Institute of Technology's Sloan School of Management and at the Harvard Business School. In addition, he held teaching positions at both Dartmouth College and the University of Virginia.

His consultancies included Ohio University, MIT, the Ford Foundation, the R. K. Mellon Foundation, the Lilly Endowment, and the American Foundation for Management Research.

As a consultant to universities, businesses, foundations, and churches during the tumultuous 1960s and 1970s, his eclectic and wide-ranging curiosity, reading, and contemplation provided an unusual background for observing these institutions.

As a lifelong student of organization—that is, how things get done—he distilled these observations in a series of essays on the theme of "Servant as Leader," the objective of which is to stimulate thought and action for building a better, more caring society.

INTRODUCTION

*Life should be leisurely, not to allow time for loafing or for slowness
of pace, but to allow for organization of the optimum life; whenever
one finds he or she cannot do the things that are most important for
want of time, something is basically wrong with the structure.*

Robert K. Greenleaf
Dream Journal, January 26, 1961

*Spend all you have for loveliness. Buy it and never count the cost. . . .
Count many a year of strife well lost, and for a breath of ecstasy
give all you have been or could be.*

*The rewards of living a full life may be measured in joyous moments
rather than in days or years. These are the treasures that return to the
mind in the quiet hours of the declining years. The moments nobly
lived, challenges met, the truth spoken, the slur turned aside, the
tumult quelled, the helping hand extended, and the simple expression
of gratitude, the burden borne; meeting life and feeling the response
of living—taking responsibility, prudently, if possible, but taking it
and leaving it joyfully once taken. Setting one's course on a star and
steering toward it, minding not the reefs that waylay.*

Robert K. Greenleaf
Journal, August 31, 1940

I

OVER A PERIOD of about seventy years, Robert K. Greenleaf set his course on a star and never minded the reefs that waylaid him along the way. His course was to do what he could in his little corner of the world, to make it a little bit better place in which to live and work. The route took him through a lifelong exploration of institutions, their missions, and the roles individuals play in determining the lives of these organizations. The star that set Greenleaf's course was a more caring society, mediated through its institutions; those institutions would be led by servant-leaders.

Servant-leadership is subject to many interpretations, but Robert Greenleaf defined it in his first examination of the topic, in "The Servant as Leader":

> It begins with the natural feeling that one wants to serve, to serve first. Then conscious choice brings one to aspire to lead. . . . The difference manifests itself in the care taken by the servant—first to make sure that other people's highest-priority needs are being served. Do those served grow as persons; do they, while being served, become healthier, wiser, freer, more autonomous, more likely themselves to become servants? And what is the effect on the least privileged in society; will he or she benefit, or, at least, will he or she not be further deprived? ["The Servant as Leader," 1991, p. 7]

Greenleaf did not always use the term *servant-leader* in his thinking, working, and writing. Nor did he talk at great length about spirituality and leadership until his later years. But his thinking over the years was suffused with the abstract notion of leading-by-serving in a spirit-filled way.

Greenleaf's ideas about servant-leadership have their roots in his upbringing in Terre Haute, Indiana, where he saw his father being a servant-leader in his labor union, his community, and, to a lesser degree, his church.

As Greenleaf frequently noted in his essays, he was a student of organizations, or "how things get done." During his long career with American Telephone & Telegraph, he was fortunate to have positions which allowed him to pursue that study in great depth. He spent much of his time there in management research, development, and education. He saw this work as one aspect of his response to the call of a sociology professor, to get inside a large institution and try to change it from within, try to make it more serving to people.

This urge to "convert" people and institutions is rooted, to some extent, in Greenleaf's Judeo-Christian background and his experiences in various Quaker communities. In addition to searching for religious or spiritual answers to societal woes, he also participated in secular activities such as the cooperative movement of the 1930s and, later, in Jungian dream analysis as a part of his quest. But he acknowledged that his thinking about servant-leadership was firmed up after reading *Journey to the East* by Hermann Hesse. Greenleaf decided to read the book because he noticed how prominent it was on college bookstore shelves in the 1960s. He surmised that it was a popular book speaking to students of that era who were discontented with various leaders and institutions. At the same time, he contracted as a consultant with several university administrators, suggesting to them ways of dealing with discontented students.

Greenleaf's first published essay on the theme "The Servant as Leader," in 1970, was initially addressed to those college students. In it, the reader was offered an alternative to mainstream modes of thinking about how institutions should operate and people should be treated. Subsequent revisions of this essay have addressed a broader audience. But the challenges to predominant ways of thinking and behaving remain.

Following his retirement from AT&T, Greenleaf was a consultant to many businesses, colleges and universities, foundations, and religious organizations in the United States and abroad. Around the time of his retirement, he gathered respected scholars and businesspeople around him to organize a center which would provide the impetus for institutional leaders, especially those affiliated with colleges and universities, to examine their operations and to consider how they might become more "ethical." Greenleaf viewed ethics as that which "is morally right." He said that "ethics in business (or anywhere else) starts with a person, an individual person."

In 1964, Greenleaf and his colleagues formed the Center for Applied Ethics. A few years later, the organization's name was changed to the Center for Applied Studies and then in 1985 to the Robert K. Greenleaf Center for Servant Leadership. This organization provided the umbrella under which Greenleaf did much of his thinking and writing. During the 1970s and early 1980s, he wrote several essays on the servant theme that were published by the center. At the same time, he pursued his many consultancies, thus providing more fodder for his writings.

Greenleaf consulted with various religious organizations, ranging from individual churches to national judicatories and ecumenical groups. In his later years, he came to feel the religious community was not fulfilling its obligations to society and to God. Nevertheless, he saw a vast untapped potential there. He said his work with universities during the 1960s led him to search "for the points of greatest influence in building strength in the social structure. Out of this came the conclusion that stronger, more influential churches were what our troubled society was mostly in need of, and that this need could not be filled until seminaries became more effective in their leadership and support of churches" ("My Work with Churches," unpublished paper, p. 9).

Out of this concern, Greenleaf wrote numerous essays on his ideas for how seminaries could serve churches, which could in turn serve communities. The essays in this volume reflect his efforts in developing these themes. As noted earlier, he felt that ethical behavior in an institution began with the individual; so, too, with the churches and seminaries. Inspired, prophetic institutional leadership begins with one spirit-filled, faithful person who will be strong enough to strike out on a different path, leading the institution down that path.

Greenleaf offers this example of an effective religious leader: "As I read the record of the life of Jesus, I do not believe that his great leadership rested as much on his knowledge of the theological roots of his tradition as it did on his belief in the dependability of the inspiration that was available to him as he faced the crises of his ministry."

". . . The faith that makes one a leader," he said at another point, "is the belief that if one ventures into the unknown, *in the situation* that [sic] the guidance to chart one's steps will be received. Faith in the heat of action is the quality that enables one, in the face of tension and stress, to remain calm and open to inspiration" ("My Work with Churches," unpublished paper, p. 16).

Greenleaf expressed his credo (described his "star") thus:

> I believe that caring for persons, the more able and the less able serving each other, is what makes a good society. Most caring was once person-to-person. Now much of it is mediated through institutions—often large, powerful, impersonal; not always competent; sometimes corrupt. If a better society is to be built, one [that is] more just and more caring and providing opportunity for people to grow, [then] the most effective and economical way, while supportive of the social order, is to raise the performance-as-servant of as many institutions as possible by new, voluntary, regenerative forces initiated within them by committed individuals, *servants*. Such servants may never predominate or even be numerous; but their influence may form a leaven that makes possible a reasonably civilized society. ["Spirituality as Leadership," 1982, p. 53]

To the end of his life, Greenleaf had his course set on his particular star. Today, his colleagues with whom he counseled, and the staff and board of the Robert K. Greenleaf Center, continue to carry his message to leaders from all walks of life. As Greenleaf noted in many of his writings, the transformation to servant-led institutions is of necessity a gradual process involving changing one person at a time. In his attempts to transform individuals and institutions, perhaps Greenleaf was hoping to help himself and others discover meaning, joy, and loveliness in their lives.

PART ONE

NURTURING THE SPIRIT

THE CHALLENGES OF RELIGIOUS LEADERSHIP

What it is in the mind of a person that stifles action, I do not know. But the world is cursed (or blessed) with an enormous amount of inertia. Tugging at people are all sorts of conflicting demands, and the one who thinks and weighs them all never (or rarely, for the genius only) breaks away down any well-marked path. That is the problem of reformers. Consequently [the reformers] must move [people] on emotion, by the kindling of a spiritual drive that overrides the intellectual inertia.

Robert K. Greenleaf
Journal, September 13, 1941

Greenleaf wrote this position paper in 1982 for a commission on church leadership of the United Methodist church. The group included seminary presidents, some bishops, staff members of the church hierarchy, and consultants working with churches. This piece summarizes many of Greenleaf's thoughts on leadership while adding clarifications and definitions of terms. In essence this is a draft of a later publication called "The Servant as Religious Leader." Greenleaf wrote in a later paper about his work with churches that the United Methodist leaders did not respond to this paper as they wanted to talk only about structure. He notes that in the later publication he did comment on structure; however, the paper presented here is the gist of that publication.

RELIGIOUS LEADERS
AS SEEKERS AND SERVANTS

THE WORD RELIGION, in common usage, has many meanings. Yet if one uses that word as it will be used here, in its root meaning of *re ligio*—to rebind—and separates any sectarian view, it may be possible to lead persons who have widely varying religious beliefs toward common ground for dealing with some of the critical problems of our times.

I am a creature of the Judeo-Christian tradition. If I had grown up in a Buddhist, Hindu, or Muslim culture, I might address the subject of religious leaders in quite a different way. But my hope is that no persons will exclude themselves from consideration of the issues raised in this paper because of their religious beliefs. My perspective in writing this paper is that of a student of organization—how things get done—not that of a scholar or theologian.

The thinking that culminates in this paper emerged during the stressful years of student unrest in the 1960s, when I was deeply immersed in the traumatic experiences of several universities in which the fragility of these prestigious institutions was exposed. Against the background of my knowledge of universities of that period, the student attitudes did not seem irrational. I wondered whether, in view of the flaws revealed in universities, our society was sufficiently caring and serving to endure. My conclusion was that if it did endure, something had to change!

Reflections on these experiences led me, in 1970, to begin to write on the servant theme. These writings were circulated among religious institutions. Also, I have had several close relationships with pastors, church administrators, lay leaders, governing boards, and congregations. In these experiences I found considerable concern for the present state of leading in churches and for a consequently diminished influence of churches on their members and on society at large. Paralleling these reported findings from within churches, I made my own observations during this period from involvement with businesses, foundations, and universities. All of these soundings, plus what is available in the news, suggest a deteriorating society with little evidence of effective restorative forces at work.

One could simply view this with alarm and join the choruses of lament that one hears from some who have made similar observations. I prefer to turn my energies to the support of efforts that might set a restorative force in motion. All that any individual can do is to make one's best effort, alone or in concert with others. The future will be whatever it turns out to be.

I begin with the assumption that the enormous resources of religious institutions in the United States could, within a generation, help turn this faltering society around and start us on a long-term constructive course if a substantial number of them, each from its own unique set of beliefs, could work toward a common goal of a "good" society.

Is it not possible that many religious institutions, as they now stand, have within them the human resources from which effective leaders might evolve who would move their institutions to become more constructive elements of a good society? Could a new, persuasively articulated, prophetic vision generate the faith required for those who have leadership potential to take the risks, to develop the strength, and to make a new and determined effort to lead? This paper is written with the hope of contributing to a dialogue out of which a solid conceptual base for such an effort may emerge.

But, some protest, is this not the age of the anti-leader? People simply do not respond to leadership in these times, so it seems. Could it be that what is needed now are new language, new concepts, new skills—all of which may be needed if we are to have a quality of leadership that will be effective in our times? Can those who are moved to make common cause pool their resources in a creative effort to produce new forms of religious leadership that will be accepted by contemporary people as realistic and useful? In the hope that others will respond and contribute, I offer what my experience suggests.

Some Definitions

It seems to me that six common terms need to be reexamined. I venture to initiate discussions that might help bring some like-minded people together by offering definitions for *spirit, leading, religion* (including *alienation*), *prophet, theology,* and *belief.* The definitions that emerge out of discussion of these terms may form a conceptual base for designing a new approach to religious leadership. In suggesting the following definitions, I am open to persuasion that there are better ones, ones that would provide more acceptable common ground among people who profess widely varying beliefs. As an opening proposition, I submit that a new approach to religious leadership should be useful to many groups, each of which is unified by a set of beliefs, but with wide variations in belief both between and within groups.

A common definition of *spirit* is that which is traditionally believed to be the vital principle or animating force within living beings. But this needs a value dimension. I prefer to say that spirit is the animating force that disposes persons to be servants of others.

I would not accept the monk in his cell or the theologian in his study as spiritual unless the fruit of their efforts finds its way, ultimately, to nourish the servant motive in those who do the work of the world. This is why churches could be so important in helping the gifts of contemplation and theological reflection become an animating force and a guide to action for those who have the opportunity to give religious leadership.

What could these two words, *religious* and *leadership*, mean, separately and together?

The common meaning of *leading* is going out ahead to show the way. I would limit it here to those situations in which the way is unclear or hazardous, or offers opportunity for creative achievement. Leading entails risk or requires a venturesome spirit, or both. Simply marching at the head of the parade, literally or figuratively, or maintaining the status quo for some situation, however large or impressive, would not qualify as leading as that word is used here.

Religious is used in the root meaning of *re ligio*, to rebind. Ours is a stressful world, and people and institutions are fragile. All but the crude and insensitive live under the constant threat of coming unbound, alienated. *Alienated*, in these pages, designates those who have little caring for their fellow humans, who are not motivated to serve people as individuals or as institutions, and who, though able, do not carry any constructive, society-supportive role, or who miss realizing their potential by much too wide a margin. Any influence or action that rebinds—that recovers and sustains such alienated persons as caring, serving, constructive people, and guides them as they build and maintain serving institutions, or that protects normal people from the hazards of alienation and gives purpose and meaning to their lives—is religious. Any group or institution that nurtures these qualities effectively is a church, synagogue, mosque, or temple. Both *religion* and *church* may have additional, or differing, meanings for individuals and groups. What is suggested is offered as a common basis for viewing religious leadership among people of many differing beliefs in separate churches.

Together, as *religious leadership*, these two words are used to describe actions taken to heal, or build immunity from, two serious contemporary maladies: (1) widespread alienation in all sectors of the population, and (2) the inability or unwillingness of far too many of our institutions to serve. Each of these maladies is seen, in part, as a cause of the other, and neither is likely to be healed without coming to terms with the other. The test of the efficacy of religious leadership is whether, directly or indirectly, it causes things to happen among people that heal or immunize them from these maladies.

The test of any kind of leadership is if leaders enjoy a mutual relationship with followers. Are these followers numerous enough and constant enough to make an effective force of their effort? The leader is always attached to an effective force of people. Among those who are normally followers are those who from time to time will also lead. The titular leader gives continuity and coherence to an endeavor in which many may lead.

I use the word *prophet* with some trepidation because of the massive history of usage that stands behind that word. But it is important here to establish a demarcation between leading and the many images that the word *prophet* calls up, some of which are closely related to leading. Although separate from the leader, but indispensable to him or her, the prophet is the one who has the ideas which, if implemented, will create the means for healing. The prophet who is not a leader is one who, regardless of the quality or utility of her or his ideas, does not attract and hold enough followers to make an effective force. Such a prophet may be literally a voice crying to be heard in the wilderness. As is often the case, this prophet is ignored in his or her lifetime, except as some contemporary leader uses the prophet's ideas and has the ability to hold together a following.

It is followers, then, who make a leader, and who may cause a prophet also to be a leader. The latter is likely to happen only under one of two conditions: (1) the prophet has sufficient persuasive power to bring followers into an effective force in the prophet's lifetime (Buddha, Jesus, Mohammed), or (2) prior to the prophet's message there are dedicated seekers who are open and waiting for a prophetic voice and who may respond even though the prophet may not be persuasive. George Fox, the great prophetic seventeenth-century voice in England who founded the Quakers, might not have been heard had there not been, for prior decades, a dedicated group of expectant seekers listening intently for a prophetic voice that would give their lives meaning and significance they knew they did not have.

Today we seem to have few prophetic voices with us. It is possible that they are here and speaking as eloquently to the problems of today as the greatest in any age. The lack in our times may be a paucity of seekers who have the critical judgment required to test the authenticity of a prophet. *Is anybody listening?* Are able and discriminating persons listening, people who are willing to work hard to get the skills, to put forth the effort, and take the risks to lead? If a prophet speaks and is not heard, and if no able leader supplies the necessary persuasive powers, the prophet's vision may wither away.

An important aspect of religious leadership is the nurturing of seekers. The religious leader may not have the persuasive ability to put power behind a particular prophet's vision. But she or he may be able to sustain the spirit of seekers and encourage them to listen so that they will respond to prophets who are speaking in contemporary, realistic, and perhaps hard-to-take terms.

Prophet, seeker, and leader are inextricably linked. The *prophet* brings vision and penetrating insight. Within the context of a deeply felt and searching attitude, the *seeker* brings openness, aggressive searching, and good critical judgment. The *leader* adds the art of persuasion backed up by persistence, determination, and the courage to venture and risk. The occasional person embodies all three. Both prophet and leader are seekers first. But in religious leadership, as that term is used here, persuasion is only as effective as the quality of the prophetic vision that inspires it and infuses it with spirit. In the end, the quality of prophetic vision shapes the quality of society. The religious leader who is not a prophet is but the instrument of that vision.

What gives "quality" to a prophetic vision is, of course, somewhat beyond the veil of mystery that the human mind cannot penetrate. But one facet of that quality is ponderable: the ability to "think straight" as far as human reason will go. This is what brings us to *theology*. There are several common meanings for theology, and I gather that among professional theologians the range of meanings is quite wide. From the available common definitions I choose, for the purposes of this discussion of religious leadership, "The rational inquiry into religious questions, supported by critical reflection upon communal concerns."

The effective religious leader, like other leaders, is apt to be highly intuitive in making judgments about what to do and what not to do. Such a leader also draws heavily on inspiration to sustain spirit. But intuitive insight and inspiration are not apt to be dependable guides in an ignorant, uncritical, or unreflective person. Careful analytical thought, along with knowledge and reflection, provides a check and a guide to intuition and inspiration, gives a solid basis for communicating with informed, prudent people, and offers a framework of assurance to those who would follow.

My definitions of religion and theology given above leave aside the question of *belief*. Belief may be explicit and well formulated or implicit and subjective; effective religious leaders may have some of both. Whether implicit or explicit, trust in the leader and the willingness to be led depend upon whether the religious leader's beliefs are understood and accepted.

This discussion of religious leadership presumes that the effective leader will have firm beliefs, whether explicit or implicit. However, no particular beliefs are postulated as a condition for being accepted as a religious leader. *Any* set of beliefs that undergirds a leader who causes things to happen among people, directly or indirectly, that heal or immunize from the two pervasive maladies named above, is accepted as having validity that warrants respect. Such acceptance permits people of good will, with widely differing beliefs, to work in concert as religious leaders on matters that make for a good society.

A Good Society

There are, as I see it, three forces that blend enabling people of widely varying beliefs to work together toward a "good" society: (1) seekers who are open to being led by servants whose beliefs they (the seekers) can accept, (2) prophetic voices that address contemporary issues in realistic ways—and are heard—and (3) religious leaders who have persuasive power that is supported by both theology and belief. Both the prophet and the religious leader (who may be one person) are seekers and servants first.

A "good" society is seen as one in which there is widespread *faith as trust* that encourages and sustains ordinary good people to become constructive influences in the world as it is: violent, striving, unjust, as well as beautiful, caring, and supportive.

Even with finite resources, many facets of a "good" society might be achieved: for instance, giving the opportunity for as many as possible, especially black and Hispanic youth, to engage in useful and remunerative work and to gain a feeling of belonging and being a part of a constructive effort where they are. When we encourage good health, protect the environment, and care for the needy, the aged, and the disabled, we give children fine preparation for a life of service. There are enough able people to give this care, and their lives would be more rewarding if they did it—*if* these able people would be brought together as an effective force. This is the essence of religious leadership: to bring them together and sustain them as an effective force.

Religious leadership is seen as crucial to building *faith as trust* under conditions in which powerful forces are operating that would destroy that faith.

Leadership Toward Faith as Trust

It may not be possible to find a basis for all people of widely varying beliefs to work together toward a "good" society, but the definitions of terms suggested here are given in the hope that enough of them can find common ground to give the culture more solidity and resiliency than it now seems to have. What is required is that enough people who hold differing beliefs accept a common definition for religion as is suggested here, that is, any influence or action that rebinds or recovers alienated persons as they build and maintain serving institutions, or that protects normal people from the hazards of alienation and gives purpose and meaning to their lives.

Theology, as it is defined here, is the rational inquiry into religious questions, supported by critical reflection on communal concerns. Such an inquiry into the influences and actions that *do* rebind, with results like those named in the paragraph above, may yield the basis for beliefs that make religious leadership possible. And what would we like to see them rebound into? An integrated, loving, caring community?

To the extent that traditional beliefs now attract and hold followers when persuasively advocated, they provide this unity of faith as trust. The disturbing lack of solidity and resiliency in contemporary society may be due to the failure of traditional beliefs to provide the basis for faith as trust in too many people, even in some who "belong" to churches and profess their creeds. Some of the latter, deep down inside, may be just as alienated as those who are openly skeptical.

The challenge to contemporary religious leaders, both those professionally or otherwise engaged in churches and those who lead in other settings, is to establish, in contemporary terms, through rational inquiry and prophetic vision, beliefs that sustain those actions and influences that do in fact rebind, heal alienation in persons, and render institutions more serving. It may be that among those who now "believe," there are some who would find greater meaning and purpose in their lives by following new religious leaders who advocate persuasively a fresh belief that is rooted in contemporary analysis of what best rebinds the alienated in these times and supports those who would be constructive influences.

The Issue of Faith in a Leader

In my essay "Mission in a Seminary," I contend that "The best trustees, especially the chairperson, will believe that a new, clear, and powerful mission can indeed result from dialogue that questions . . . will induce. Further, trustees will believe that mission will evolve in such a way that faculty and executives grow in the process. It is the kind of faith that people who move institutions of any kind have to have."

Faith is a many-faceted concept, a subtle and complex notion. It is discussed here only in relation to leadership. What can it mean in a leader who is successful in bringing and holding together an effective force of people? It may be that it is communicated confidence that a mutually agreed-upon goal can be reached and is worth achieving. This confidence sustains the will to persevere and contend with the inevitable vicissitudes. Such a definition would, of course, fit the successful leader of a gang of thieves. One large step away from the broad definition would insert some clear dimension of justice or mercy as the goal. But would such a qualification, by itself, merit the label religious? I think not. How can we define religious leading without specifying a particular theology or set of beliefs? It may require an operational definition such as I suggested earlier for *religious*. "Any influence or action that rebinds—that recovers and sustains alienated persons as caring, serving, constructive people, and guides them as they build and maintain serving institutions, or that protects normal people from the hazards of alienation and gives purpose and meaning to their lives—is religious. Any group or institution that nurtures these qualities effectively is a religious institution, regardless of the beliefs it holds to."

This definition involves the word *serve*. In my first essay, "The Servant as Leader," I suggested that the servant-leader is servant first. It begins with the natural feeling that one wants to serve, to serve *first*. Then conscious choice brings one to aspire to lead. Such a person is sharply different from one who is *leader* first, perhaps because of a need to assuage an unusual power drive or to acquire material possessions. . . . The difference manifests itself in the care taken by the servant, first to make sure that other people's highest priority needs are being served.

The following two sections from the essay "The Servant as Leader" are offered as having a bearing on *faith* in religious leaders.

A Sense of the Unknowable: Beyond Conscious Rationality

The requirements of leadership impose some intellectual demands that are not measured by academic intelligence ratings. They are not mutually exclusive but they are different things. The leader needs two intellectual abilities that are usually not formally assessed in an academic way: one needs to have a sense for the unknowable and be able to foresee the unforeseeable. The leader knows some things and foresees some things which those one is presuming to lead do not know or foresee as clearly. This is partly what gives the leader his or her "lead," what puts him or her out ahead and qualifies the leader to show the way. . . .

As a practical matter, on most important decisions there is an information gap. There usually is an information gap between the solid information in hand and what is needed. The art of leadership rests, in part, on the ability to bridge that gap by intuition, that is, a judgment from the unconscious process. The person who is better at this than most is likely to emerge the leader because she or he contributes something of great value. Others will depend on the leader to go out ahead and show the way because his or her judgment will be better than most. Leaders, therefore, must be more creative than most; and creativity is largely discovery, a push into the uncharted and the unknown. Every once in a while a leader finds himself or herself needing to think like a scientist, an artist, or a poet. And the leader's thought processes may be just as fanciful as theirs—and as fallible.

Intuition is a feel for patterns, the ability to generalize based on what has happened previously. The wise leader knows when to bet on these intuitive leads, but he or she always knows that s/he is betting on percentages—his or her hunches are not seen as eternal truths.

Two separate "anxiety" processes may be involved in a leader's intuitive decision, an important aspect of which is timing, the decision to decide. One is the anxiety of holding the decision until as much information as possible is in. The other is the anxiety of making the decision when there really isn't enough information—which, on critical decisions, is usually the case. All of this is complicated by pressures building up from those who "want an answer." Again, trust is at the root of it. Has the leader a really good information base (both hard data and sensitivity to feelings and needs of people) and a reputation for consistently good decisions that people respect? Can he or she defuse the anxiety of other people who want more certainty than exists in the situation?

Intuition in a leader is more valued, and therefore more trusted, at the conceptual level. An intuitive answer to an immediate situation, in the absence of a sound governing policy, can be conceptually defective. Overarching conceptual insight that gives a dependable framework for decisions (so important, for instance, in foreign policy) is the greater gift.

Foresight: The Central Ethic of Leadership

Machiavelli, writing three hundred years ago about how to be a prince, put it this way. "Thus it happens in matters of state; for knowing afar off (which it is only given a prudent man to do) the evils that are brewing, they are easily cured. But when, for want of such knowledge, they are allowed to grow so that everyone can recognize them, there is no longer any remedy to be found."

The shape of some future events can be calculated from trend data. But, as with a practical decision mentioned earlier, there is usually an information gap that has to be bridged, and thus one must cultivate the conditions that favor intuition. This is what Machiavelli meant when he said that "knowing afar off (which it is only given a prudent man to do)." The prudent person is one who constantly thinks of "now" as the moving concept in which past, present moment, and future are one organic unity. And this requires living by a sort of rhythm that encourages a high level of intuitive insight about the whole gamut of events from the indefinite past, through the present moment, to the indefinite future. One is at once, in every moment of time, historian, contemporary analyst, and prophet—not three separate roles. This is what the practicing leader is, every day of his life.

Living this way is partly a matter of *faith*. Stress is a condition of most of modern life, and if one is a servant-leader and carrying the burdens of other people—going out ahead to show the way—one takes the rough and tumble (and it really is rough and tumble in some leader roles), one takes this in the belief that, if one enters a situation prepared with the necessary experience and knowledge at the conscious level, *in the situation* the intuitive insight necessary for one's optimal performance will be forthcoming. Is there any other way, in the turbulent world of affairs (including the typical home), for one to maintain serenity in the face of uncertainty? One follows the steps of the creative process which require that one stay with conscious analysis as far as it will carry one, and then withdraw, release the analytical pressure, if only for a moment, in full confidence that a resolving insight will come. The concern with the past and future is gradually attenuated as this span of concern goes forward or backward from the instant moment. The ability to do this is the essential structural dynamic of leadership. . . .

The failure (or refusal) of a leader to foresee may be viewed as an *ethical* failure, because a serious ethical compromise today (when the usual judgment on ethical inadequacy is made) is sometimes the result of a failure to make the effort at an earlier date to foresee today's events and take the right actions when there was freedom for initiative to act. The action which society labels "unethical" in the present moment is often really one of no choice. By this standard a lot of guilty people are walking around with an air of innocence that they would not have if society were able always to pin the label "unethical" on the failure to foresee and the consequent failure to act constructively when there was freedom to act.

Foresight is the "lead" that the leader has. Once one loses this lead and events start to force his or her hand, one is leader in name only. He or she is not leading; they are reacting to immediate events and probably will not long be a leader. There are abundant current examples of loss of leadership which stem from a failure to foresee what reasonably could have been foreseen, and from failure to act on that knowledge while the leader had freedom to act.

There is a wealth of experience available on how to achieve this perspective of foresight, but only one aspect is mentioned here. Required is that one live a sort of schizoid life. One is always at two levels of consciousness: one is in the real world—concerned, responsible, effective, value oriented. One is also detached, rising above it, seeing today's events, and oneself deeply involved in today's events, in the perspective of a long sweep of history and projected into the indefinite future. Such a split enables one better to foresee the unforeseeable. Also, from one level of consciousness, each of us acts resolutely from moment to moment on a set of assumptions that then govern one's life. Simultaneously, from another level, the adequacy of these assumptions is examined, in action, with the aim of future revision and improvement. Such a view gives one the perspective that makes it possible to live and act in the real world with a clearer conscience.

The two preceding sections, "A Sense of the Unknowable" and "Foresight," suggest dimensions of the inner resources of a leader that support self-confidence and build confidence in followers. Why would anyone follow the leadership of another unless one has confidence that the other knows better where to go? And how would one know better where to go unless one had a wider-than-usual awareness of the terrain and the alternatives, and unless one's view of the future was more sharply defined than what most people have? Also, confidence in a leader rests, in part, on the assurance that stability, poise, and resilience under stress give adequate strength for the rigor of leadership. All of the above, of course, stand on a base of integrity and dedication to service that supports faith as trust.

Faith as Trust

Earlier it was suggested that faith might be viewed as communicated confidence that a mutually agreed-upon goal can be reached and is worth achieving; such faith builds the sustaining will to persevere and contend with inevitable vicissitudes. These may be subliminal things. And they may breed in followers a feeling of trust in the dependability of the inner resources of the leader. Is not *faith as trust* in a religious leader therefore rooted in a firm sense of the dependability of the inner resources of one who, as we have said, influences or takes actions that rebind; one whose actions recover and sustain alienated persons as caring, serving, constructive people; one who guides them as they build and maintain serving institutions; one who protects normal people from the hazards of alienation and gives purpose and meaning to their lives?

Could we say, then, that the religious leader's own faith is trust in his or her own inner resources? If one is to take the risks of leadership (and all significant leadership entails venturing and risking), one needs to trust that inner resources will, *in the situation,* give the guidance that will justify the trust of followers. One cannot know *before* one ventures to assume leadership what the markers on the course will be, or that the course one will take is safe; to know before would make the venture risk-free. One has confidence that, *after* one is launched in the venture, the way will be illuminated. The price of some illumination may be the willingness to take the risk of faith. Followers, knowing that the venture is risky, have faith as trust in this communicated confidence of the leader.

Some may speculate on what lies beyond the inner resources of the leader, but leader and follower may or may not share these speculations. For faith as trust to be real, even in a religious leader, it suffices that the inner resources of the leader are known by both leader and follower to be dependable. The test: a leader feels strong and is accepted by followers as being stronger than most people.

I have listened in recent years to many in responsible positions in religious institutions as they discussed what they called their leadership problems. The following are some of my impressions:

○ Change a few words, and they sound no different from the harried executives in other institutions that I have been listening to all my life.

○ Most of what they call *leading* I would label *managing, administering,* or *manipulating.* I am not aware of much leading as defined here.

○ The main problem revealed, as I see it, is a lack of faith as it would relate to leading. What they call faith seems to me to be mostly belief in certain doctrinal positions. There is little evidence of deep inner resources that they trust and that others would trust.

○ This trust would be the basis for confidence in their ability to attract and hold followers in a high-risk venture. They are mostly "safe" people.

In short, too many of these good people have seemed to lack enough faith to lead.

The Religious Leader as a Person

If we accept such definitions as those given above, what can be said about the person who might be giving effective religious leadership today?

Anything said in answer to the question is indeed speculation. Religious leaders in the future, like all sorts of leaders in the past, will probably be many different types of people. And they may evolve in ways that we cannot now foresee. They are more likely to emerge if there is an expectancy, an awareness and acceptance that they may not resemble any type that we can now imagine. Let me select descriptions of two quite dissimilar examples of historical figures whose work impresses me as I reflect on the question above. These comments are taken from the essay "The Servant as Leader," as written in 1970.

John Woolman

Leaders work in wondrous ways. Some assume great institutional burdens; others quietly deal with one person at a time. Such a man was John Woolman, an American Quaker, who lived through the middle years of the eighteenth century. He is known to the world of scholarship for his journal, a literary classic. But in the area of our interest, leadership, he is the man who almost single-handedly rid the Society of Friends (Quakers) of slaves.

It is difficult now to imagine the Quakers as slaveholders, as indeed it is difficult now to imagine anyone being a slaveholder. One wonders how the society of two hundred years hence will view "what man had made of man" in our generation. It is a disturbing thought.

But many of the eighteenth-century American Quakers were affluent, conservative slaveholders and John Woolman, as a young man, set his goal to rid his beloved Society of this terrible practice. Thirty of his adult years (he lived to age fifty-two) were largely devoted to this. By 1770, nearly one hundred years before the Civil War, no Quakers held slaves.

His method was unique. He didn't raise a big storm about it or start a protest movement. His method was one of gentle but clear and persistent persuasion.

Although John Woolman was not a strong man physically, he accomplished his mission by journeys up and down the East Coast by foot or horseback visiting slaveholders. . . . The approach was not to censure the slaveholders in a way that drew their animosity. Rather the burden of his approach was to raise questions: What does the owning of slaves do to you as a moral person? What kind of an institution are you binding over to your children? Person-by-person, inch-by-inch, by persistently returning, revisiting, and pressing his gentle argument over a period of thirty years, the scourge of slavery was eliminated from the Religious Society of Friends, the first religious group in America formally to denounce and forbid slavery among its members. One wonders what would have been the result if there had been fifty John Woolmans, or even five, traveling the length and breadth of the Colonies in the eighteenth century, persuading people one-by-one with gentle nonjudgmental argument that a wrong should be righted by individual voluntary action. Perhaps we would not have had the war, with its six hundred thousand casualties and the impoverishment of the South, and the resultant vexing social problem that is at fever heat one hundred years later with no end in sight. We know now, in the perspective of history, that just a slight alleviation of the tension in the 1850s might have avoided the war. A few John Woolmans, just a *few*, might have made the difference. Leadership by persuasion has the virtue of change by convincing, rather than coercing. Its advantages are obvious.

John Woolman exerted his leadership in an age that must have looked as dark to him as ours does to us today. We may easily write off his effort as a suggestion for today on the assumption that the Quakers were ethically conditioned for this approach. All people are so conditioned, to some extent— enough to gamble on.

Nikolai Grundtvig

Nikolai Frederik Severin Grundtvig, whose adult life was the first three quarters of the nineteenth century, is known as the father of the Danish folk high schools. To understand the significance of the folk high school one needs to know a little of the unique history of Denmark. Since it is a tiny country, not many outside it know this history and consequently Grundtvig and his seminal contribution are little known. A great church dedicated to his memory in Copenhagen attests to the Danish awareness of what he did for them.

At the beginning of the nineteenth century Denmark was a feudal and absolute monarchy. It was predominantly agricultural, with a large peasant population of serfs who were attached to manors. Early in the century reforms began which gave the land to the peasants as individual holdings. Later the first steps toward representative government were taken.

A chronicler of those times reports:

> The Danish peasantry at the beginning of the nineteenth century was an underclass. In sullen resignation it spent its life in dependence on estate owners and government officials. It was without culture and technical skill, and it was seldom able to rise above the level of bare existence. The agricultural reforms of that time were carried through without the support of the peasants, who did not even understand the meaning of them. . . . All the reforms were made for the sake of the peasant, but not by him. In the course of the century this underclass has been changed into a well to do middle class which, politically and socially, now takes the lead among the Danish people.

Freedom—to own land and to vote—was not enough to bring about these changes. A new form of education was designed by Grundtvig explicitly to achieve this transformation. Grundtvig was a theologian, poet, and student of history.

Although he himself was a scholar, he believed in the active practical life and he conceptualized a school, the folk high school, as a short intensive residence course for young adults dealing with the history, mythology, and poetry of the Danish people. He addressed himself to the masses rather than to the cultured. The "cultured" at the time thought him to be a confused visionary and contemptuously turned their backs on him. But the peasants heard him, and their natural leaders responded to his call to start the folk high schools—with their own resources.

"The spirit (not knowledge) is power." "The living word in the mother tongue." "Real life is the final test." These were some of the maxims that guided the new schools of the people. For fifty years of his long life Grundtvig vigorously and passionately advocated these new schools as the means whereby the peasants could raise themselves into the Danish national culture. And, stimulated by the folk high school experience, the peasant youth began to attend agricultural schools and to build cooperatives on the model borrowed from England.

Two events provided the challenge that matured the new peasant movement and brought it into political and social dominance by the end of the century. There was a disastrous war with Prussia in 1864, which resulted in a substantial loss of territory and a crushing blow to national aspiration. And then, a little later, there was the loss of world markets for corn, their major exportable crop, as a result of the agricultural abundance of the New World.

Peasant initiative, growing out of the spiritual dynamic generated by the folk high schools, recovered the nation from both of these shocks by transforming their exportable surplus from corn to "butter and bacon," by rebuilding the national spirit, and by nourishing the Danish tradition in the territory lost to Germany during the long years until it was returned after World War I.

All of this truly remarkable social, political, and economic transformation stemmed from one man's conceptual leadership.

Grundtvig himself did not found or operate a folk high school, although he lectured widely in them. What he gave was his love for the peasants, his clear vision of what they must do for themselves, his lone articulate dedication—some of it through very barren years, and his passionately communicated faith in the worth of these people and their strength to raise themselves—if only their spirit could be aroused. It is a great story of the supremacy of the spirit.

And Now!

These two examples from previous centuries illustrate very different types of leadership for the common good. They are not suggested as general models for today, although some useful hints may be found in them. What these examples tell us is that the leadership of trail blazers like Woolman and Grundtvig is so "situational" that it rarely draws on known models. Rather it seems to be a fresh creative response to here-and-now opportunities. Too much concern with how others did it may be inhibitive. One wonders, in these kaleidoscopic times, what kind of contemporary leadership effort will be seen as seminal one hundred years from now.

What Can Be Taught About Leadership?

It may be that leaders are "born and not made," but some things can be taught to those who are "born" to the role. The most effective teaching of leadership I have seen was with mid-career executives who, in somebody's estimation, had demonstrated the potential for leading. The course was taught by a very wise and perceptive professor, John Finch, chairman of the department of English at Dartmouth College. His course had an alliterative title, "The Language and Literature of Leadership." After some consideration of the structure of language, the professor moved on to the principal subject matter of the course, four Shakespearean "history" plays: Richard II, Henry

IV parts I and II, and Henry V. These were employed as case studies of the use of language by kings, with the language artistry of Shakespeare as the central focus. (Most effective leaders of any sort have a unique language artistry.)

After watching this unusual teaching of language usage to midcareer executives, I wondered whether it might be possible to employ this approach with college-age people, and whether such teaching might have the effect of bringing some young people to an awareness of their potential to lead and to establish their sensitivity to language as an art form for effective leaders.

Part of a religious leader's role as consensus finder is constant inventiveness with language and avoidance of a stereotyped style. One leads partly by the constant search for the language and the concepts that will enlarge the number who find common ground. The leader thus strives to bring people together, and hold them together, as an effective force. An experimental approach to language is part of this skill.

Part of the success of consensus leadership is faith, confidence that the language exists that will provide the needed common ground *if* one will persevere and communicate this confidence to all involved. Faith cannot be taught in a didactic way; but it can be communicated.

The Problem of Organizational "Gimmicks"

The opprobrious label *gimmick* is applied to any organizational procedure that is introduced with the hope of accomplishing what only better leadership will do, or that will not be effective long-term because it is not in harmony with the prevailing quality of leadership. Such nostrums claiming to reduce institutional pain (which most institutions have some of) or boost organizational effectiveness are abundantly available. Too often the result is an "aspirin" effect, not the path to long-term health for either person or institution. Well-led institutions are not good customers for gimmick salespeople. Those institutions either evolve their own procedures, or they learn from other well-led situations. They are not in the market for aspirin.

I hear the anguished cry, "What does one do when the organizational pain is intense?" My response is, "Attend to the quality of leading, unless you want to spend the rest of your organizational life living on aspirin!"

In my work with AT&T, I had the opportunity, almost from the beginning, to follow closely the "Hawthorne" researches that culminated in a landmark book in 1939, *Management and the Worker*, and, in 1966, *Counseling in an Organization, A Sequel to the Hawthorne Researches.*

This research, and the employee counseling program that grew out of it, were done in the Western Electric Company's Hawthorne plant in Chicago, a huge factory with twenty-five thousand workers and a long record as a very productive place with fine human relationships. It had had the benefit of unusually able management for several years before the research started. The research revealed, among other things, that employee preoccupation with personal problems was a significant element in satisfaction and productivity with work. There ensued from this finding a substantial program of employee counseling, probably the most ambitious effort to serve an industry and its people in this way that has ever been undertaken. The report in *Counseling in an Organization* notes that there were five employee counselors on the staff in 1936. This number rose to fifty-five in 1948, but by 1955 it was down to eight.

Why did this work rise and then decline? And why did the effort fail when employee counseling was introduced into several other Western Electric plants and operating telephone companies? The conclusion of close observers, including myself, was that it declined at the Hawthorne plant when the last of the succession of great managers retired in 1952 and new managers who had different ideas began to question the program. The justification during the program's peak years was philosophical rather than statistical. It was simply one of the appropriate things to do in a factory with the exceptional leadership that the Hawthorne plant had long enjoyed. It "paid off" because it was part of the right way to run a factory. It was not introduced as a gimmick. Rather it evolved in a natural way as an appropriate thing to do. When the counseling program was introduced at other locations with great care, sometimes using staff from the Hawthorne plant to head it, it was done with the intent of fostering the benign and productive circumstances at Hawthorne. It was a gimmick promptly rejected in five other locations, like an inappropriate skin graft.

Later, after I retired from AT&T and acquired a much wider view of institutions, I noted that the occasional exceptional institution was usually free of gimmicks. Exceptional institutions, I concluded, are astutely administered and wisely led. They learn from other experience, but their procedures evolve out of their own experience and they are congenial to the local culture.

Physical technology is readily transferable; but organizational technology is culture bound, and any institution imports it at its peril. Any effort to improve organizational performance should attend first to the quality of leadership, and then evolve organizational procedures congenial to that leadership. In organizational performance it is the quality of leadership that governs. Procedures are important, but they are subordinate to the way the institution is led.

The Growing-Edge Church

In 1972 I wrote an essay on "The Institution as Servant" in which I made a comment on the growing-edge church. Such a church, I suggested, is "one that accepts the opportunity all churches have to become a significant nurturing force, conceptualizer of a serving mission, value shaper, and moral sustainer of leaders everywhere." Since then I have not made a systematic study, but I have kept a close watch and I have not found a church that I think qualifies as a growing-edge church in these terms. Why? Are the criteria unrealistic? Do any really want to be growing-edge churches, or is something standing in the way?

I have concluded that it is the latter. If so, what is standing in the way?

As I get about among churches and church-related institutions, I am impressed by the extent to which they employ commercial consultants to advise them and by the presence in their work of procedures I would label as gimmicks. Both, it seems to me, are evidence of inadequate religious leadership. If this is a valid judgment, might it not account, in part at least, for the inability of churches to achieve the healing influence they might have on the two pervasive problems of alienation of persons and failure of institutions to serve? Why would one look to any church for moral and spiritual guidance if that church is seen, even to a small extent, as simply a broker between those in need and abundant facilities elsewhere capable of serving that need? Further, how can a church in this posture infuse religious leadership, a critically needed quality, into the whole fabric of society?

A church might choose another mission than to become a growing-edge church by the criteria I have given. But if it aspires to that distinction, then I submit that recourse to consultants and gimmicks will stand in the way.

Let me speculate on why some churches may have turned to consultants and gimmicks because they are not clear about their mission or have not thought through its implications. Could it be that this diversion to do the "in" thing and to look for "answers" from experts is an unconscious escape from the much tougher and more demanding course of nurturing seekers? Seeking is an opening to prophetic vision which could have disturbing consequences, and not many are likely to undertake it unless they are given exceptional nurture and leadership.

Also, to be a seeker one must first acknowledge that one does not know all, one does not "have" it. Finally, one must be open to inspiration as the ultimate source of strength if one is to live effectively in these turbulent times.

I have followed one thread of this diversionary influence in churches for thirty-five years. In the summer of 1947 I attended the very first group development conference, at Bethel, Maine. This was to be the launching of a major research effort by Kurt Lewin, who came to this country as a refugee scholar in the 1930s. But Lewin died suddenly on the eve of this first session, so it was carried on by his students.

Lewin was a rigorous experimental psychologist. I registered for this session on the urging of a close friend, Karl Hovland, who was then chairman of the department of psychology at Yale. Karl felt that this work might be a breakthrough of great practical consequence.

Alas, in my judgment, Lewin's students who carried on his work did not share his careful scientific temperament and skill. My view was confirmed by the abrupt termination of the tenure of Lewin's Research Center for Group Dynamics at Massachusetts Institute of Technology. I have since often wondered where we would be today if Lewin had lived a normal life span. I am quite certain that the cultish movement that took off from that session I attended in 1947 would not have materialized. I promptly dissociated myself from it; but some churches bought in on that one and other diversionary activities in a big way.

These are called "diversionary" activities because they divert churches from what I believe should be their central concern, *inspiration*. They divert churches to techniques and procedures. Differing contexts of belief illuminated by a range of theological reflections suggest many meanings for the word *inspiration*. But I doubt that any of those meanings would embrace techniques and procedures that have the flavor of gimmicks or the advice that most commercial consultants would give.

This is not intended as a diatribe against consultants; in my more active days I was one myself. But once I evolved the views I have expressed about consultants to churches, and their wares, I no longer accepted money for consulting services to a church. I gained some perspective on this from Alcoholics Anonymous. One of its principles is that the essential work of AA, one recovered or partly recovered alcoholic helping to recover another, may not be done for money. The phenomenal success of AA rests in part, I believe, on strict adherence to this principle.

A church in which inspiration is the prime source of guidance may safely pay a lawyer, accountant, architect, or others for rendering ancillary service. But if a church is uncertain about the inspiration that guides it, then it had best turn to seekers who are not paid. The priceless skill of the religious leaders, that which stands above all others, may be the nurture of seekers. What the world of institutions needs from churches is not preachment about leadership, but clear and convincing models. Every institution, within the scope of its mission and opportunity to serve, needs its own equivalent of seekers to keep it on a true course as servant and to ensure its survival. And it is just as difficult to sustain such persons in a business, unit of government, or university as it is in a church. Are other institutions likely to learn to evolve, support, and encourage these people unless churches hold up the model for them? Any church that is a clear and convincing model as a harborer of seekers will, in my judgment, distinguish itself as a growing-edge church. Its effective religious leadership will be confirmed.

An interesting aspect of leadership is that, whereas administrative responsibility in institutions can be assigned, authority given, and resources allocated, *anybody can lead!* Anybody can lead who can bring together and hold followers as an effective force. While the logical place for leadership of churches may be in seminaries, such leadership may come from anywhere. If one strong, growing-edge church emerges, *it* may lead the seminaries of all denominations into the role of servant of the churches, from which position seminaries might evolve into significant leaders of churches.

Religious Leaders: A New Frontier

The prime challenge to those who would be religious leaders in our time may be to create and sustain an effective force among those who can be led in making ours a more caring civilization. Civilization-destroying forces are at work all the time, and some resources need to be devoted to identifying and opposing them. But the creative aspect of religious leading is affirmative: it is healing and preventing alienation and building more serving institutions.

I think of religious leading as a new frontier because it seems not to have been prominent in the concerns of religious thinkers as an explicit goal. What then is the new opportunity? Is it not to make of existing religious institutions—churches, synagogues, temples, mosques, seminaries—laboratories for preparing leaders for a more caring society? Will not the first step be to prepare strong leaders for the work these religious institutions have to do, and then to share their mature experience with institutions generally? How will we do that? Let them begin with William Blake's dictum: "What is now proved was once only imagin'd." And what will nurture their imagination? Let me suggest three subjects for reflection that have been prominent in this essay.

Persuasion

The move away from the "control" model that comes down almost unchanged from Moses in the hierarchic principle and toward the "servant" model about which much remains to be learned might begin with cultivating the attitudes that will permit the shift from coercion and manipulation to *persuasion* as the predominant modus operandi in institutions. Elsewhere I have written that on arrival at a feeling of rightness about a belief or action one is persuaded through one's own intuitive sense, checked perhaps by others' intuitive judgment. But, in the end, one relies on one's own intuitive guide. One takes that intuitive step, from the closest approximation to certainty that can be reached by conscious logic to that state in which one may say with conviction "This is where I stand." This takes time! The person being persuaded must take that step alone, untrammeled by coercion or manipulative stratagems. Both leader and follower respect the integrity and allow the autonomy of the other. Each encourages the other to find an intuitive confirmation of the rightness of the belief or action. Persuasion stands in sharp contrast to *coercion*: the use, or threat of use, of covert or overt sanctions or penalties, the exploitation of weaknesses or sentiments, or any application of pressure. Persuasion also stands in sharp contrast to *manipulation*, guiding people into beliefs or actions that they do not fully understand.

The religious leader will be persuasive and, insofar as humanly possible, will avoid any taint of manipulation or coercion. This is suggested as an indispensable condition of being trusted by followers or colleagues. Unilateral actions by leaders in emergencies, with later explanations, are more likely to be accepted as appropriate if the relationship is predominantly persuasive. But in an imperfect world, there will be exceptions. And no matter how it seems to the leader, some may see manipulation or coercion when the leader thinks they are not there. Perhaps discussion of the realities, in which lapses are acknowledged as failures, may be the most open course. But persuasion, when exercised by a leader, is not passive. It is dynamic, sustained, and challenging. It may repel some who might be followers of a less insistent leader. The leader will be prepared for rebuff and failure and will need a sustaining spirit.

Seekers

Earlier it was suggested that prophet, seeker, and leader are inextricably linked. Sometimes two or three are merged in one person. But prophet and leader are seen as seekers first, who later evolve into other roles. What does the seeking role bring to the fusion? Perhaps it is openness, aggressive searching, and good critical judgment—all within the context of the deeply felt attitude that one has not yet found it!

The seeker contributes ever-alert awareness and constant contact with available spiritual, psychological, and material resources. Also, the seeker helps guard the religious leader against becoming trapped in one of those closed verbal worlds in which one's influence is limited to those who share one's exclusive vocabulary.

Seeking is also waiting, expecting, and working with a sustained listening group that is ready to receive a prophetic vision. The group will have prepared itself to make discerning critical judgments about what they hear. Seekers are religious in that they share a discipline which sustains them as persons who are always prepared to respond to a new, carefully examined rebinding influence. An important role of religious leaders is to provide the sustenance for seekers.

Prophet

The prophet, in William Blake's terms, is one who imagines what will later be proved. Seekers, under the shelter of religious leaders, will adduce the proof and carry the new idea into the work of the world so that it helps both to recover and protect people from alienation and builds more serving institutions.

Earlier I noted the prophetic vision given by Nikolai Grundtvig to the people of nineteenth-century Denmark; it resulted in a remarkable social transformation when the spirit of Danish young people was so aroused that they found a way out of a stagnant culture by building a new social order. It should be noted that in this nineteenth-century Danish experience, Bishop Grundtvig did not offer a model of the folk high school, nor did he himself found or direct such a school. He gave the vision, the dream; he passionately and persuasively advocated that dream for over fifty years of his long life. The indigenous leaders among the peasants of Denmark responded to that vision and built the schools with no model to guide them. They knew how to do it! They were, in effect, the seekers of their time and place. Grundtvig gave them the prophetic vision that inspired them to act on what they knew.

Our restless young people in the 1960s wanted to build a new society too. But those elders who could have helped prepare them for the task just "spun their wheels." As a consequence of this neglect, a few of those young people, in the sixties, simply settled for tearing up the place. In the absence of a new prophetic vision to inspire the effort to prepare our young people to build constructively, some of them may tear up the place again! Do not be surprised if they do just that. The provocation is ample. Some among the older generation could prepare today's young people to live productively in the twenty-first century.

A serious deficiency of our time may be the presence of prophets who are not sufficiently realistic, inspired, and persuasive, and of seekers who are not sufficiently humble, open, and dedicated listeners. As a consequence, too few of those in a position to be religious leaders are servants.

Leading Versus Governing

We live in an age in which there is much talk about leading. In recent years I have had several occasions to listen to discussions among those who head churches or church-related institutions who were convened to talk about leadership. Yet they seemed to me to be talking mostly about governing (managing, administering, even manipulating). All of this connotes control.

Leading, as I use that term, is a bid for a wholly voluntary response. It is going out ahead to show the way when the way is uncharted and entails some risk. It calls for both imagination and foresight, which reside in the deep resources of the leader and are the basis of the self-confidence that will sustain the leader's venturing-risking spirit, and the confidence of followers in the leader with whom they share the risk.

Institutions in which there is little urge to do other than what has been done before usually do not need leaders; able governance will suffice. But if, either out of necessity for survival or because they wish to serve better or more creatively, institutions want to do something that neither they nor others have done before, then leaders who are capable of prudent venturing and risking must emerge.

If followers are to respond voluntarily and with spirit, these leaders must have dedication to persuasion, and they must have the language skills that will elicit this response from followers. People respond voluntarily and with spirit when something from the deep inner resources of the leader comes through to them. Competent and inwardly strong leaders who are by nature servants, inspired by *re ligio,* can be the most influential of all when they have the gift of appropriate language, if they will address the interlocking problems of alienation in persons and the failure of institutions to serve. The need for such religious leaders is urgent.

There are many ways to lead, and many possible promises that support a leadership strategy. The premise here is that of the servant-leader: *those being served grow as persons; while being served, they become healthier, wiser, freer, more autonomous, more likely themselves to become servants. The least privileged person in society will either benefit, or, at least, not be further deprived. No one will knowingly be hurt, directly or indirectly.* If this premise is to embrace the meaning of *religious,* then, it seems to me, some terms should be defined. At the outset six definitions were suggested, for *spirit, leading, religion* (including alienation), *prophet, theology,* and *belief.* If not these, then other definitions should be supplied because language, ideas, and skills are critically important to one who leads. If religious leadership is to be effective in our time, then new language, new concepts, and new skills may be required.

Could this not be a golden opportunity for religious leaders—for those who will be seekers first?

These observations written by Greenleaf in the late 1980s illustrated the importance of having visions or profound ideas in his own life. The essay which follows develops his thinking about the importance of visions or ideas in nurturing the individual human spirit, which in turn will lead to more serving individuals in more serving institutions.

The following piece combines two short essays Greenleaf wrote for a book draft. The combined essays are "Reflections on the Idea of Servant as Nurturer of the Human Spirit," written on January 8, 1986, and "The Idea of Servant as Nurturer of the Human Spirit," written on March 21, 1986. This writing pulls together many threads of Greenleaf's thinking connecting the individual with the institution. Perhaps his own words best express what is happening here: he is connecting "prophecy with the people."

THE SERVANT AS NURTURER
OF THE HUMAN SPIRIT

*Five ideas seem to me to have shaped the course of my life work.
They were the servant model of my father in my early years; the
advice of my professor to get into a large institution, stay there, and
become a meliorative force; at age twenty-five, beginning to read
E. B. White, sensing his great art of seeing things whole, and learning
to practice that art; the advice of Elmer Davis at age forty to begin
then to prepare for a useful old age; and at age sixty-five reading
Hermann Hesse's* Journey to the East *and seeing the vivid
dramatization of the servant as leader. These ideas sustained me
in my work from youth onward and have had increasing force as
I have grown older.*

*We live in a veritable babel of communication, much of it
originated by hucksters in pursuit of a fast buck rather than by
those who carefully weigh what is important to say. Far too much
of it is put forth by plausible, intelligent, and articulate people who
are both entertaining and titillating, but whose words do not leave
an impact of pithy, significant ideas.*

Robert K. Greenleaf
"The Primacy of Visions in Nurturing the Human Spirit"
(unpublished, undated; the Greenleaf Center)

I SUPPOSE ONE'S VIEW of the relative importance of this subject depends on how one sees our society and its needs, both now and in the future, ranging from one extreme where everything is okay and has an assured future to the other where everything is precarious and fragile and urgently in need of strengthening. If one chooses the first position, there is nothing to discuss. If one stands anywhere near the second position (as I do), there is much to discuss.

In nineteenth-century Denmark, Nikolai Grundtvig regarded his society as urgently in need of strengthening; he passionately advocated schools of the spirit for the peasant youth, who were, in our terms, alienated. Able and resourceful potential nurturers of the spirit (latent leaders) responded, building and operating the schools of the spirit. The result was that those once-alienated youths as mature adults took the initiative to build and operate new institutions that assured a sound, durable future.

There were four basic elements of Grundtvig's philosophy: (1) the primacy of nurture of the human spirit, (2) the living word in the language of the peasants, (3) poetry and song being central, and (4) the spirited life of the peasants as the strength in a culture. One hundred years after Grundtvig's death, his ideas are still working. [See the essays "Religious Leaders as Seekers and Servants" and "The Servant as Gradualist" for more complete accounts of Grundtvig's work.—Eds.]

I see our society as urgently in need of strengthening. Awareness of the pervasive alienation among contemporary young people in our country suggests that nurturing the human spirit could become a unifying idea. With all of the diversity of religious beliefs and nonbeliefs, there is a chance that substantial consensus could be achieved in searching for a basis for this unifying idea in our own history and myth. Among our contemporaries who have the gifts of poetry and song, there may be some who with spirit meet the challenge to create the "living word with power" for our times.

Perhaps one cause of the alienation is a plethora of mediocre institutions—schools, churches, businesses, governments, philanthropies—that fall much too far short of the service to society that is reasonable and possible with available human and material resources. I believe our society could be made much stronger and more durable if the now-able people in our midst, who see themselves as responsible, would take initiatives and risks to inspirit these institutions and lead them to be more serving. Inspirited people who take risks and initiatives lead more fulfilled lives.

The process could begin if some of these more able people would catch the vision that they could be nurturers of the human spirit in the way that Pope John XXIII was nurtured by the three great mentors of his youth. [See "Pope John XXIII: Nurturer of Spirits" in Part Two of this book.—Eds.] There are opportunities for nurturing the spirit in every human contact. Those who see themselves as servants will be alert to these chances.

These nurturers of individuals thus become the people who care for the people who care for institutions, just as Pope John XXIII nurtured the Roman Catholic church into its greatest period of innovation in several hundred years. He left it with problems of adjustment with which they are still struggling, but he made of it a much more serving and influential institution. Institutions thus inspired evolve traditions that free future participants to work creatively and in a sustained way as a force for good.

But there comes a time when institutional traditions are no longer adequate, the cutting edge is lost, and the institution faces atrophy. Then another servant must nurture the human spirit of one who will lead a transformation process to a new level of performance from which new traditions emerge. The big questions are: what is our tradition? What sources of history and myth will form the ground on which a new thrust to nurture the human spirit in the young will rest? There are subsidiary questions, but these need to be answered first. The durability of a society rests in part on the continuous presence of servants who will nurture the potential servants of the future (especially among the young) that this cyclical renewal process requires.

My faith is rooted in confidence that the means for healing, preventing pervasive alienation, and building a more caring society are within our grasp if a few of us who see ourselves as servants will take the risk of reaching for those means. Nurturing the human spirit in those few, those who are aware of their servant natures, is the challenge.

If there had been a Grundtvig in Germany at the close of World War I, someone to launch a movement to inspirit German youth, it is possible that there might not have been a Hitler in the 1930s. What if a similar inspiriting movement could have reached American youth in the depression years of the 1930s; would there have been a Joseph McCarthy in the 1950s? If a similar inspiriting movement could be launched today among young people anywhere in the world, what would be the future consequences regarding such primary concerns as peace, justice, and compassion?

In my view of the world, there are people whom I would call "spirit carriers." It is difficult for a prophet like Grundtvig to reach the large masses for whom just hearing the message is not enough; they need sustained tutoring, as the peasants of nineteenth-century Denmark did.

I am confident that a similar latent leadership is present in our late-twentieth-century U.S. society, waiting to be inspirited. This latent leadership could be brought to life with a force equal to what Grundtvig's vision generated, if only the nurture of the human spirit in the young could become a dominant idea in our time. In our large and fragmented culture, a single, prophetic voice may not speak to all of us. But many prophetic voices may speak messages of hope that will stir a ferment that could bring this seminal idea to power.

Solon (the ancient Athenian statesman and lawgiver) must have been supported by spirit carriers; just his advocacy of freedom would not have been enough to set Athens on a new course. Would the message of Jesus have had its lasting effect if the disciples, and people like Paul, and those who followed Paul, had not mediated it in a sustained way?

The record is clear in nineteenth-century Denmark. Spirit carriers, the resolute people who built and led the folk high schools, gave the sustained tutoring that was required to change the lives of the peasants. Without their work, Grundtvig would have been a crier in the wilderness.

I see our nation as dispirited because spirit carriers are not emerging to reach people in sufficient numbers and in sufficient depth to make a difference. What are these needed spirit carriers like? They have the motivation to work hard and long. They know a good inspiriting vision when they see or hear one. They have the will, the courage, and the ability, and they can marshal the resources to carry their message on a sustained basis to large numbers.

Such spirit carriers are probably good listeners. When George Fox gave his great message that founded the Quakers in seventeenth-century England, he had been preceded for one hundred years by a group called the Seekers. This was a small band of religiously motivated people who met regularly to listen for a prophetic voice that would nourish their spiritual hunger. If the Seekers had not been there to respond and become spirit carriers, Fox too might have been only a crier in the wilderness.

A few years ago, I formed a plan for faculty members to become volunteer spirit carriers to students; I took the plan to a friend on the faculty of a large college. His immediate response was that he would not take this on, and he didn't believe there would be one faculty member who would. Later I talked to the college president about my friend's response. The president said that the students were hungry for spiritual leadership; but the faculty members would not do anything they weren't paid for, and even then, they would not do something unless it added to their professional standing.

In a conversation with the head of a theological seminary, I made the suggestion that he personally offer a not-for-credit seminar on leadership to seminary students. His prompt response was that he would not want to do that because the faculty would think he was trying to set the students against them. What a sad commentary on the state of an important institution, one that is training pastors for the future.

Servants who nurture the human spirit are spirit carriers. They serve to connect those who do the work of the world, or who are being prepared for that role, with vision from both past and contemporary prophets. Those servants find the resources and make the intensive effort to be an effective influence. They don't just make speeches or write books as the prophet does. They are spirit carriers; they connect the prophecy with the people so that it changes their lives.

The spirit is power, but only when the spirit carrier, the servant as nurturer of the human spirit, is a powerful and not a casual force.

This essay appeared in *Studies in Formative Spirituality* (February 1982). Greenleaf reiterates many of the ideas he presented in other writings on leadership and the roles of religious institutions in making a more caring society. In this particular essay, he focuses more on the role of the theologian and the monastic in further influencing others to make this a more caring society. Also, he adds a line to his classic credo in response to those in the church who accused him of being a "romantic."

SPIRITUALITY AS LEADERSHIP

WE ALL HAVE OUR OWN particular windows on the world. No two of us may have the same view of what is out there. My window, through which I contemplate everything, including the subject of *spirituality as leadership,* is as *a student of organization—how things get done.* I am not a theologian, nor am I versed in the ways of monastics; but I appreciate the roles of both in the scheme of things, and I believe that each occupies a strategic place from which to wield a constructive influence on this troubled world; and each has great, perhaps largely unrealized, potential to serve us all. That both of them *do* serve us all, and serve us well, is the central concern of the essay.

My credo for some time has been expressed thusly: "I believe that caring for persons, the more able and the less able serving each other, is what makes a good society. Most caring was once person to person. Now much of it is mediated through institutions—often large, powerful, impersonal; not always competent; sometimes corrupt. If a better society is to be built, one more just and more caring and providing opportunity for people to grow, the most effective and economical way, while supportive of the social order, is to raise the performance as servant of as many institutions as possible by new voluntary regenerative forces initiated within them by committed individuals: *servants.*"

Because some church persons have responded to this by suggesting that I am a *romantic,* I have recently added a sentence: "Such servants may never predominate or even be numerous;

but their influence may form a leaven that makes possible a reasonably civilized society."

As a student of organization, how things get done, I am interested in *all* institutions, including churches, church-related institutions, seminaries, and monasteries. I am especially concerned that those who presume to guide, direct, administer, manage, or *lead* any of these institutions are effective in helping their institution to serve well everyone who is touched by it, both those within and those without the institution.

Origins

My introduction to *spirituality as leadership* came early in life. I was very close to my father, who stands as a model to me now. He was a true servant. With only a fifth-grade education and working as a skilled artisan most of his life, he managed, with his limited opportunities, to leave a little corner of the world a bit better than he found it. I was aware, when I was young, that he was both leader and spiritual, but I would not have used those terms until I was old.

Then, in my senior year in college when I was still without a clear vocational aim, I had the good fortune to have a wise professor of sociology who helped me shape one. He told us that ours was becoming a nation of large institutions and that they were not serving us well. "You can stand outside and criticize as I do," he said, "but nothing of substance happens until someone who is inside and has his hands on some of the levers of power and influence decides to change something. Some of you ought to make your careers inside these big institutions and become a part of the influence that changes them for the better." This advice settled my goal: I would get inside the biggest business that would hire me. That turned out to be the biggest—American Telephone and Telegraph Company.

Soon after graduation I was digging post holes with a line construction crew and in a couple of months I was shifted to the engineering department. After a few months of that . . . I

Power

To a student of organization, how things get done, the problem of power in institutions begins with the account in Exodus 18 when Moses' father-in-law, Jethro, comes to visit him and finds him bogged down by details of his office. Jethro gave Moses advice: *Organize it,* he said. "You shall represent the people before God . . . choose able men . . . as rulers of thousands, of hundreds, of fifties, and of tens. . . . Every great matter they shall bring to you, but any small matter they shall decide themselves. . . . Then you will be able to endure, and all these people will go to their place in peace." Jethro did not say that this was a more effective arrangement or that it would make a better society; he said only that Moses would endure and that the people would go their way in peace.

In short, said Jethro, "You, Moses, become chief who makes the big decisions, and spread the burden of little decisions through the hierarchy below you." This is commonly accepted organizational theory to this day.

Then later, as we know, the Lord was displeased with Moses and fired him, citing as his main reason that incident of drawing water from the rock. In effect the Lord said, "You, Moses, told the people that *you* drew that water from the rock. *I* drew it. In other words, you, Moses, acted as if you were God. I am putting in a new chief."

Now, the act in which Moses assumed that he was God may have been the tangible incident that provided the proximate cause for his dismissal. Is it possible that the ultimate cause was that stupid advice that Moses accepted from Jethro? *Anybody* who is set up as the single chief over a vast hierarchy (or even a small one) is vulnerable to the illusion that he or she is God!

"How would *you* organize it?" the faithful often ask. "Not *that* way," is my firm reply. Anyone who is placed in the position of unchecked power over others is vulnerable to the corrupting influence of that power and may fall victim to the illusion that one is God. *No one, absolutely no one, should be given unchecked power over others.*

That much quoted assertion of Lord Acton, Professor of History at Cambridge University and a plain-speaking Catholic layman, "Power tends to corrupt and absolute power corrupts absolutely," was written in the course of his active and vocal opposition to the assumption of Papal infallibility. A significant, but less quoted, sentence followed: "There is no worse heresy than that the office sanctifies the holder of it." These ideas were not new with Acton, though his expression of them is the more quotable. William Pitt made the same contention in the House of Lords one hundred years earlier, "Unlimited power is apt to corrupt the minds of those who possess it."

A person may lead by persuasion and be free from that corruption. I say "may" because some charismatic persuaders may be so powerful as, in effect, to coerce and be corrupted. But, if one holds, in one's hands alone, the sanctions that permit one to compel others, one is vulnerable. One can never know, if one holds power over another, whether the assent to one's leadership is voluntary.

Is there a discipline that one might practice to relieve one of that vulnerability? To reduce it, but not eliminate it?

In my book *Servant Leadership,* I argue the case for shared power with colleagues who are equals as a preferable alternative to the concept of single chief. And in a later essay, "Servant, Retrospect and Prospect," the suggestion is made that young people who aspire to be servant leaders should be advised never to accept a role in which they wield power over others *unless* that power is shared with close colleagues who are equals—and equally strong.

Such a collegial group will have a leader, but that leader is empowered to lead by one's colleagues, not by a superior power.

Money

When Jesus drove the money changers out of the temple, he quickly purified the temple, by his standards. But he did more than that. He provided theological justification for coercion, for those who want or need it. Then, by that act, he affirmed the stigma of *profane* on money which persists to this day in such epithets as "filthy lucre" and "the root of all evil."

What if Jesus had chosen instead to leave the money changers *in* the temple and then had undertaken to persuade them to bring their practices within the embrace of the sacred? It might not have made much difference in the simple economy of Jesus' day. But in our complex money-dominated civilization, even if he had been only partly successful, it might make the difference between survival or collapse of our civilization.

Another aspect of money that concerns the quest for spirituality as leadership is the problem of those who have more money than their legitimate needs require, thus giving them power over those who have less money than they think they need, including large numbers at or below the poverty level. The power exists whether they loan the money at interest, invest it for the return of rent or dividends, speculate in some venture, hide it in the mattress, or give it away. And some of the power of money is near the absolute—*even in the giving of money!*

Scripture tells us that it is more blessed to give than to receive. My quite extensive experience with the giving of money by foundations suggests some exceptions—blessed to whom? Alms can corrupt both giver and receiver, and sometimes it is one or the other. Sometimes one person controls a foundation by having as fellow trustees friends or relatives who defer to one's personal judgment. This makes the power of one person absolute, and it is corrupting (absolutely, as Lord Acton says it is). Even if one is a member of a foundation staff, in dealing with grant applicants where one's role is to give or withhold the recommendation to make a grant, one has power in one's own hands alone that is near the absolute. And it is corrupting. I speak from personal experience.

What is the corruption that flows from absolute (real or near) or unchecked power? I believe that it is *arrogance,* being overly convinced of one's own importance, and all of the evils that stem from that aberration in judgment.

Competition

This is an interesting word, *competition.* In its root meaning it has more of the flavor of strive together for some goal—a cooperative venture. But in common usage it means contend with others for supremacy over them in some sort of win-lose contest. In a sense, the winner gains power over others.

Is the widespread disposition to compete an inborn tendency or an acquired trait? We are all raised in a culture that is so competitive from infancy onward that it is difficult to know what humans would be like if all were conditioned by a noncompetitive culture.

All sorts of institutions may compete: schools, churches, hospitals, governments, foundations, and businesses. Businesses in the U.S. are required to compete by law—with stiff criminal penalties. It is an interesting sign of the times that some astute culture watchers are now recommending that the antitrust laws be repealed. This may mark the beginning of a fresh examination of competition, both competition between institutions and between persons, and a new searching may be opened into related issues of power and money. Will leadership rooted in spirituality have an influential voice in these examinations?

The answer to this question depends, I believe, on whether a significant number of persons in monasteries and seminaries become more spiritual—in the sense that I have defined it—and take a more affirmative leadership role than most have chosen so far; and whether churches, with the leadership thus provided by those in seminaries and monasteries, will become effective formative influences that build and sustain spirituality in as many as possible of the legions who lead in the complex affairs of the world.

Spirituality as Leadership and the Matter of Faith

I have chosen to digress on the three-headed issue of *power, money, and competition* because I believe that if spirituality as leadership (as I have defined it) is to become a major force in producing a more caring society (and I hope it will), then the process of spiritual formation will need to reach the large numbers who do the work of the world. These people are deeply involved with power, money, and competition and, unless they lead split lives, an unfortunate state, their spirituality must be reconciled with the realities of the world they live in. Many need help.

I have noted that common attitudes regarding power and money have clear biblical roots. A literalist would say that competition is also biblically sanctioned: I Corinthians 9:24, II Timothy 2:5–6. I cite these not to argue a theological case, but simply to emphasize how old and deep in our Judeo-Christian heritage these issues are, and how massive is the task of achieving even a modest advance in spirituality in the everyday affairs of most people.

I said at the outset that I would not accept the monk in his cell or the theologian in his study as *spiritual* unless the fruit of their efforts is such that it finds its way to nourish the servant motive in those who do the work of the world. Where does this stipulation leave us? Is there any basis for hope for the future? I think there is. Let me state briefly what I see as a basis for hope.

If one is to be hopeful, it seems to me, one must be able to answer "yes" to the following three questions:

1. Can the large numbers who suffer alienation in our times be helped to find themselves at home in this world as it is—violent, striving, unjust as well as beautiful, caring, and supportive—by accepting and nurturing their servant natures?

2. Can those who now lead and carry the burdens and take the risks and absorb the tensions of showing the way to others, whether in large affairs or small, be helped to find a sustaining level of spirituality that gives them some detachment from, and perspective on, their burdens so that they can carry on with clarity of vision, compassion, and grace—qualities of life that only a lift of spirit is likely to make possible?

3. Will some among us be open to receive the gift of spirituality as leadership and then, with that gift, make a mission of healing alienation and assisting the spiritual formation of established leaders—in the terms of (1) and (2) above?

If one is to be hopeful, one must have faith (as trust) to answer "yes" to these three questions. Not belief that some miraculous intervention will rescue our present low-spirit culture, but belief—as trust—that a long series of painstaking steps by normal, competent, dedicated people will bring this present society, in time, to a conspicuously higher lever of spirituality. What might some of those steps be?

These steps begin, it seems to me, with the reader and the writer of this essay. Do *we* believe that a small movement toward a more spiritual society will result from steps that *we* take with our own personal efforts? If the readers of this [essay] will not make that effort, who will?

The first step for those of us who resolve to make this effort may be to focus our effort on one or more of the primary sources of knowledge about spirituality and how that precious quality grows: monasteries, whose creative power is in contemplation, and seminaries, whose creative power is in theological reflection.

Individuals who are involved in the world of affairs and who need spiritual nurture cannot be expected to identify and conceptualize their need and reach back through the churches to seminaries and monasteries for the substantive help that would serve them. Rather the opportunity is for seminaries and monasteries to lead—to initiate actions that are mediated through churches, and that have the effect of nurturing spirituality wherever there is a chance for it to grow.

Is any significant number of persons in seminaries and monasteries prepared and disposed to lead in this way?

They seem not to be. Most seem primarily concerned for maintaining churches as they are (or to recover what they have been), not to lead them to what they have the potential to be as servants of society. If one listens to discussions among trustees and staffs of churches and church institutions (as I have at length), the evidence of the effort to lead them from monasteries and seminaries is not there. Churches manage their affairs conscientiously, but there is little incentive for leadership to go out ahead where the path is not marked and entails risk. They lack spirituality as leadership. They choose, rather, to stay with the tested and tried. When a new idea is proposed, they ask, "Where is the model? Where is it being done successfully?" Someone else is expected to lead and to mark a safe, risk-free path. In a word, they lack faith. They do not trust their own experience regarding what can be achieved with both people and institutions in the uncharted future.

The central problem of the world of organized religion may be that the two key institutions, monasteries and seminaries, that should infuse spiritual vitality into churches do not lead and seem not to have the faith that all effective leadership requires.

Leadership in the Spiritual Life

Can these two institutions be brought to a position of leadership?

"No way," the cynic will say. "You can't possibly move even one of those seminaries or monasteries, as they are, into the affirmative leadership role that your vision requires. They don't have it in them. You will have to build new institutions with new people."

"True," we respond, "they don't have it in them. All the evidence confirms it. But we have a problem with the idea of new institutions with new people. Have we contributed anything if we should do that, assuming that new money and new people can be found? Those new institutions will become 'old' sooner than you think because we would not have learned how to build and sustain spirituality as leadership in old institutions. No, dear cynic, we have something that you do not have. We (the reader and the writer) have faith. We believe in the possibility of transforming old people and old institutions. We have faith that will sustain us in the long, patient process that this transformation will require. Faith is the stuff that spirituality is made of. To lead with spirit is to transform.

"As to the time required for spirituality, thus engendered, to make a noticeable impact on the culture, we are not underestimating the enormous obstacles in difficult issues like those of power, money, and competition, and their deep penetration into churches and church institutions. And we are not concerned about time. We, and those who will follow us, will continue to give leadership, spirituality as leadership, into the future of time unknown."

I stated my bias at the outset: I am a student of organization, how things get done. I use the word *student* advisedly because, fortunately for humankind, one never has mastery; one is always searching. Further, I believe that, in a society in which so much caring for persons is mediated through institutions, the most open course to build a more just and caring society is to raise the performance as servant of as many institutions as possible by new regenerative forces initiated within them by committed individuals: *servants*. And who will nurture the servants who make this commitment? I believe it will be churches that are inspired and guided by spirituality as leadership that emerges from contemplation and theological reflection.

The prime formative challenge of our times, of all times as I see it, is the nurture of servants.

This essay is dated June 1, 1987. Greenleaf's own introduction offers his goals for this piece. As he noted, the essay is intended for young people who might "see themselves as reformers" someday. In some ways, the idea of gradual change reflects Greenleaf's own method of operating in his career at AT&T and in his consultancies. This piece relates very closely to other writings in this volume on theology of institutions, the Institute of Chairing concept, and the important roles of trustee chairpersons.

THE SERVANT AS GRADUALIST

THE FOLLOWING PAGES are not so much a connected discourse on a theme as they are a series of short essays dealing with the contrast between what I see as *gradualism* and the quick-fix process that is called *confrontation*. These essays are mostly written to encourage those entering maturity to weigh carefully the tactic they will employ if they should sometime see themselves as reformers. John Woolman and Nikolai Grundtvig are presented as examples of gradualists. They are contrasted with Martin Luther and Mohandas Gandhi, who are seen as confrontationalists. All four stand out in history as successful reformers. The consequences of the two quite different approaches are assessed in the hope that those who would effect change for the better can make a rational choice of their preferred tactic early in life. My own preference for gradualism is clearly signaled, but I concede that it is not congenial to some temperaments. A long-term gradualist strategy for building a more effective and more humane society is presented at the end.

○

I learned early to be a gradualist, and I was not aware that I was different from the norm. It was just my natural way of working. Only lately have I reflected on this very important tactic that I have been practicing for over sixty years. I share some of my reflections here.

My career aim was set by my sociology professor's remarks about the United States becoming a nation of large institutions which were not serving us well, and that nothing would change until someone with access to power and influence decided to change something. I decided to get inside the largest business that would hire me, stay there, and try to get into a position from which I could act on my professor's advice. I quickly determined AT&T was the largest, so I chose it for that reason alone. I never came to have the power to order anybody to change something, but I wielded a lot of influence, sometimes more than the people who had that power. And I changed some things with influence alone. I believe I accomplished some of what my professor advised.

There were a couple of bosses in my early years who were great mentors on gradualism. And I quickly learned that a confrontational approach was rarely effective, at least not for me. Once in a while I made waves, but not often. Effectiveness, not heroism, became my watchword. When I retired at age sixty, I was well prepared for a more adventurous second career; in some respects, the years from sixty to seventy-five were my most rewarding. But the thirty-eight years as a disciplined organization man, a thoroughly trained gradualist, were absolutely essential for my very satisfactory, sometimes exciting, second career. Now I am in my third and final career, in which I am collecting my thoughts and sharing them with fellow seekers.

○

Gradualism, as I see it, is more a disposition than a method. One is comfortable with a slow pace and accepts taking opportunities when they come, rather than trying to batter down offending walls that are not ready to give way. One can anguish about injustice and yet accept that it cannot quickly be eradicated without incurring side effects whose long-term hurt cannot be calculated. And one can take comfort in the judgment of John Milton: "They also serve who only stand and wait." I have done a lot of waiting. And I have pushed over some offending walls by waiting for the right moment. Some of the waits were long.

Gradualists, because they are slow and willing to wait, run the risk of being mistaken for do-nothingers. But the difference is profound. The do-nothinger does not ever intend to push the wall over. The gradualist fully intends to push the wall over when it is prudent to do so, which may take a long time. The confrontationalist, on the other hand, intends to push it over right now. Damn the torpedoes!

I have no quarrel with the rapid-action people who sometimes (at great cost) break down an offending wall that is not ready to give. For myself, I have no grand strategy for changing the world, and I grant that confrontational strategies, with which I would not be comfortable and for which I have no skill, may be more appropriate than gradualism in some situations. Such strategies sometimes call for heroism and are more likely to make history than the quiet, time-consuming ways of gradualists. In summing up my reflections, I simply want to make the case for gradualism in the hope that it may be made known to those whose lifestyles have not yet been set and who are open to a fundamental choice of direction in their lives. There may be some oldsters who are tired of trying to batter down walls that do not want to give, and who would welcome a fresh start. I would like to share with them too.

It is in this spirit of sharing that I reflect on some events in history in which heroic changes were made swiftly—sometimes at great cost of life and property—and ask disconcerting questions. What if skillful gradualists had been more influential than confrontationalists in those situations? How might the quality of the resulting society have been affected? I give a couple of examples of gradualists who stand tall in history as great achievers, with little or no negative consequences attached to their efforts.

I address these questions and examples from the perspective of my special calling, that of a student of organization. I have been an institution watcher since I was twenty-one, when I began with a critical look at the college I was in. It did not come off very well despite its high ranking among colleges of its kind. Every chance I have had, I have critically examined institutions. Rarely have I been able to give any institution high marks when I ask what service would be reasonable and possible for that institution given its available resources, human and material. Very few institutions, including the most prestigious, score above mediocrity. The opportunities for dedicated gradualists in this world are limitless.

I do not submit my role of institution watcher as being a platform superior to others for discussing the issues that follow. It is simply one way, my way. Whether their lives have been spent observing flowers, antiques, or paintings, those who pursue their fields with concentration are apt to see things that the casual observer might miss. So it is with an institution watcher. What I hope to show about the role of gradualism is how it looks to a student of organization who is prepared to raise some questions about celebrated events and actions where a "solve it quick" tactic of confrontation was used.

One result of a long commitment to gradualism is a belief in the reconstructability of our many institutions. This will happen if an ethic can emerge that encourages more strong people to resist the temptation to go immediately for the quick fix and at least reflect on the slow, but sometimes more effective, gradualist approach.

○

Early in my career as an institution watcher, as a non-Catholic, I became interested in the Roman Catholic church as the largest nonpublic institution in the world. I have read a good deal of its history, and I have watched closely its development as an important contemporary institution, one whose quality affects the lives of us all. I have been particularly interested in the Reformation period, the splitting off of the Protestant movement under Martin Luther (1483–1546). And I have looked at the intriguing role of Erasmus in that period.

Erasmus (1466?–1536) was a Roman cleric, like Luther. He probably was the leading classical scholar and theologian of his day, moderate and conciliatory by temperament. While he shared much of Luther's criticism of the church of that day, he remained aloof from the controversy that ensued over Luther's confrontational attacks on the church and refused to align himself with Luther's aggressive campaign. Since most Europeans of that period wound up on one side of the controversy or the other, by remaining neutral Erasmus didn't fit anywhere and spent his last days in virtual exile. It is difficult to know whether Erasmus can be identified as a gradualist; would he have taken gradualist reform steps within the church had not the turmoil of the Reformation dominated his mature years?

What would have been the result if Luther, with his great mind, creative powers, and energy, had dedicated his life to gradualist reform and had stayed within the church as Erasmus did? Luther probably would not have the heroic place in history he now occupies, and there would not have been a Protestant movement, at least not at that time. As a gradualist reformer within the church, Luther might have been able to elicit Erasmus's support. Since both were priests, together they might have made a real dent in the church. And the defensiveness within the church, which persists to this day and probably contributes to its being a predominantly negative force, might have been mitigated. Other gradualist reformers might have been encouraged to follow Erasmus and Luther, and the church might have emerged in the twentieth century as a quite different and more influential institution. For instance, the silly assumption of papal infallibility in the 1870s might have been avoided since it may have been a product of the pervasive defensiveness.

From the perspective of a gradualist, five hundred valuable years have been lost as a result of the Reformation. I believe that the church as it is today is reconstructible into the major culture-shaping force that it has long had the potential to become. But that will take a large amount of gradualist energy and time.

The Protestant movement could enjoy a lively defense of the great contributions it made that might never have come if Luther had been a gradualist and had stayed in the church. A good case can also be made for the harm that came from the Protestant separation. I submit the issue of Luther's decision to any who are weighing the choice of which course to take when they have reform of something as their goal.

○

I have in mind the lives of two great culture-shaping gradualists as I weigh this issue of reform style.

The first of these is John Woolman, an eighteenth-century American Quaker of humble origins. [See the detailed introduction of Woolman in the essay "Religious Leaders as Seekers and Servants."—Eds.] Largely self-taught, he was dedicated to keeping a now-classic journal. His claim as a great culture-shaping gradualist rests on his work to free the Religious Society of Friends of slaves. He was definitely not a forerunner of the fiery nineteenth-century abolitionists who, in the judgment of some historians of the period, created a clamor that helped make the war inevitable. The slightest alleviation of the tensions in the 1850s might have avoided that awful war.

Woolman's approach was to reason with the Quaker slaveholders, one at a time, manifesting his love for the slaveholder as well as the slave, which made slaveholders welcome his visits. Over a period of thirty years, while he earned a modest living and supported a small family, he traveled the East coast, visiting and revisiting slaveholders, pressing his gentle, nonjudgmental, but firm argument.

Others joined the effort, and by 1770 the Religious Society of Friends became the first religious group in America formally to denounce slavery and forbid its practice among its members. Woolman was willing to wait. Appointed a minister by his Quaker meeting, he never ventured forth without approval from the meeting. One of his several memoranda on slavery lay before the meeting for fourteen years before they acted on it and it could be published.

What if there had been more than one John Woolman? They might have made the difference and prevented a civil war. Woolman stands to me as the model of the gentle persuader, gradualism at its best. Notwithstanding their ethical conditioning, the eighteenth-century Quaker slaveholders were numerous and a conservative lot. They were not pushovers for Woolman's approach.

○

The other culture-shaping gradualist who comes to mind is Nikolai Grundtvig, the Danish pastor and bishop, poet, historian, and hymn writer whose adulthood spanned the first three quarters of the nineteenth century. [See the detailed introduction of Grundtvig in the essay "Religious Leaders as Seekers and Servants."—Eds.] In the last fifty years of his long life, his great mission was passionate advocacy of the folk high schools that significantly raised the quality of life of his country and left a lasting imprint on all of Scandinavia.

Grundtvig began his adult life with a very contentious temperament. He was intelligent, articulate, creative, and a competent theologian. But he waged such a vigorous war on contemporary theologians that at one point he suffered a legal judgment for libel and was placed under court censure for twelve years. At about age forty the Danish church "sent him to the woods" and assigned him to a "safe" spot as chaplain in an old ladies' home. For the next fifty years, he launched a gradualist movement to remake the failing Danish culture.

He created a vast literature, writing fifteen hundred hymns which still dominate the Danish hymnal. His home was the spiritual center for the rapidly growing folk school movement. Out of his tumultuous beginnings there emerged in Grundtvig a firm faith in the wisdom and hardihood of the Danish peasants that would remake the Danish culture, if only their spirits were aroused.

He conceived the folk high schools for Danish youth as "schools of the spirit." These were residence courses of a few months for farm youths. They were taught in Danish at a time when the so-called cultured people spoke and wrote in German and were abandoning their own culture. Those cultured folk saw Grundtvig as a confused visionary and contemptuously turned their backs on him. But the indigenous leaders among the peasants heard him and responded to his vision. They built the schools at first with peasant resources, but later with government subsidy.

The teaching was all oral, in what Grundtvig called "the living word." There was much singing, with most of the songs written by Grundtvig. He personally did extensive research to recover and make available the ancient Nordic myths that, along with Danish history, gave to these eager farm youths the solid background in their culture needed for their later creative leadership as adults. No social or economic ideology was taught, and no blueprint for a future design for Denmark was suggested. Grundtvig, a man of deep Christian faith, advocated that the schools should not be explicitly Christian. Such faith, he believed, could only find a congenial place in the psyche of one who was thoroughly grounded in his culture. Although Grundtvig never founded or operated one of these schools, he gave and sustained the vision.

The consequence of Grundtvig's fifty years of passionate advocacy of his vision was that the farm youths, who had been inspirited and culturally rooted by the schools, remade the rural economy with producer and consumer cooperatives on a model taken from England. They became a new political force in assuring a sane society. Over one hundred years after Grundtvig's death, there are four hundred active folk high schools throughout Scandinavia.

As I reflect on Grundtvig's life, his last fifty years are seen as an example of the power in an idea when it is passionately advocated and supported with spirit as the central focus of a life. Again, gradualism at its best.

○

A near contemporary of Grundtvig was Mohandas Gandhi, who may have been the greatest leader of the common people the world has ever known. He was a major force in bringing down the British Empire and ending colonialism in the world. While he personally eschewed violence, much violence came in the wake of his effort. His tactics were clearly confrontational. I would like to speculate on what the course of events might have been if Gandhi, with his great vision and dedication to reform, had been a gradualist.

First, a comment on where he stands in history. There are heroic statues of him all over India, where he is much appreciated as a national symbol. But a close examination of the record reveals Gandhi as a tragic figure, which he himself acknowledged at the end. He had a great dream of a simple handicraft society, but he was used by the politicians who led the revolution in India. As in most revolutions—possibly to some extent in our own—an important driving force is the urge of out-of-power politicians to displace the incumbents and install themselves. Gandhi was used by those politicians, led by Jawaharlal Nehru, to put over their revolution. They had no intention of being guided by Gandhi's great dream in building the resulting nation. Instead, when they got into power, they proceeded to build India as fast as they could into a modern industrial nation, which Gandhi would have abhorred.

What if Gandhi, as a young man, had been a gradualist? He might have stayed in England, where he was studying law, and devoted his life to persuading the British gradually to move India to dominion status, like Canada. If Gandhi had devoted his life to this tactic, its consequences might have been considerable. If the British Empire had remained intact, and if persuasive reformers had led it to modify itself into a family of nations with limited sovereignty, there would have been three great powers in the world instead of two—a safer arrangement. Furthermore, by ending colonialism rapidly, many new sovereign nations emerged at a time when absolute sovereignty was coming into question as a tenable, long-term idea. A continuing core of a strong British Empire would have offered a basis for a viable world federation, which even the proud United States ultimately might have joined.

The above scenario assumes that Gandhi could have found his life satisfaction in the slow process of persuasion—and that the British could have been persuaded. Those who were close to Gandhi, near the end, report that he went out of this world a sad, disillusioned man. Such is seldom the fate of a gradualist, for whom expectations for what can be accomplished in one lifetime are not very great.

○

Gradualism, as I suggested earlier, is more a disposition than a method. Certainly it is not an ideology, and it is equally applicable to all the ideological frameworks I know about.

I understand the reservations that victims of injustice have about gradualism. If I were ground down by some oppressive injustice, I would probably not be responsive to the suggestion that by going slowly things might come out better. However, as one who has led what I regard as a privileged life but has some disposition to be a reformer, I stand my ground in asking that people think of the consequences before they launch an attack to wipe out injustice in a hurry.

My first perspective on gradualism came from what I learned from the Quakers. When I was thirty years old, and eight years into my career as an institution watcher, my wife and I moved into an old Quaker community north of New York City, where I worked. We immediately became attracted to the Quaker meeting there, because of its worship service and the style of its business meeting. In due course we joined the meeting. I had many years of active service in the local meeting and in larger bodies. Later I wrote extensively for *Friends Journal*, a Quaker magazine.

I was particularly intrigued by the business meeting, in which there was no voting; they moved only by consensus. I have watched many meetings and done some chairing. (The Quakers call it *clerking* to avoid any implication that the one who sits in the chair is in charge.) The Quakers are human, like the rest of us, I discovered. I have been in a few meetings where people got mad and called each other names. But they never voted. That seems very solid in the tradition. I have watched particularly the art of clerking as conducted by myself and others. And I have been careful to observe which tactics and behavior by the clerk seemed to facilitate consensus and which seemed to hinder it.

First, there seems to be a critical quality of faith, a firm belief by the clerk that consensus is achievable no matter how deep the divisions seem to be. Any manifestation of anxiety by the clerk, either by manner or facial expression, no matter how subtle, practically assures that the meeting will get hung up. Then there is the art of stating and restating a possible basis for consensus, inventing and reinventing both ideas and language. Proceeding toward consensus on a controversial matter is slow, sometimes requiring adjournment for several sessions. It is true gradualism; it can take a lot of time and patience, especially by the clerk. But the end result is worth it.

My most extensive, and interesting, experience with the process, however, has been in my business life. In any meeting on a contentious issue, whether I was in the chair or not, I often emerged as the consensus finder by manifesting faith in the process and searching for the unifying ideas and language. In my later years at AT&T, I was occasionally invited into a situation where the organization was at loggerheads. Near the end of my tenure I sometimes either initiated, or was asked to serve on, a task force of senior managers who had the assignment to find an answer to a critical question. Consensus was important because a task force report with a minority opinion attached was not of much value. The same qualities were required to facilitate a task force report: faith that consensus was realizable if we stayed with it and applied creativeness in inventing the ideas and language. I am grateful to the Quakers for giving me the opportunity to gain confidence and skill in the process before I took it into the sometimes highly charged business environment.

I was not self-conscious about my tactic at AT&T. I learned it gradually through my work with the Quakers, and it just became a part of my normal way of working, wherever I was. I don't recall that I have made an explicit statement about this process before. I just practiced it consistently. Ultimately, I believe I was judged "different" in a controversy and was allowed to function in my natural stance.

The large corporate staff of about twenty-five hundred people consisted mostly of specialists of one sort or another; nobody stood out. At the top of the pyramid was a single chief executive, who made an attempt to preside alone over this vast business of over one million employees, a very complex technology, and a huge investment.

Notice of my kind of gift must have percolated up to the top man, because one day I found myself in his office listening to a long tale of woe. He had been unsuccessful in initiating a particular action he wanted to take. I realized that what he wanted done was something the bureaucracy probably didn't want to do, and they had subtle ways of proceeding without getting caught. This particular chief had been a high-level manager for a long time. He had come to his present post from being chief of a subsidiary and really didn't know this particular bureaucracy well. I debated in my mind, while I listened, what I could say to him. I knew there was nothing I could say to him in a few words that would be helpful. So when he finished I said to him gently, "As I see your dilemma, your problem is that you don't understand the problem. And the only course I see available to you is to set in motion a process of inquiry so that you will get a better understanding of the problem. Then you will see clearly what to do about it."

As I was making my little speech I could see the color rising in his neck, and I knew that when I finished I would catch it. And I did. He gave the desk a resounding crack with his fist as he literally shouted, "God damn it, I don't want to understand anything. I just want to know what to do about it—now!"

This encounter with the chief executive of what was then the world's largest business is an important example because it reveals one of the flaws in contemporary society. All of our institutions tend to be governed (on paper at least) by a single chief atop a pyramidal bureaucracy. This particular chief, who didn't want to understand his problem so he could move on quickly to another one, was able, honest, intelligent, and hardworking, with good personal habits. He had all of the virtues one would like to see in such a person, except for the desire for understanding. He didn't have time to be understanding; he had never had that kind of time in a busy, unreflective life. He was surrounded by a staff of able but unreflective managers like himself. There was really no way a gradualist could help him except to write an occasional speech for him which he would deliver with spirit and conviction as if he were revealing his innermost thoughts. But it would be a speech that he could not possibly write.

During the tenure of another chief, I proposed a study to try to find an answer to a vexing problem of that day. Ultimately I found myself in that chief's office to defend my proposal. After listening a bit, he turned it down. "Takes too much time," he said. "The need is too urgent." "OK," I said. "I will make you a wager. Let's each put some money in an envelope and give it to your secretary to be opened in a year. I will wager that if you do not do this project, or something of equal depth, in a year this problem will still be here, just like it is today." He wouldn't bet. But I would have won, because in a year the problem was still there.

On another occasion, my proposal was accepted for a major study of a critical problem; ten able managers from around the system were appointed as a task force to work on it. The study took about three months, and the final report was devastatingly critical of the way a certain aspect of the business was being run. The bureaucracy was caught where it hurts, and they did not like it one bit. There was quite an uproar and I was accused of brainwashing the task force. (I really hadn't done an adequate job of preparing the study team to defend it as their report.) So we were at an impasse, because we needed an answer the organization would accept.

I proposed that we do the study again with a new team. This time, I proposed further, when the new team members were appointed they were to be carefully briefed to keep them from being brainwashed by me. The result was a group of ten quite hostile and defensive people. But I played it straight. The report writing took a longer time because of my repeated insistence that this was their report and they would have to defend it. It came out exactly where the first group had landed. Such is the life of a gradualist in a key research spot in a huge bureaucracy. You win some and you lose some.

o

There may be very few cases of a pure gradualist or pure confrontationalist. In my own experience as predominantly a gradualist, I have occasionally swung fast on something and later regretted it. But on two occasions when I really made waves, on reflection I felt good about it. I have not produced any clear criteria that would guide a gradualist in making an exception. I can only counsel that if there is time, think about the consequences before you act. As in certain moral choices, one is well advised to think about consequences and predetermine one's response before the occasion presents itself.

In emphasizing a sharp distinction between the two styles, I want to make a special point for those who see themselves as servants. I hope they give careful thought to what consequences their acts will have on all of the people touched by the action in any way. I also caution them to be wary that when they reform something in a hurry, they should be sure that the remedy is long lasting and, hopefully, that it is spirit nurturing.

Spirit. What are we talking about? As I have discussed it elsewhere, dictionaries are not helpful because of the wide variety of meanings that are in common usage. Spirit is used here as the drive behind the urge to serve, the force that takes one into an active role as servant. One who has the urge to reform something is more likely to nurture the human spirit in those touched by the reform action if one's predominant tactic is gradual, rather than confrontational. This contention is based on the record of the four great reformers cited here. Woolman and Grundtvig seem more clearly to nurture the human spirit than did Luther and Gandhi, who accomplished great change but whose spirit impact is less clear. I believe that the Quaker tradition of consensus is more spirit-nurturing to participants than what is accomplished in those church bodies that vote on issues.

The gradualist as reformer seems to manifest more respect for the person than does the confrontationalist, who is more likely to push some people around. In voting, a minority may be pushed around, whereas in consensus everybody's position is respected. So much of the influence on the young in our culture comes from history-making events that do not favor the likelihood of young people being drawn to Woolman or Grundtvig as models. Luther and Gandhi are much more attractive models to those who are drawn to the heroic and the spectacular. There is little that is spectacular about human spirit, which may be very subtle in even its most powerful manifestations.

As the driving force behind the urge to serve, spirit may be a profound manifestation of the deep good and strength in a person. It may also be a primary ingredient that makes a civilized society possible. We have as good a society as we do because enough choose to serve to offset the influence of those who use our society for self-aggrandizement.

At the root of my faith is the quite certain feeling that the potential for a person being guided by human spirit (as defined here) is quite prevalent at birth, but some persistent virus limits it or kills it off. In the quiet of my reflective years, I have wondered about this destructive virus. If we know what it is, can we curb it? Out of my wondering has come the suspicion that this virus is how the use of power has evolved while we have become as civilized as we are. (Power is the means, in the hands of some, to push other people around, maybe in a consciously exploitative way, maybe with a benign intent, but pushing around just the same.)

I learned very early about power when I dropped out of college for a while to earn some money. At age nineteen, I found myself jettisoned into a powerful, if small-scale, management job. There I had a large enough dose of that virus to last a lifetime. Then, at twenty-two, when I entered AT&T, I quickly resolved that whatever I did I would not become a manager. It took some fast footwork in my early years to avoid being pushed into a manager's job. I am deeply grateful that this huge power-centered company allowed me to live my life the way I wanted and to evolve ultimately into accepting a position of great influence without using power.

Evolving as our society has from a very long era of despotic governments with their armies and police, I suppose it was natural that when other types of institutions began to evolve, power-centered control with a hierarchy and somebody as king would be the accepted means of moving the institution toward some sort of goal. We have lived so long with this assumption that, destructive of human spirit as it appears to be, there is little capacity to think about a better, more spirit-nurturing way for institutions to function.

When I wrote my essay "The Institution as Servant" some years ago, I sharply challenged the conventional wisdom of a single chief sitting atop a pyramidal bureaucracy; I urged in its place a governing group of equals with a *primus inter pares* as their leader. I was only able to make this modest suggestion because I knew of several large and successful European businesses that were organized that way. They too have their problems, but they have taken a small but significant step away from what I see as a patently destructive idea. In organizational ideas we seem hung up on certain assumptions just as mathematicians were hung up for two thousand years on Euclid's assumptions, until some bold mathematicians began to experiment with contradictions to the assumptions and found they had new mathematics that could deal with phenomena that Euclid could not interpret.

When the framers of our government designed our present federal structure two hundred years ago, out of revolution rather than out of a gradual process of change, they had only the model of a king as the primary leader. They chose to elect their king, rather than allowing hereditary succession, and they imposed some restraints on the office. But they left enough sovereign autonomy so that one person, on his or her own, could get into a lot of trouble at the expense of the nation. Clearly the concept was still that of a king with some quite absolute powers.

Other federal systems that have evolved more gradually have tended toward a parliamentary form in which the key leader is responsible to her or his peers—not perfect, but a superior idea as I see it. If we had had such a parliamentary structure during the Iran-Contra episode, the government probably would have fallen; we might have quickly gotten a new one and gone on our way. The Founding Fathers, in their revolutionary haste, seem not to have been as wise and far-seeing as they are generally credited with being.

It seems an unrealistic pipe dream even to think about organized human activity without giving power to some people to push other people around. Heavy-handed or benign, I suspect that both holding and using power as it is commonly accepted are destructive of human spirit in both the powerholder and the subject. If we are to move toward a more servant-led society, it is imperative that we find a better way to assign power (if we have to assign it at all) than we have traditionally done and are doing. Otherwise, these institutions of ours will continue to grind down human spirit on a mammoth scale. We will not have many servants, and we will have a weaker society.

How will we find a better way? A long-term gradualist approach is suggested, one that will take at least a generation to make a slight dent in the problem. Making the United States alone into a less power-ridden society may take several generations of gradualist effort. But the effort to take that first step may be a necessary thrust in preserving and enhancing our free society and enabling us to give some leadership to a faltering world. A first step is suggested. The course of subsequent steps will emerge from a successful beginning.

<hr>

My personal goal as a gradualist reformer is progress, however small, toward a more caring and less power-ridden society. The two goals are linked. Our society is not likely to become more caring until it becomes less power-ridden. These goals are proposed in the belief that a national society that is more caring and less power-ridden will be stronger, in all assessable dimensions of strength, because it will favor the flowering of the human spirit. Therefore that society will better hold its own in a contentious world.

The most feasible first step in moving toward these two goals, as I see it, is imparting new, strong, visionary leadership in the persons who chair the trustees or directors of our legions of institutions, one institution at a time. A governmental edict in this regard would probably not be helpful. It will best be done by the slow process of persuasion. Three imposing obstacles stand in the way of getting this strong, visionary leadership in the strategically placed persons who chair trustees and directors:

- In the for-profit sector, chairing has largely been assumed by the chief executive officers. These CEOs will be loath to yield to a visionary who is independent of management control.

- In the not-for-profit sector, while board chairs are usually independent of the management of the institution, their roles are often nominal. These largely honorary chairpersons will be loath to take on "visionary leadership" even if many in those positions are indeed capable of it. As one executive of a not-for-profit remarked, off the record, "They are mostly cheerleaders."

○ Perhaps the most formidable obstacle is the common assumption in both sectors and in society at large that "management is all." This belief holds that the people who get things done have all the gifts required to make our institutions effective and desirable. Managers, the people who get things done and assure good performance day-to-day, are important people, and we need many of them. But without adequate purpose, direction, and far-sighted vision, the ablest managers can (and do) bring institutions to ineffectiveness or failure. In the nature of their predominant work, managers are generally incapable of producing indispensable visions. It is not realistic to expect it of them. We have taken on a formidable task if we are to change the common wisdom that management is all and substitute it with the idea that vision from another source is indispensable. The trustees, especially their chairpersons, are suggested as the other sources because they are involved enough to know, and detached enough to see the institution in perspective.

These three obstacles would seem insurmountable to anyone but a dedicated gradualist. It will require a lot of sustained, painstaking effort and patient waiting. But I am hopeful, because I believe that there are among us able, influential people who are latent gradualists in whom hope can be aroused. And with hope nothing is impossible.

I want to suggest a difficult but feasible first step that could provide a solid basis for hope. If a first step is taken prudently, it may open the way for the next steps in the long, slow movement toward a society that is more caring and less power-ridden.

If seminaries would first create, under their corporate wings, Centers for the Study of a Theology of Institutions and then, under those auspices, establish Institutes of Chairing, they could begin by convening seminar groups of existing chairpersons in order to assess the state of the art of contemporary chairing. With this resource of experience, they could expand the content of these courses until enough is learned about what contemporary chairing might be so as to begin to formulate *a theology of chairing*. From this knowledge base, it may then be possible to move to seminars for undergraduates and graduate students on the leadership opportunities in chairing, so that a vision for a better society might begin to be shared with young people in their formative years. With this involvement, seminaries might begin to attract the quality of students they do not now have, who, as later pastor-leaders, will help bring churches into a more vital, culture-shaping role.

What is envisioned here is not just a stirring of the waters, a new fad that will soon be replaced by a newer fad. Rather, what is envisioned is the start of movement toward a profound change in society's structure, in which trustees and directors emerge as people of great strength and influence, to be originators and purveyors of visions that give direction and purpose to our institutions. The chairpersons of these processes will be seen as the leaders in shaping the future course of our economy and our culture. The consummation of these achievements will be slow and deliberate. But in the long test of history, this may loom as revolutionary change. The spirit nurturing of trustees and chairpersons may come to be a major mission for churches, supported by seminaries that may become important conceptual resources for the advancement of our civilization.

---

o

Such strength as we now have in our institution-bound society is managerial. And, as I have argued, the managerial mind is incapable of generating visions. Businesses fail under the impact of this, and nonprofits—which are designed not to "fail"—become ineffective. Over the years I have watched several conspicuous cases in which strong managers overrode weak trustees who might have given a little vision but had no strength. They gave little other than legal shelter to the institution. To an institution watcher there is only one word for this: tragic!

———— o ————

An overriding vision for seminaries may be reaching for the opportunity to become what the root meaning of their name implies: *seminal,* the place of all places from which seminal ideas emerge. When seminaries become oriented to seminal ideas, a core concern may come to be grappling with the means for building greatness in both people and institutions as the focus of a long, sustained effort that would establish seminaries as the prime generators of visions in a vision-starved society. Gradualism at its best.

I have tried to give some perspective on gradualism as I have experienced it in my own life, as I have gleaned it from history, and as I project reform ideas into the long-range future. I have done this in the spirit of Walt Whitman, as he described it in his "Song of the Open Road":

> Allons! the road is before us! It is safe—
> I have tried it—my own feet have tried it well—
> be not detain'd!

> (Whitman, [1867] 1987, pp. 178–189)

Let me close with the words with which Ralph Waldo Emerson closes his essay on "The Uses of Great Men":

> . . . [G]reat men exist that there may be greater men. The destiny of organized nature is amelioration, and who can tell its limits? It is for man to tame the chaos on every side, whilst he lives, to scatter the seeds of science and of song, that corn, climate, animals, men may be milder, and that the germs of love and benefit may be multiplied. [Emerson, 1876, vol. 4, p. 38]

Greenleaf wrote this speech for the National Conference of Catholic Laymen Person/Team meeting on October 16, 1973, in New Orleans. This meeting was one of five "tracks" organized for the first National Council of Catholic Laity National Assembly. As noted in Greenleaf's speech, the person/team name was selected to "emphasize the individual importance of the person as well as the small support group in the vitality of the larger diocesan or national organization." With this as the foundation, Greenleaf developed a presentation of many of his well-known thoughts about leadership, service, and even the theology of institutions. In addition, he presented interesting ideas about how each person in a group assumes a special leadership role, and he distinguished the roles people assume in groups. He also emphasized the importance of distinguishing between healing and wholeness, and change or correction, when approaching group problems.

Greenleaf commented on his experience at this meeting in a letter of October 30, 1973, to his long-time friend Edward Ouellette. He wrote that this was a "most interesting experience . . . laymen very friendly. Clerics a little reserved—not sure what to make of me."

TYPES OF LEADERS

"PERSON/TEAM." This is an interesting theme that you have chosen for this section of your conference. It has prompted me to think, in ways that are new to me, about a problem we all share: how to make the organizations we work with both more effective and more humanly satisfying. I hope that this theme has also stimulated you to fresh thinking. Because I will be speaking out of my own experience and my own tradition, which may be quite different from yours, I ask you to help build the bridge between them.

Let me begin by relating an experience of several years ago, when I was visiting a large state mental hospital in the company of a staff psychiatrist. In the course of the visit, we entered a locked ward, a large room in which there were about fifty men in the charge of two orderlies. It was a startling scene to one such as I, not accustomed to seeing mental illness en masse. These patients were sullen and hostile looking. They were standing or sitting as isolated beings with no apparent interaction among them. We spoke to the orderlies briefly and went on our way. As we left, I said to the psychiatrist, "That was scary to me. Are those two orderlies safe in there with all of those hostile looking men? Isn't there a chance that the patients might gang up and jump them?" His prompt reply was, "Not a chance; those orderlies are quite safe. You see, it is part of the illness of those poor patients that they cannot get together on anything."

The scene in that ward, and the psychiatrist's answer to my question, have stayed with me as one of my vivid memories because, I have come to believe, what I witnessed there was an extreme form of a pervasive illness in society. The more I understand of myself and my fellow humans, the more I am convinced that most of us are a little bit crazy, and what separates us from those I saw locked up in that ward is simply a matter of the degree of the illness. Our inability to get together and work together on matters of mutual concern and for the common good is a widespread problem.

I relate this incident and make this observation as an introduction to what I want to say this morning because, as I understand the Person/Team theme as expressed in the literature on this conference, there is a basic attitude needed to build the relationship you want. I believe that if enough people feel deeply and reflect that attitude, it creates a climate within which a team is possible—a team being any organization in which any of us may be involved. The team, thus nurtured, then wields a growth-building influence on its members.

As I see it, we are concerned with a circular process: the person builds the team and the team builds the person.

The basic question we have in this session is, How can any one of us, as an individual, break into this process to facilitate this continuous interaction between persons and teams so that each nourishes the other: people growing as persons and in their capacity to build strength in teams, and teams using that strength to nourish growth in persons?

Let me repeat some of the language I have found in your publications so as to establish a common ground. Here are a few isolated phrases and sentences:

"How can we learn to make the Christian life work?"

"New ideas for lay training and personal spiritual growth." "Working together in parish councils and lay organizations."

"The name *Person/Team* was selected to emphasize the individual importance of the person as well as the small support group in the vitality of the larger diocesan or national organization."

If one compares this language with what I have just said in my own way about the Person/Team theme, the main difference is that I will be speaking out of my own experience in general, non-theological (but I hope not nonreligious) terms.

The big question is how an individual can break into this circular process in which persons and teams are interacting, when they may, in part, be neutralizing one another, or worse still, they may be actually pulling one another down. How can one enter this process and become an influence so that both persons and teams are raised up by the interaction? I have said that one begins with a firmly held attitude. And I told the story of my experience in the mental hospital to suggest that the inhibiting condition that keeps person and team from mutually building one another up is an *illness,* rather than an *error.* The difference in terms is important because *illness* suggests a condition to be healed, whereas *error* suggests a condition to be changed or corrected, and the two processes to me are poles apart: *healing* versus *changing or correcting.*

I once had the opportunity to sit in as an auditor on a two-day seminar on the subject of *healing.* The participants were twelve psychiatrists of all faiths and twelve pastors and theologians of all faiths. It was an off-the-record conversation. There was no agenda, and no papers were read. They had just a one-word theme, *healing,* and they simply talked informally about it for two days. It was a fascinating experience for me, a layman, sitting back in the corner as the only auditor.

The most interesting part of it happened at the beginning. The chairman, a psychiatrist and a very wise man, opened the seminar with this question: "We are all healers, whether we are psychiatrists, priests, rabbis, or ministers. Why are we in this business? What is our motivation?" A good question. Why would anyone want to be a healer?

There followed ten minutes of one of the most interesting conversations I have ever listened to. In that short time they reached a unanimous judgment—all twenty-four of them. They agreed: *"Our motivation is our own healing."*

Healing is an interesting word, with its meaning "to make whole." What I learned from this seminar is that one never fully makes it. It is always something sought. Perhaps, as with the pastor and the doctor, one who enters the person-team relationship as an intervenor who seeks to make it better by his presence might better see *his own healing as his motivation.* Something subtle is communicated to one who is being served if explicit in the compact with one who serves is the understanding that the search for wholeness is something they share. It is a never-ending search because the concept of wholeness seems enshrouded in mystery, along with other mysteries that we will probably never fully understand.

Therefore, if you enter an organization with the intent of helping the circular process between person and team so that each will build the other in a continuous, mutually reinforcing process; if you enter it with the hope that your intervention will help the relationship to better serve all concerned, then I urge that you consider what your attitude is toward the impediments you will surely find, because those impediments are found wherever there are people. Will you regard these impediments as *error* that you are called upon to *change* or *correct,* or will you regard them as *illness* in which your relationship is that of *healing agent?* If you see the impediment as error that you are called upon to change or correct, then you risk being led to assume "I have it; I will give it to you," either overtly or covertly. If you see the impediment to group effectiveness as *illness,* you have a chance to enter the relationship as *healer,* as one who seeks to make whole—to make everybody whole, including yourself, the healer—so that *all* may see more clearly where they should go and how they should get there.

I am not arguing the general proposition that there is no error that needs to be changed or corrected. My only point is that it is a sounder attitude to enter the person/team relationship as healer rather than change agent. Not only is it a more effective approach, but one is much less likely to fall into the trap of playing God.

Let us examine a common problem of teams, or groups, or institutions, to see where this attitude of healing might lead one in practice.

Many organizations are floundering because their goals are not clear, or they are the wrong goals, or they do not stretch the organization far enough. This is a very common condition, and it may be common for several reasons. Some people are *activity-oriented* rather than *goal-oriented*. Some prefer hazy goals because they are less demanding. Some are just fuzzy in their own thinking. Some want the goal stated precisely in their favorite terms or they won't buy it. Then, it has never occurred to some that it makes any difference whether they have goals or not. As I see it, a clear goal is a precondition for organizational effectiveness, and the lack of one can be a serious matter of organizational health. What does one do in the face of these conditions, say, the lack of clear goals due to a combination of reasons such as I have just stated?

The best prescription, it seems to me, is to *listen intently,* with the genuine wish to learn without judging every motive, every attitude, every reason. And one must regard what one hears—which may not be pretty in some cases—as manifestations of illness to be healed rather than error to be corrected. It is amazing what problems will melt away when all one does is listen intently, with the attitude of healer. It is possible for a parent to take the heat out of a child's temper tantrum in a matter of seconds by listening.

Let me tell you a story that is close to our common interests here. Last summer I received a call from a stranger who introduced himself as the pastor of a Protestant church that was governed by its own trustees. The pastor told me that he had read some things I had written on trustees and asked if I would be willing to attend a one-day retreat with him and his board. They had the usual problems that such bodies have, including unclear goals. I agreed, because this process interests me.

The pastor and I spent a couple of hours talking about it ahead of time and agreed that we would ask the retreatants to consider two questions: first, what do you trustees, as individuals, want from this church? The assumption was that they were typical of the membership and that by stating their personal wants they would provide the basis for a goal statement for the church. The second question, assuming that these expectations would define the goals, would be: what do we as trustees have to be in order that we can help lead a church that can achieve these goals?

When we settled down after dinner for our first session, the pastor asked them, "What do you as individuals want from this church?" (I then said I just wanted to listen to what they had to say.) In that time, a great deal came out. These trustees, as individuals, wanted many different things. At the end of three hours, we all knew that if this church were to serve its present members it had to be a combination of several things, that the process was going to be difficult, taxing the trustees giving leadership to such a church. But for the first time, it was clear what they wanted. This revelation came, I believe, because somebody *listened* and *believed* that it would come.

The next day was equally interesting, as I listened for long stretches and only made occasional brief comments. The result was not a radical transformation; a lot more than a one-day retreat would be required for that. Reports I have suggest that, initially at least, the meetings were more difficult. But their chairperson reports that they have largely stopped voting. (Out of my Quaker background, I had chided them about their practice of voting. I argued that nine people do not need to vote, and that the time they waste on parliamentary procedures could better be spent on working for unanimity.) Further, there were some indications that individual trustees were beginning to search for appropriate leadership roles, not leaving it all to the chairperson, as I had urged. They listened to me because I listened a lot more to them. There were nine of them, and I listened a lot more than nine times as much as I talked.

I have stressed listening because I believe that a disciplined approach to listening is one of the best approaches to a healing attitude. Great as I believe the healing power of listening to be upon the one who is talking, a much greater healing takes place with one who learns and assiduously practices *listening*.

It is not my intent here to give a lecture on listening. Learning to listen isn't helped much by lectures about it. But let me make this one observation, which I believe is pertinent in this particular gathering. Listening isn't just keeping quiet; and it isn't just making appropriate responses that indicate one is awake and paying attention. Listening is a healing attitude, the attitude of intensely holding the belief—faith if you wish to call it thus—that the person or persons being listened to will rise to the challenge of grappling with the issues involved in finding their own wholeness. In the case of my listening to the church trustees, there was an intensely communicated faith that these nine people could raise their sights and lead a church that would be significantly more helpful to its parishioners.

I have used the word *faith* advisedly. I believe that each of us can put that term in whatever theological framework we embrace, and that we can work together, despite theological differences, on the common problems of the person/team relationship that everybody faces when wanting to do what we can to help all of our institutions better serve our very needy society.

Let me turn now to the question of leadership. When future historians take the full measure of the times we live in, they may refer to ours as the age of the anti-leader. When John Gardner wrote his final report as president of the Carnegie Foundation a few years ago, as he left to become secretary of health, education, and welfare in Washington, he appended an essay with the provocative title "The Anti-Leadership Vaccine."

In this essay he castigated colleges and universities generally—they had been the principle beneficiaries of Carnegie Foundation grants—for administering this anti-leadership vaccine wholesale to their students. Based on my own rather intimate involvement with universities, I would concur that faculties do have large quantities of such a vaccine, and they administer it quite freely. One faces an uphill job in trying to deal with recent college generations on the question of leadership.

Part of the problem is that a stereotype has emerged. The leader is seen as the person at the head of the parade with the flag, or the single chief atop the pyramid of a big organization. We have mistakenly confused leadership with ego display, covert manipulation, and the overt use of coercive power.

Let us redefine leadership in broader terms. Everyone who feels responsible, who feels some obligation to help some part of society function a little better, or whose own creative urges prompt him or her to want to build something anew, is a leader. It isn't the scope of the task that makes a leader. Leadership is what one does if one wants to wield a healing influence on society. The leader is one who goes out ahead to show the way.

We are indebted to contemporary work in group dynamics for making us aware of the many roles that leaders play in group effort. Only one of these is *headship*. Some of the more important leader roles that have been identified in group ventures both large and small are:

○ *Mediator:* intervening in a dispute where two people or two groups have locked horns, and working out a basis for resolving the difference so that the task of the group can go on. This is usually a subtle and inconspicuous role, but one of inestimable value.

○ *Consensus finder:* that rare experimental person who keeps trying to state the consensus idea that will resolve an issue. Often this means the constant search for words on which agreement can be reached.

○ *Critic:* the person who finds the logical flaws so they can be dealt with. Sometimes the critic bluntly states that what is going on does not make sense, or makes a wry remark pointing to an obvious flaw. There is, of course, the problem of the destructive critic who hurts more than helps. The critic's performance is best viewed as revealing evidence of illness.

○ *Meliorator:* the persons who by their evident love for others and the warmth this generates are reducers of tension and prompters of good feeling. With as many abrasive people as there are around, nothing would move without the meliorators.

○ *Keeper of the conscience:* those whose constant effort is to hold the work of the group solidly within a context of values and belief that all accept as necessary for the work they want to do.

○ *Process watcher:* those whose predominant interest is to watch the total process. All of the roles of leadership are closely scrutinized; the absence or malfunction of any one of them is noted, and some quiet action is taken to see that it gets into place and functions properly.

○ *Titular head:* chairperson, chief, or whatever. This person is needed because some things can be routinely decided and it is important to have it understood who will do it. Someone should be spokesperson for the group. If parliamentary procedures are used, this calls for a presiding officer. Usually all of these duties are carried out by the titular head. *But if all the other roles are well cared for, the titular head may be a quite nominal role.*

This concept of many roles, all of them essential and equally important, provides leadership opportunities for any who want to assume them by taking roles that are appropriate for their experiences, skills, temperaments, and interests. Leadership is thus seen as many parts played by many people in which all who feel responsible for the quality of the group effort take a part. If these several roles are carried well, the actions by any one person may be so unobtrusive that his or her contribution is scarcely recognized. The group just moves quietly on its course. Such a group may seem to be *leaderless*. But, in fact, such a group or team may be the most intensely led of all.

The ideal resolution of the person/team issue, it seems to me, is building a feeling of responsibility in all or most of the team members for the optimal functioning of the group toward a clearly defined goal. With this general feeling of responsibility, it is then possible to help people to an awareness of the many leadership roles that responsible people play, and to encourage everyone to find a role or roles that are congenial. A good process watcher is then essential to see that they all function. Everybody who wants to and is willing to cultivate the awareness and competence to do it, can lead. All lead and all follow.

What I have read in your literature about the person/team section mainly centered on the functioning of lay organizations within the church. This has caused me to wonder whether you are taking a broad enough view of your mission.

I take it that you see your church as a great institution that stands in need of its own healing, or else you would not be concerned for the person/team. Perhaps to the extent that you as a church organization are in need of healing, your own healing will be measured by the progress of your healing mission to the whole institutional structure of our society. You may not be able to heal yourself alone. You may only be healed in proportion to your effectiveness as healers in the world at large.

Your church is potentially the most powerful healing force in the world. It is within your power as laypersons in the church to mount a new healing mission to the major institutions that shape our society and its values. I know that you have a deep and abiding concern for values. But few churches, even when they are as large and powerful as yours, are any longer an important direct influence on the values of individuals, including their own members. The predominant value-shaping influence on the great majority of us is the combined effect of other large institutions (business, school, labor union, media, political party, government, philanthropy) which do not seem to have a sufficient concern for their value-setting influence.

Much of the power of churches has shifted away from being a predominantly direct influence on individuals. I believe that the potential power of the churches remains undiminished, but that it needs to be turned into new channels to be realized as a social force. The opportunity that is open is a new mission of healing to the whole institutional structure of society. An enormous value-shaping leverage can thus be placed in your hands. What can be yours is a brand new role of trustees to society (trustees in the full meaning of that term) in a way that greatly strengthens your influence on the values of individuals—all individuals.

In summary, I have tried to contribute to the theme of your conference, the person/team, from my own relevant experience and within the context of the traditions in which I am at home. Regarding the always present impediments to effective groups and teams, I have urged that these impediments be viewed as *illness* to be approached by the attitude of *healing,* healing that brings wholeness in the deepest religious sense to both healed and healer. *Listening,* intense listening that communicates faith in the capacity of the one talking to heal himself, is advocated as the basic attitude-builder for the healer. *Leadership* roles are suggested for all who feel responsible for the performance of the team. Finally, team, parish, diocese, and church probably cannot be healed for their own internal work except as each of them mounts an effective healing mission to the world, a mission that accepts that institutions must be cared for before persons can be cared for.

It is a large order. Do not underestimate the task. Also, do not underestimate the joy you will have if you take it on with spirit and faith. If one is to love the world as persons, one must now love the institutions through which most of the caring for persons is mediated. I do absolutely believe that within most of the major institutions of the world there are latent, self-regenerating forces that are capable of bringing the institutions to stature as dependable servants of society, and that they are waiting only for a new healing force to actualize them. Who will be among the healing forces? Perhaps you? Perhaps you as an individual? Your team? Your parish? Your diocese? Your church?

No matter how impossible the task, or how seemingly insurmountable the obstacles, or how great the odds are against you, if you are reasonably sure of your goals, just put your head down and keep on going.

This piece probably was written in the mid-1960s. Greenleaf presents several themes which pervade his writing: persuasion, listening, communication, spirit. Here, as in several other pieces, he offers practical suggestions for implementation of his ideas. This piece includes all of the draft of "A New Religious Mission," which is also in the Andover Newton Theological School's Greenleaf archives.

AN OPPORTUNITY FOR A POWERFUL
NEW RELIGIOUS INFLUENCE

THIS IS WRITTEN in the hope that with the right combination of ideas, resources, and people, a new religious force will be released in the world. Ours is a predominantly Christian society. The opportunity is for initiative by conservative, responsible people—older people—who are dedicated Christians, but who will venture to give leadership to a new religious force which probably will not be exclusively Christian and which, while ultimately conservative (because it will work to assure the future), will have the initial impact of being disturbing and unsettling to older conservative people.

I make three assumptions concerning this initiative. First, a new religious force of any significance will work primarily through the emerging spiritual power of young adults. Older people may offer counsel and share their inspiration and their resources, but the power and direction will come from rapidly maturing young people. Most of the great religious movements of the past have come this way. Young adults today know that this is where the power is and that any new force that moves the world will be propelled by their power. The only real question is, Will the older, the more responsible, the truly conservative people deal with this power so as to balance the release of its potential as a constructive force?

A second assumption concerns the prophetic voices among the emerging young adults, which might generate a new religious force of great healing dimensions. Many people arriving at early maturity have great potential power but never wield their full influence in a way that will initiate a significant new religious force because their first efforts to communicate the intensity of their religious feeling are not met with a sufficiently encouraging response from the responsible and the conservative among their contemporaries. They become criers in the wilderness, and the inspiration wanes. A prophet is made as much by the character of the response of those who hear him or her as by the quality of the inspiration she or he receives and strives to utter. An obligation of the responsible and the conservative is to be ever alert to hear and to respond to new prophecy from the emerging young adult.

A third assumption is that the great religious prophets of the future will not necessarily be theologians, philosophers, or people of literature. They are as likely to be lawyers, doctors, businesspeople, scientists, or politicians. And they will carry out their prophetic roles while functioning at a high level of excellence in their professional field. In fact, unless significant prophecy emerges in all of these places, the vision, without which the people perish, will not be sufficiently evident. The world society in which we are all inextricably involved is far too complex, it is in too revolutionary a mood, and it is fast becoming too literate and aware of its sources of expertise for very much of the prophetic wisdom it needs to be uttered by ministers, scholars, or writers. These will, of course, continue to serve, but more on a par with those who are more immersed in the ongoing work of the world. Businesses, government bureaus, law firms, clinics, and scientific laboratories have not only become large, sophisticated institutions and important sources of new knowledge, but they are just as likely to harbor a philosopher, a prophet, or a saint as is the monastery or the university. This is a new condition in this century, and it shapes everything. The dependable prophecy of the future will come from the whole spectrum of human ability, including "little" people in remote places and "big" people in conspicuous places. It must come from many people, and if these people are to serve us well, a new kind of effort will be required to release these prophets.

In some ways the emergence of the prophet must have been easier in earlier times, when people were not so bombarded with communication as we are today. So much of the communication in which we are engulfed is strident and artfully contrived, with subliminal implications. In self-protection, sensitive people must tune out most of it because there is neither the time nor the discernment to sift out the true from the false, the real from the spurious. Consequently, when the tentative prophetic voice is raised by a young person of great promise, who is to hear him or her? Where will the encouraging response come from that is necessary for the growth and sharpening of his prophetic powers? Do we know enough about the necessary conditions so that an affirmative effort can be made by a group of older, concerned people to make an explicit effort to find the emerging prophetic voices among the young and give them the needed encouragement? The answer is yes, we do know enough. We do not know all, but we know enough to give us hope that if the effort were made with great singleness of purpose, it would have a good chance of making a difference. But there is much that will only be learned by dedicated effort.

Such a group of concerned older people will begin by acknowledging that their most important task is to help the young prophetic voices find their way and gain the strength to influence their times as a constructive force. The concerned people will also begin by searching their own motives, to be sure that their sole interest is to find, encourage, and support the powerful release of the prophetic strivings of exceptional young people regardless of their chosen professional fields. And, they, the older generation, must be scrupulously careful not to impose their old ways upon it. Those who seek to give this encouragement to the young will need to be exceptional people, able, wise in their years, and representing the bulwark of responsibility in the modern world. And they need to be crystal clear in the compact that binds them together in this work because they may (and they ought to) represent quite a spectrum of differences. They have a tremendous obligation not to encourage the demonic. (For instance, Hitler was demonic, but as a young man he must have given some evidence of his great charismatic powers and might therefore have come to the attention of such a dedicated group as is proposed here. Thus the danger of encouraging the demonic must be squarely faced.)

But what also must be faced is the quite likely prospect that a new religious force that gives hope to the world will be deeply disturbing to the old, the conservative, and those who yearn for the comfort and certainty of a kind of world view that passed with the nineteenth century. Is there a group of mature, responsible, and truly conservative people who will accept the obligation as bounded by these considerations? There are such people, and their own fulfillment in this life requires that they undertake such a mission. But it will take a great act of faith, not faith in a conventional doctrinal sense, but rather faith as Dean Inge [William Ralph Inge, Lady Margaret Professor of Divinity at Cambridge University, England.—Eds.] once defined it: the choice of the nobler hypothesis. It is the choice to act upon those assumptions about the nature of people and the world that will release an optimal contemporary force to lead people to be religious in the root sense of that word, that is, "bound to the cosmos," at one with the great creative force. A religious person in this sense stands above and beyond dogmas and creeds and one's limited capacity to conceptualize and articulate. It is religion at the level of awe and wonder as one contemplates the great mystery of all creation and of one's own significant being. Despite other differences, faith at this level will give a small group of able, dedicated, responsible, truly conservative people the common ground from which to proceed with assurance.

In order to bring this new religious influence to fruition, this small group of dedicated leaders will incorporate their venture under a governing board which will be sufficiently representative of the major facets of American thought that there can be no question of its determination to proceed within a framework of purpose as discussed above. To bring such a group together and keep the singleness of purpose which this mission requires will, of course, be difficult. But it is a necessary condition for the accomplishment of this mission. The initial funds should be sufficient to maintain an office, to support at least one sensitive and creative staff person, and to carry on an intensive consultation program with educators and others in order to persuasively reach potential donors as well as those whose support is needed to identify the outstanding young people who should be involved. Also, the initial effort should excite the interest of those distinguished persons who will respond with enthusiasm to the opportunity to join the faculty of the new institution set up for this purpose. The next step would be to raise the funds to establish the institution, to recruit a distinguished faculty, and to begin the recruiting selection of the young people who should be attracted to the idea.

Those selected for support and encouragement will be young college-aged men and women, mostly from the United States but from the world as well, who are judged to be exceptional, who have good intelligence; emotional stability; a well-developed value system that builds upon but goes beyond the traditional; and good work habits supported by achievement, drive, and a strong pull toward the inward spiritual experience. Those selected will be offered the opportunity for summer programs while still in college and a one- or two-year program upon graduation that will be financed to the extent necessary by the new institution. It will be difficult to persuade young people to add a year to professional preparation that already takes too long, and it may not always be necessary. But at the start, there is no other way.

What will the program be? The complete design would, of course, emerge only out of further study and opinion gathering. In the absence of such a firm basis now, preliminary thinking about it suggests the following criteria for judging the individual accomplishment of young people who undertake this work (and even the most exceptional young people with the best of modern education often fail to meet these criteria):

1. Effective interpersonal relations, including the disposition to persuade and to be persuaded in normal human encounters.

2. The ability to reason logically and exercise good critical judgment about current critical issues in the nation and the world.

3. Exceptional speaking and writing ability coupled with the tendency to listen intently.

4. Extraordinary sensitivity to the great symbolic meaning in the Judeo-Christian tradition as seen in the context of the essential teachings of world religions.

5. A high level of self-understanding and awareness of one's relatedness to the cosmos; a feeling of belonging in the world as it is.

6. Relaxed and open acceptance of the inward promptings of the spirit.

7. The disposition to order one's life, regardless of one's chosen vocation, so as to live optimally as a person of strong affirmative religious influence and ethical sensitivity.

8. The disposition to work closely with a small dedicated group in a sustained effort to wield a powerful constructive influence upon one's immediate society and the world.

9. The solid experience of being heard as responsible adults, both by their contemporaries and by their seniors. If they have a prophetic voice, they will know it and their obligation to develop it will be clear.

10. The goals of a career image of greatness in professional accomplishment and of religious influence as distinguished public citizens.

The first question that might be asked about criteria such as these is whether they duplicate the claims made for undergraduate education as it now exists. Those claims are made somewhat in these same terms, but the undergraduate accomplishment falls far short (as many thoughtful educators know), especially with those who have great potential for leadership. The remedy is simple: in the undergraduate years, do for those who give evidence of great potential as spiritual leaders what is now done for potential scientists and mathematicians, namely, find them early and give them exceptional opportunities to grow, opportunities in scale with their potential for growth. A Sputnik revolution in the late 1950s was required to bring scientific and mathematical training into this priority. What kind of incentive will be required to do the same for spiritual leaders who are both scarcer and more urgently needed than scientists? The two categories are not mutually exclusive; a scientist might be a spiritual leader (and some have been). To bring the same priority of development to religious leaders within the undergraduate college will require another kind of challenge. The one suggested here is to create a new institution to demonstrate that it can be done. There is no point in pressuring the colleges if, plain as the need is, they do not see it. But they probably will see it, and rise to the challenge, if a new institution starts to do it with conspicuous success. This suggestion is made in the belief that there is no quicker way to bring the colleges to this position.

But then, one may ask, where are the teaching resources to bring about the ten results named above? These teaching resources exist, but they are dissipated among those of high and low potential alike. Many great teachers would respond with alacrity to the opportunity to concentrate some of their good years in the training of those judged to be exceptionally gifted for religious leadership. Furthermore, truly great teachers usually emerge out of the opportunity to work with exceptional students. An opportunity like that conceived here, in which men and women destined for great careers in law, medicine, business, education, government, and the church are assembled, is rarely offered to the greatest teachers.

Finally, how would one who would support a venture like that described here have the assurance that she or he was releasing a force for good? They would be assured because they would be investing their energy and resources in one of the most dependable of the affirmative qualities in human nature: the capacity of young people to rise to an idealistic challenge. If, added to this, the skills for effective leadership are matched with the environment of the great power and wisdom of the Judeo-Christian tradition as seen in the context of world religions, and if the best of our ethical teachers are drawn into the service of such a program, there is as much certainty of releasing a force for good as any human venture in this world is likely to achieve.

A great creative thrust that commands our best inspired people will be required to develop a program that wields these influences. However, if one in four of these young people who become deeply involved in this program is significantly matured in these ways, and if one in a thousand becomes a great religious figure, the effort will justify all of the investment of material and human resources that can be marshaled for it. If this initiative encourages exceptional young people to form the gathered communities of two or three where, we are promised, the strength and the power will really generate, this effort can change the world.

PART TWO

LEADERS AS INSPIRITED PERSONS

No person is to be trusted with any aim unless he or she has some contact, however tenuous, with ultimate purpose and unless his or her involvement is substantial at the level of symbol and essence.

Robert K. Greenleaf

There are two drafts of this short fantasy piece in the Greenleaf archives at Andover Newton Theological School. The first draft might have been written tongue in cheek as Greenleaf suggests that wars and the presence of too many lawyers led to the demise of society. The second draft reflects more accurately his concern with religious leadership. What follows is the second draft of this fantasy.

THE COLLAPSE OF CIVILIZATION:
A FANTASY

IF OUR CIVILIZATION does not make it, and there are prophets of doom around who say it won't (but I don't believe anybody knows), the following event may take place some day.

———— o ————

Historians, archaeologists, theologians, and other interested
folk are gathered in the year 3200 A.D. to take note of the one
thousandth anniversary of what is generally agreed was the
final gasp in the collapse of the civilization that preceded theirs.
They were further agreed that the basic ingredient that makes a
civilization possible is the prevalence of a sufficient level of
order so that most people can live in peace most of the time.
There are embellishments and detractions from this that make
peaks and valleys in the quality of the civilization, but the basic
requirement is order.

   Good historical records of the pre-2200 civilization had sur-
vived and been preserved. Working with these and current as-
sessments, the scholars had several aims. Among them were: (1)
make careful comparisons of the two civilizations; (2) try to understand causes of the collapse in 2200 and how it might have
been averted; (3) trace the development of the current civilization and try to explain how it came to be so different from its
predecessor, since the two human natures seemed about the

same; (4) learn more about the vulnerabilities in their contemporary society so that they could launch needed protective measures; and (5) identify any significant lessons to be learned from the collapse in 2200 that would guide them in designing ways to conserve their civilization. There had been many signs of deterioration long before the ultimate collapse into disorder, and there was a long and painful decline before the collapse. From the perspective of 3200 A.D., the signs of the imminence of that collapse were unmistakable, but they were ignored, as they always had been prior to previous collapses.

But, those people in 3200 A.D. asked, was there an ultimate cause, was there a big lesson to be learned that would enable just a few prudent people to set in motion restorative forces in the fourth millennium to avoid the calamity that befell their predecessor civilization? They concluded that there was such an ultimate cause, one big lesson from which they could profit. That single cause was a failure of religious leadership.

This was not a sudden failure that marked an abrupt decline. Throughout recorded history powerful and persuasive prophetic voices had occasionally emerged, and the quality of civilization, here and there, had surged forward—for a time. But ultimately, the influence of all of them declined even though large numbers continued to adhere to a "faith." What doomed the civilization that ended in 2200 was the long-term absence of caring concern among the faithful that nurtures leaders in every generation, those whose sustained disposition to care forms the "glue" that holds a civilization together, in opposition to the destructive forces that were ever-present then and still are in the year 3200. The failure was that those who held the "faith," in all ages and in all sectors of the globe, did not husband the tradition that continually replenished the "glue." Great civilization builders emerged from time to time; if they had not, that earlier civilization would not have lasted until 2200. But their emergence was sporadic and unpredictable, and as a consequence, civilization was always precarious.

The ultimate failure in 2200 was called, by those assembled in 3200, a failure of religious leadership because of the root meaning of the word, *re ligio,* to rebind—in the preceding metaphor, to renew the glue that holds the civilization together. The word *religion* had been appropriated by the faithful, whose primary concern was caring for persons, not so much for society and its institutions.

The conferees in 3200 were puzzled that neither in the previous civilization nor in theirs did those who adhered to a faith seem to nurture the essential religious leadership that continuity of any civilization requires. They noted that, from the available evidence, the decline of that previous civilization did not appear irreversible until about the year 2000. Prior to that critical date, it would have been possible to recover from the long neglect of the nurture of religious leaders.

Why, those in 3200 asked, did those twentieth-century people, with their vast resources for education, neglect the preparation of religious leaders who would be so vital to the continuity of their culture? Clearly, it had never been in the structure of society to explicitly prepare leaders of any kind. The focus of preparation, which became so intense in the twentieth century, had been on the intellect and on skills. One of the times that religious leadership had been attended to in an explicit program, they noted, was in the nineteenth century, when Bishop Grundtvig in Denmark devoted his life to advocating the folk high school, an educational venture that remade the dying culture of his small country.

Despite that notable example with its conspicuous success, nothing seemed to have been learned from this. Why? The reason seemed to be that his was not a scholarly venture. Bishop Grundtvig spoke passionately over his long life (he did not write) to the indigenous leaders of the peasant class. He inspired them with a vision that they could, with their own resources, remake the culture—and they did, by conducting schools for young adults to prepare them for religious leadership. But it was not a scholarly thing; it did not produce a literature. The accomplishment in nineteenth-century Denmark was spectacular, but since the twentieth-century educational system was based on the intellect, rather than experience, the achievement was not communicated. Another Grundtvig in the twentieth century might have produced a preparation for religious leadership appropriate for that century and thus might have checked the decline then so evident. But that person did not appear. Great people emerged: William James, John Dewey, both of them titans. But they did not have Grundtvig's gift to arouse those who would set up the programs to prepare young people for religious leadership.

Why, it was asked in 3200, as the point of irreversibility approached near the end of the twentieth century, was not some heroic measure produced to check the trend? Apparently the people of the time did not know that that was where they were. It was just another crisis, and they had been through crises before. They would muddle through this one as they had done many times in the past. Anyhow, at that point, even if they had known their peril, they would not have known what to do. Only adequate resources of religious leadership could have devised, and persuasively advocated, the heroic steps that would have been needed. And they did not exist; so the end came.

Greenleaf wrote this reflection on October 15, 1983. A note on the draft paper indicates this was a response to a question from Robert Wood Lynn. For many years Greenleaf and Lynn were in almost daily communication on topics such as the one covered in this piece.

REFLECTIONS ON SPIRIT

HOW TO TALK ABOUT SPIRIT?

Carl Rogers once opined, "If you have something important to communicate and if you can possibly manage it, put your hand over your mouth and point."

It would be a little difficult to point to spirit. Perhaps the next best thing is to describe manifestations of it.

Many years ago a friend from Madison, Wisconsin, told of a meeting of a local women's club that she attended when Frank Lloyd Wright (whose studio was at nearby Spring Green) was invited to speak on the subject "What Is Art?" When he was introduced, he acknowledged the introduction, took from his pocket a little book, and proceeded to read Hans Christian Andersen's fairy tale about the little mermaid. Wright was a large, impressive man with a good voice and stage presence. He read it very well. When he finished, he closed his book, paused as he looked at his audience, and said, "That, my friends, is Art." And he sat down.

I suspect that one of the problems in helping seminaries to be more effective servants of society is that there is too much talking and not enough pointing.

Spirit is generally defined as the animating force in living beings. I open my essay "The Servant as Religious Leader" with the statement, "Part of my excitement in living comes from the belief that leadership is so dependent on spirit that the essence of it will never be capsuled or codified." Later in the essay I add, "Part of that essence lies beyond the barrier that separates mystery from what we call reality."

"Spirit," I then said, "as the animating force in living beings is value free. Hitler had spirit; he was a great, if demonic, leader. Putting value into it, in my judgment, makes it religious." But I leave it to the reader to judge what I value, from the total import of the essay. And so it is (for me) with spirit. It has meaning as an aspect of individual lives; distillation into an abstract definition does not add much. One must look at individual lives and learn from them.

Many years ago I was invited as a resource person to a gathering of the Roger Williams Fellowship at the Divinity School of the University of Chicago. This was a group of liberal Baptist ministers. In the closing session I sat with two or three other resource people in a sort of summary session. In the course of this I received a question something like: "You come from New York. Do you know Norman Vincent Peale, and if so, what does he have that we don't have?" My response was, "Yes, I do know him and have heard him preach several times. But I don't know what you don't have."

I have a close friend who was a college classmate of Peale's and a lifelong friend. Through him I met Peale shortly after he came to New York as a young preacher and I have had occasional lunches with him. I think I understand why he is a great preacher (not profound like Harry Emerson Fosdick, whom I also heard on occasion) but a warm, kindly man, easy to know, and a great story teller. He has a very informal preaching style. He doesn't use a pulpit; he just stands up and talks. His usual sermon starts with the description of a common problem and the observation, "Now, I have this problem, and you probably have it. Let's talk about our problem." There follows about twenty minutes of stories and anecdotes to make the problem and approaches to it vivid. Not spectacular sermons at all, but they tend to reach people where they are and give them courage to go on.

I think that the secret of Peale's success as a preacher and writer was that, in very simple terms that reached large numbers, he communicated spirit. I suspect the Baptist preacher who asked the question, and others in the group for whom he may have been spokesperson, are lacking in spirit or else the question would not have been asked. People who have plenty of spirit usually are not too concerned about the performance of others who seem to be doing better.

Ultimately I distilled my thinking about spirit into the word *servant*. It came to me as I was driving with my wife, Esther, from Prescott, Arizona, to San Francisco after a bad experience with students at Prescott College, one of the radical new colleges of the 1960s. I decided that I would need new language if I was going to communicate with students of that generation. It was a fortunate choice because I was able to build more around the word *servant* than I could around *spirit*. It enabled me to distance myself from those to whom I could not talk and to draw closer to those with whom I can talk. Life has been much more pleasant after that choice.

But I have had some curious encounters with church people around the word *servant*. At a meeting of ministers of largely evangelical churches in Washington, I was challenged on its use. To one participant, I asked what Jesus' words in Matthew meant to him: "... whoever wishes to be great among you must be your servant, and whoever wishes to be first among you must be your slave; just as the Son of Man came not to be served but to serve. ..." (Matthew 20:26–28). His frank answer was, "I have never thought of it!"

I find it helpful to stay with a "consequential" definition of *servant* rather than an abstract one. As I wrote in 1970 the test rests with the care taken by the servant, who is the first person to make sure that other people's highest priority needs are being served. "Do those served grow as persons; do they, *while being served*, become healthier, wiser, freer, more likely themselves to become servants? And what is the effect on the least privileged in society; will he or she benefit, or at least not be further deprived?" I concede that this is a very difficult test to administer. But one who aspires to be servant may come closer to achieving this result by keeping this consequential definition foremost in all thinking.

As I reflect on spirit and the servant idea, the most spectacular single incident in my thirty-eight years with AT&T comes to mind.

I was fifty-four years old (six years before I retired). The public relations staff at AT&T, from whom I instinctively kept my distance, convened a meeting to consider a proposal from a public relations consulting firm for an economic education program for AT&T and its affiliated company employees. There were about twenty-five officers of AT&T and affiliates in the meeting, mostly PR people. I was low man on the totem pole in the meeting. The plan was that the two representatives of the consulting firm would present and discuss their proposal in the morning. Then we would lunch in the conference suite and convene in the afternoon to consider whether we wanted to buy the proposal.

About ten minutes into the meeting, these two fellows didn't smell right to me. I went out to the phone and called one of my staff and told him what was happening. I gave him the names of the two fellows and their firm. Then I asked him to put everybody on it and find out as much about them as they could by noon; I would call again for their report.

The presentation was well polished. The two fellows were able and facile. But the content of what they wanted to put on was shocking to me (the kind of stuff Ronald Reagan must have offered in the years he was a free-enterprise lecturer for General Electric, when they were on their binge of saving the world for capitalism).

When I called my office for a report, my worst fears were confirmed. These two salespeople were notorious hucksters. In two hours, my staff had produced a report that the combined resources of the FBI and the CIA could not have duplicated. These were clearly people with whom we should not work. The documentation to support this position was detailed and verifiable.

My problem then was what to do with what I knew. I decided to sit tight and see what the judgment of the conference would be.

When we reconvened, the consensus was not long in forming that this was a good idea and we ought to buy it. When it seemed to me that they were about to firm up a judgment to buy this program, I entered the discussion.

I suggested that before firm judgments were made, I wanted to report what my staff had found when they checked up on these fellows. In a few crisp sentences I summarized their findings, which were quite conclusive. These were not folks we should get involved with on a program like this that would go to all employees. Even if they had turned out to be reputable, I had serious questions about the content of the program.

This was Mickey Mouse economics, I said. They might get away with it if they showed it only to management people. But if they should expose our nonmanagement people to it, the unions would cut them to ribbons. It would be a disaster. What interest of the business would they advance by doing this? For the life of me, I said, I could see no rational reason for wanting to do this. They were being taken in by a couple of smooth hucksters.

I had two main concerns about what was going on there. Where was their intuition? Why was it up to me alone to smell something wrong with this deal? How did the idea ever get this far without anybody asking whether this was the consulting company they wanted to have dealing with our employees? My second concern was more serious. Where in the hell was their judgment? That this number of assembled brass would buy a sleazy idea like this shook my confidence in the future of the business. I said I thought I would sell my stock!

There was a moment of strained silence, and the meeting erupted in indignation with everybody talking at once—some of them shouting. The party got noisy when a friend, Jack Joseph, woke up from a nap. He rolled his eyes and quickly concluded that it was Greenleaf against the field (I was having a great time fending off all of the assaults I could). Jack was a big man with a shock of white hair, a good voice, and a commanding presence.

He pulled up his chair, took a quick measure of the issues and, in a loud voice, started pitching on my side. He was promptly nailed by one of the conferees, who shouted, "Jack, what goes on here? You've been back there asleep. You don't even know what this fight is all about."

Jack drew himself up in great hauteur and started tapping on the table with his fingers as the meeting got quiet. Finally (still tapping his fingers) he said slowly and with emphasis, "I know I've been asleep; I know I don't know what this fight is all about; but there's one thing I do know. I know which side I'm on!"

There was a roar of laughter. The person chairing the meeting said he could see we were not going to settle this matter, so he adjourned the meeting. The subject never came up again. That was the end of it.

As I said, all present were officers of AT&T or affiliated companies. The officer group had a good grapevine of their own, so the report of this episode got around. The reason I have so clear a memory of what I said there is that, in my remaining six years in the business, as I met with officers alone I was likely to be asked what I had said to those fellows when I torpedoed that silly economics-course idea.

Within the past year, a business friend told me of meeting one of the young officers of the local Bell company and asking him whether he knew me. He replied that he didn't know me, but he knew of me, and that I had been retired a long time. He said, "We don't have a Bob Greenleaf in headquarters anymore, and we need one."

Shortly after the episode related above, I had lunch with Norman Vincent Peale. (Jack Joseph was a college classmate of Peale's and the lifelong friend who introduced me to him.) I told Norman of the incident and Jack's part in it. Norman was very reflective about it and said, "That was an outstanding characteristic of Jack's from when I first knew him in college. No matter what the controversy was, he always knew which side he was on. As you know, his lifelong motto has been 'Often in error, never in doubt.'" I knew that well.

Somehow I feel this is an aspect of spirit. People with spirit are not likely to be fence sitters.

I could, of course, find many examples in my experience where I feel spirit was manifested; those with different experience would probably cite examples that are quite different from mine. The important consideration here is not whose conclusions about spirit are valid and whose are not, but to recognize spirit as an essential ingredient of leadership, and that it moves different people in different directions, depending on their strengths and *values*.

Spirit in a leader is the quality that leads him or her into risk and venture; this is communicated to the timid and the less venturesome, who are energized to follow. Spirit directs the leader when the going is rough, uncertain, or hazardous and gives strength and assurance to the less hardy. Spirit sustains the leader in long, depressing periods when things are not going well. Spirit armors the leader for the stress of crisis and the unexpected. Spirit is an aspect of inner strength.

From my limited view of things, folks in the full spectrum of belief and nonbelief, from atheists and humanists to the most orthodox evangelicals, possess these qualities. I can't see that it makes much difference. But neither am I assured that anywhere in this spectrum is there positive encouragement for the growth of these qualities. Nor am I aware that those I have known who seemed to be effective leaders found churches influential in shaping the values that guided them. Their values, of course, were shaped by the culture, and the presence of churches had an impact on that. But that is not a sufficient influence for churches.

Some people are known as "great spirits" because they exude the stuff. I venture the opinion that if churches are to have a formative influence on spirit among their parishioners, pastors should be great spirits. If one reads carefully a report on a meeting of Catholic seminaries, they do not have at present students who will exude spirit as priests. More likely (as the report comments), they will continually need the shoring up of somebody else's spirit. Not a good outlook for the future.

And I suspect that if we had a similar opinion on students now enrolled in Protestant seminaries, the judgment would be the same: bad!!! It is not likely to get better until seminaries attract great spirits (or potential great spirits) as students. And this is not likely to happen until great spirits join the faculty and see to it that there is a curriculum that attracts these folks. And that is not likely to happen until the seminary gets a trustee chairperson who gives the place a vision that requires it!

I come back to the Danish folk high school because it is the only explicit *school of the spirit* (and they used that term) that I know about. It had a profound effect on the quality of Danish society. But it would not have happened if Nikolai Grundtvig had not devoted fifty years of his long life to its advocacy. Grundtvig was truly a great spirit.

There is little to learn from the Danish folk high school as a model. Mostly what can be learned from the Danish experience is the following:

- A great spirit as leader can cause things to happen.
- A school of the spirit was then, and probably still is, a practical idea.
- The format of a school of the spirit (whether in a seminary or elsewhere) will need to be attractive to contemporary young people who have the potential to become great spirits.
- There are people in the United States today (as there were in nineteenth-century Denmark) who know how to build attractive schools of the spirit. They need some prophetic leadership, as the builders in nineteenth-century Denmark needed. Nothing has changed except the people. Dispirited people need to be replaced by great spirits. Then things will happen!

How to get a few great spirits into the right places is the problem. How to get a few great spirits as trustee chairpersons of seminaries is the immediate challenge.

Greenleaf wrote this short essay in the mid-1980s. Its contents came in two parts. One piece is in the Andover Newton Greenleaf archives, and the other is in the book draft Greenleaf was working on in the 1980s. Together, these pieces present the "bottom line" of his thinking. As he says here, seeing things whole is the builder of and derivative from the human spirit, which is the "ultimate moving force in all human endeavor."

SEEING THINGS WHOLE

SEEING THINGS WHOLE! This is one of those seminal ideas that, depending on the circumstances, can be either simple or complex. I was first alerted to this idea when I was twenty-five and started to read E. B. White. Through the ensuing fifty-seven years of reading and rereading Mr. White, the significance of seeing things whole has grown to impressive proportions in my view of affairs. Some time was required to grasp it, but when I got it, it was a profound idea. I have not received answers to any of life's dilemmas from reading Mr. White, but through the years I have been constantly aware that if I will but know where I am (and where I, and others with similar dilemmas, have been), and if my direction is right (well thought out and uncluttered with zany ideas), I will always know better what to do now.

I am not aware that in literature or elsewhere the significance of seeing things whole has been adequately developed, except in Matthew Arnold's sonnet, "To a Friend," someone "who saw life steadily and saw it whole" (Allott, 1979). I am not aware that in the course of my formal education I heard anything about this idea. But with the perspective I got in my early years, and as I have watched closely my own experiences and observed others in action, I have evolved my own view of the central position of seeing things whole in human affairs of all sorts. And as I have reflected on the human spirit as the "bottom line," the ultimate moving force in all human endeavor, I have come to regard the gift of seeing things whole as both a builder of, and derivative from, that spirit. People who have a strong charge of spirit are more likely to see things whole. The practice of seeing things whole tends to nurture the human spirit, both in oneself and in others who are closely related to one's effort. I see spirit and seeing things whole as separate but interacting qualities.

Let me give some examples.

My father was sustained by great spirit and had the habit, in any situation, of looking first to see things whole. He was a skilled machinist who had the ability to take drawings and make a whole machine. He had a special skill in building inventor's models. He also had the reputation in our town as an expert diagnostician of ailing stationary steam engines, which in the early years of the century powered the machines in factories. Occasionally on a Sunday, he would be asked to inspect someone's ailing engine. I recall two occasions when I accompanied him on these missions.

The first was a paper mill that made heavy brown craft paper. This big, long mill produced paper in large, wide rolls. The mill was powered by an enormous engine. Its flywheel (as I recall it) was about fifteen feet in diameter and the shaft a foot through. The problem with this engine was that when it started or stopped, it vibrated heavily and really shook up the place. Once carrying its load, it ran fine.

I recall Father just standing there looking at the engine and saying "start 'er up" or "shut 'er down," not listening to the chatter of the folks who were trying to tell him all of the analytical approaches they had taken to try to solve this problem. After about five minutes of watching intently as this engine was started and stopped, he asked for a sledge hammer. When this was brought, he crawled in beside this big flywheel and gave a few sharp cracks to the keys that locked the wheel to its shaft. He crawled out and asked them to start 'er up—and she purred. All that was wrong was that these keys had worked loose so that whenever the engine started or stopped, that big flywheel shifted a little bit on its shaft and really shook up the place.

On another Sunday, Father was called to a dairy that had a new steam pump with an engine problem. This pump had a small engine that had come from the factory in a crate and had been connected to the live steam by a local plumber. When the steam was turned on, the engine made no response at all—a curious reaction for a steam engine that would be expected to make some movement, even if it did not work well.

I remember Father just standing there and looking at that engine for several minutes and, again, not listening to the chatter of the operators of the dairy. Finally, he said, "Unless somebody has invented an engine the likes of which I have never seen, this is the first steam engine I ever saw that had a bigger intake than it had exhaust." All that was wrong was that they were putting the live steam into the wrong end of the engine. ["My Life with Father," the Greenleaf Center, 1988, out of print, p. 8]

The above are examples of visually seeing things whole. Some fail to do this when it would be helpful, because they have not disciplined themselves to be quiet and undistracted so they can intently look and reflect on what they see. If seeing is taken in the wider sense of total perception—awareness of the whole of what is to be experienced, as I learned as a young adult reading E. B. White—is the process basically any different from examples I have given of visual seeing? I suspect that it is not.

Let me give an example of seeing things whole in the wider sense of total perception. My boss in my early years at AT&T saw things whole. He saw an immediate question as a larger social issue in which a long-term trend was clear. His advice during the 1935 dispute over the National Labor Relations Act was a prime example of his seeing things whole. [See the complete account in "Critical Thought and Seminary Leadership."—Eds.]

In the 1960s I had considerable involvement with colleges and universities during the period of student unrest. This brought me into a close relationship with radical students, whom I concluded were not all irrational. When measured against the opportunities they had to help these students mature into strong responsible people, colleges and universities of that period seemed not to have served them well. I gather that the influence of higher education today in this regard is pathetically meager. Because of a poverty of both spirit and vision among faculty, administrators, and trustees, not much seems to have been learned from those trying times of the sixties.

One of my most interesting experiences of that period was at my alma mater, Carleton College. In the fall of 1969, just before the opening of school, the college chaplain, Prof. David Maitland, convened a two-week seminar of student leaders and a few faculty to talk about the problems of operating the college in those difficult times. I spent two days with them as a resource person.

The part that stands out in my memory now is that I read them E. B. White's essay "The Second Tree from the Corner." It describes a man named Trexler in a routine session with his psychiatrist. This session dealt with Trexler's fears, and a question the doctor repeatedly pressed: "What do you want?" In the course of the session Trexler turned the question on the doctor: "What do *you* want?" And the doctor, caught short, stammers, "I want a new wing on my house on Long Island."

Before reading the essay, I reminded the group that Mr. White had just turned seventy. In the course of an interview with a *New York Times* reporter who visited him on that occasion at his home in Maine, White observed that he was born scared, and that he was still scared. I asked the group to bear this in mind as I read the essay because I felt that it might be somewhat autobiographical.

When I finished reading, I said that I believed White's literary strategy seemed somewhat the same as the one Camus had in writing *The Stranger*. Camus takes one hundred pages to tell

the story of a relationship, a murder, and the trial and sentenc-
ing to death of the murderer. It seemed to me that this story
was told to set the stage for a conversation between a priest and
the murderer on the eve of his execution. White, with much
greater economy of language than Camus, told his story in five
pages to set the stage for two paragraphs at the end in which
Trexler, as he walks down the street from the doctor's office,
muses on the question, "What do you want?" I then reread
those two paragraphs.

It was an evening of clearing weather, the Park showing
green and desirable in the distance, the last daylight apply-
ing a high lacquer to the brick and brownstone walls and
giving the street scene a luminous and intoxicating splen-
dor. Trexler meditated, as he walked, on what he wanted.
"What do you want?" he heard again. Trexler knew what
he wanted and what, in general, all men wanted; and he
was glad, in a way, that it was both inexpressible and unat-
tainable, and that it wasn't a wing. He was satisfied to remember that it was deep, formless, enduring, and
impossible of fulfillment, and that it made men sick, and
that when you sauntered along Third Avenue and looked
through the doorways into the dim saloons, you could
sometimes pick out from the unregenerate ranks the ones
who had not forgotten, gazing steadily into the bottoms of
the glasses on the long chance that they could get another
little peek at it. Trexler found himself renewed by the re-
membrance that what he wanted was at once great and mi-
croscopic, and that although it borrowed from the nature
of large deeds and of youthful love and of old songs and
early intimations, it was not any one of these things, and
that it had not been isolated or pinned down, and that a
man who attempted to define it in the privacy of a doctor's
office would fall flat on his face.

Trexler felt invigorated. Suddenly his sickness seemed
health, his dizziness stability. A small tree, rising between

him and the light, stood there saturated with the evening, each gilt-edged leaf perfectly drunk with excellence and delicacy. Trexler's spine registered an ever so slight tremor as it picked up this natural disturbance in the lovely scene. "I want the second tree from the corner, just as it stands," he said, answering an imaginary question from an imaginary physician. And he felt a slow pride in realizing that what he wanted none could bestow, and what he had none could take away. He felt content to be sick, unembarrassed at being afraid; and in the jungle of his fear he glimpsed (as he had so often glimpsed them before) the flashy tail feathers of the bird courage. [White, 1984, pp. 102–103]

I have noted that seeing things whole and spirit are interacting qualities, each nourishing the other. Confidence to act on anything in the world of affairs is bolstered by the assurance that one sees the situation whole. Willingness to follow the leadership of another rests somewhat on the belief that the other person sees things whole and is likely to be dependable. The quality of seeing things whole is to me an element of faith as trust—trust in oneself, trust in others, and trust in a doctrinal position.

Robert Greenleaf wrote this short essay in the mid-1980s. It offers his opinions on people he regarded as great spirits and complements the previous, more abstract, pieces on the human spirit.

IMAGES OF GREAT SPIRITS

THE MOST SERIOUS THREAT ever in the history of our precarious democracy came, I believe, in the Joe McCarthy period of the 1950s. This was part of the aftershock of World War II. We had a similar threat after World War I, but it was not so serious. The first war was not as disruptive to us as the second.

Sen. Joseph McCarthy of Wisconsin was a bright and articulate, but demonic and destructive, man. He had become chairperson of the U.S. Senate Committee on Security, a powerful spot. His witch-hunting investigative tactics were mean and brutal; they destroyed some good people. He had the country in his terrible grip because a large number of our citizens, perhaps thinking of themselves as patriotic, supported him and seemed to approve of his aims and tactics. In the face of this massive support the majority of the Senators (who were of his party) seemed either to approve or were too timid and impotent to challenge him. His spell was broken by the widely televised hearings investigating security risks in the U.S. Army, represented at the hearings by a great lawyer, Joseph Welch.

A dramatic moment came in those hearings after McCarthy had charged that a member of Welch's law firm was pro-Communist. This brought a comment from Welch that was sharply recorded on television. "Up to this moment," he said, with tears in his eyes, "I think I never really gauged your cruelty or your recklessness. Have you no sense of decency, sir, at long last?"

Joseph Welch was an eloquent man. There was more to his statement at that point, and much more followed in the Army hearings. But I believe that that one incident touched enough people to turn the tide. It was widely replayed in that day on prime-time television.

This vivid portrayal of McCarthy at his worst, and of Welch's dramatic challenge, seemed to connect large numbers of people with a deep fragment of their heritage. For a brief moment, many Americans had a sense of history; from that point McCarthy's influence went downhill. He died a couple of years later, almost forgotten.

I am exceedingly grateful for the U.S. Constitution and the court system, which lawyers cooperate to maintain, and which produce an occasional Joseph Welch. Something goes on in the legal system that connects human experience with history, something that seems not to happen on a sufficient scale in other callings, except perhaps in the military.

Another towering figure of the McCarthy era was Sen. Ralph Flanders of Vermont, a businessman by profession, who was the first senator to challenge McCarthy and led the fight that brought the Senate's ultimate censure of him. It was my privilege to meet Senator Flanders in his old age and to have the opportunity to thank him for his yeoman service. And I am grateful to the vocation of business that produces an occasional Ralph Flanders.

My reflections on this disturbing period suggest that the veneer of our civilization is quite thin and that, in critical periods, what we do have is sustained by manifestations of the human spirit in stalwarts like Joseph Welch and Ralph Flanders. These stalwarts in high places, plus legions of lesser-known people, meet the civilization-destroying crises that emerge everyday with imagination, courage, and force. Their actions are supported by a sense of history, a vital connection with the long struggle from barbarism to what occasionally, if fleetingly, comes through as a great civilization.

The McCarthy period of the 1950s was scary, not so much because McCarthy himself was scary; his kind shows up in every generation. But the support of such large numbers at that time, enough to paralyze a timid government, was the real threat to our democracy. For the nation, it was a close call, perhaps our closest.

I think of Joseph Welch and Ralph Flanders as great spirits I have seen in action, in high places, in my time. I have known several who have not been conspicuous as public figures, but who were just as great.

When I think of the human spirit, these vivid images of greatness come to mind. My hope for the future is that we will have more of these people to cope with the stifling, destructive influences that seem ever present, and who will work hard on the civilization-building influences that are urgently needed and for which there are abundant opportunities. I also hope that what is written here will stir some latent servants into action as nurturers of the human spirit.

I am, however, deeply dismayed that neither business nor law, nor any other calling, produces nearly as many people with this spirit in their mature years as I believe are latent in every generation of young people.

"Deeply dismayed" correctly describes my feeling because the Danes demonstrated over one hundred years ago that it is possible to nurture the spirit of young people so that, when they reach their mature years, enough determined leaders will emerge to reconstruct a faltering society and to sustain a good one. I see our contemporary American society as faltering.

This essay on Pope John XXIII was written on October 17, 1986, for the book Greenleaf was writing in the last years of his life. Most of Greenleaf's impressions and information for this piece came from his reading of *John XXIII: Pope of the Council,* by Peter Hebblethwaite.

POPE JOHN XXIII:
NURTURER OF SPIRITS

THE LIFE AND WORK of Pope John XXIII continues to grow as a source of spiritual insight for the world as doubts about the impact of Vatican II among conservative elements of his church are surfacing with greater frequency. Those conservative folk in the church will be contending with the consequences of that historic event for as long as any of us are around. But the new breath of spirit that John bequeathed to the world stands apart from and above the dilemma of those Catholics who do not resonate to John's vision and who want the church to remain in the mold that John believed had no future.

As a non-Catholic, I regularly read a local Catholic diocesan weekly newspaper that carried good reports on the larger issues in the church. It seems clear that after several years, many thinking Catholics, both lay and cleric, have a firm grip on the legacy of Pope John XXIII that no subsequent papal edict is likely to disturb. It is for the John-related members of the church and non-Catholics of like mind to savor together the memory of John the person, whose spirit was sustained through many years of adversity. That spirit supported him as he became the disciplined, historically rooted seeker that his life so beautifully modeled—and that we who survive him have the option to emulate.

Not by might, nor by power, but by my Spirit, saith the Lord of hosts. (Zechariah 4:6)

The day that John died (June 3, 1963), I was teaching a class of young business executives at the Sloan School of Management at Massachusetts Institute of Technology. Those hard driving, ambitious young executives eagerly responded to my suggestion that we devote that class period to a discussion of what could be learned from the great man's life that would be useful to anybody who was trying to lead anything. It was a profoundly moving session. I recall somebody quoting a press report of a conversation with John when death was imminent. John was asked what he thought about death, and he replied, "Any day is a good day to be born. Any day is a good day to die." This may be part of the great mythology, but it is true to the image I have of John.

As a student of organization, I have long had an interest in the Roman Catholic church as the largest, most influential nongovernmental institution in the world. The most distinctive features of its central organization are its titular leader, the pope, who is elected for life by a two-thirds majority plus one of the assembled cardinals, and the quality and tenacity of what is, in effect, its governing bureaucracy, the Curia. The Curia gives the church continuity and stability through its day-to-day governance, while the pope stands as its spokesman and symbolic head and has the opportunity to give leadership that in turn gives the institution responsiveness to changing conditions. It is clearly a design for a long life. Between the two of them, they have held together, over many centuries, a widely dispersed assemblage of disparate parts comprising many ethnic and national constituencies, each of which seems to embrace the whole range from liberal to conservative. They occasionally have lost a part, as in the Protestant Reformation and the split-off of the Eastern church. But they have never lost hope that they will get those departed brethren back into the fold. Their hope is that the common bond of Christian faith will do it.

To an outsider looking in, the prime concern of these two central agencies seems to be to hold this vast array together with a common faith, the articles of which are strictly and rigidly enforced, while making prudent adaptations to keep it viable and growing in numbers and influence through wars, revolutions, and kaleidoscopic change. As an outsider I would say they have been quite successful. Just when they seem stuck in a rut and doomed to decline, they produce a great leader who lifts them out of the rut and starts them on their way again. Such a man was John XXIII, pope from 1958 to 1963.

One of the titles of the pope is the Servant of the Servants of God. The life of John XXIII, who reigned as pope from age seventy-seven to eighty-one and one-half, is to me one of the best examples of all time of the servant as the nurturer of the human spirit. He is also a great example of John Milton's dictum that "they also serve who only stand and wait." Pope John waited a long time for his great opportunity. He not only kept spirit alive and growing through long and difficult years that would have been devastating to most spirits, but he managed to have it blossom at age seventy-seven, when most of us have signed off. And with his spirit, vision, and astute leadership, he lifted the spirits of many millions and left an irreversible imprint on the Catholic church. His model gives courage to people everywhere who are contending with bureaucratic inertia. If one has the ability, the stamina, and the spirit, nothing is unchangeable.

Angelo Giuseppe Roncalli was born in 1881 in the little village of Sotto il Monte, in northern Italy, near Bergamo. He was the fourth (and first son) of thirteen children of poor sharecropper farmers who were devout Catholics. His ancestors had lived in this village for five hundred years. His was truly a peasant boyhood in this very large, very poor family. There was sort of an extended family in which a bachelor uncle was the senior male and "in charge." Uncle Zaverio took Angelo to the church, bundled in a blanket, to be baptized on the wintry day of his birth. He gave Angelo most of the parental care he received as a child.

The priest of the village was Don Francesco Rebuzzini, a dedicated and cultivated man who was to become Angelo's first model. On the wall of Father Rebuzzini's study was a motto that found its way into Angelo's journal (*Journal of a Soul . . .*, 1980, p. 440, as cited in Hebblethwaite, 1984, p. 14):

> Peace within the cell; fierce warfare without.
> Hear all; believe a few; honor all.
> Do not believe everything you hear;
> Do not judge everything you see;
> Do not do everything you can;
> Do not give everything you have;
> Do not say everything you know.
> Pray, read, withdraw, be silent, be at peace.

Angelo's biographer notes that it was the perfect formula for a Vatican diplomat, a role in which he spent much of his life.

After a few misadventures in getting educated (third grade was the height of usual achievement in Sotto il Monte at that time), Don Rebuzzini, who recognized Angelo as an exceptional youngster and a potential priest, tutored him from age ten to prepare him to enter junior seminary at twelve in nearby Bergamo. There Angelo quickly became committed to the moral life and chose "the better of the best," according to the Ignatian formula. There he also worked out his own rules for his life, rules that stayed with him. He also became a faithful journal keeper.

Angelo was sixteen when his revered Don Rebuzzini died in his presence. This humble priest remained Angelo's model for life and probably was responsible for his always regarding himself as a pastor and not an administrator or a diplomat. This pastoral image of himself remained with Angelo right through to the end of his papacy.

Angelo's seminary studies were interrupted by a year of compulsory military training that exposed him for the first time to the raw edges of life. He emerged a sergeant. This was an important chapter in Angelo's maturing experience.

In 1900, at age nineteen, Angelo passed an examination for admittance to seminary in Rome, where he had the opportunity to develop his research interests, observe the pope, and be in close contact with ceremonial life—which he greatly enjoyed. Important in his Rome seminary experience was his work under Monsignor (later "grand inquisitor") Umberto Benigni, professor of church history. Angelo's lifelong interest in history, and his own extensive historical researches, probably date from that influence.

In Rome he became interested in the Mary Immaculate Club, of which Monsignor Radini Tedeschi was chaplain. In 1905 Radini Tedeschi became bishop of Bergamo and Angelo, who was now a priest at age twenty-four, was made his secretary. He served for ten years, later writing Radini Tedeschi's biography, *My Bishop*.

These ten years were a crucial developmental period. Bishop Radini Tedeschi "was authoritarian and something of a martinet" (Hebblethwaite, 1984, p. 49), in sharp contrast to the gentle style of (then Don) Roncalli. But the new bishop knew what he wanted and insisted on discipline. Don Roncalli wrote of him in his biography, "He did not concentrate on carrying out reform so much as on maintaining the glorious traditions of his diocese, and interpreting them *in harmony with the new conditions and needs of the times*" (Hebblethwaite citing Roncalli, *My Bishop*, p. 48). This was Don Roncalli's own ambition, which he expressed in the same language when he became pope fifty years later. Bishop Radini Tedeschi's first pastoral letter on Catholic action in the social sphere (which the young priest no doubt had a hand in writing) stated principles Don Roncalli held for the rest of his life. It was a remarkable formative period for a person of such high potential.

At age twenty-five, in addition to his duties as secretary, Don Roncalli was made professor of church history at Bergamo Seminary. In browsing an old library in Milan, he came upon thirty-nine volumes on St. Charles Borromeo (1538–1584), archbishop of Bergamo, founder of Bergamo Seminary, and one of the great reformers of the church. The study of St. Charles was to become a major life mission. In his coronation address as Pope John XXIII, he said of St. Charles, "The Lord's church has had its moments of stagnation and revival. In one such period of revival Providence reserved for St. Charles Borromeo the lofty task of restoring ecclesiastical order. The part he played in implementing the Council of Trent (1545–1563), and the example he gave in Milan and other dioceses of Italy, earned him the glorious title of "teacher of bishops. . . ." (Hebblethwaite, 1984, p. 296). He may have been announcing that he intended to carry on the reform work of St. Charles. A line of thought that was begun at age twenty-five and sustained throughout his life may have been the vital force that enabled John XXIII to launch, at age seventy-seven, the church's greatest reform movement in nearly five hundred years.

Bishop Radini Tedeschi died in 1914. By 1915 there was mobilization for World War I. Roncalli was called up as a hospital orderly, in effect a chaplain, and spent the wartime period in Bergamo. In 1918 he was assigned by the bishop to be warden of a student hostel at the seminary in Bergamo. In 1919 he was appointed the seminary's spiritual director, a position of great trust. In September 1920 he gave his most important speech to that date at the National Eucharistic Congress in Bergamo, establishing himself as a forceful orator. This brought an invitation from Cardinal William van Rossum to become national director of propagation of the faith in a department of the Curia.

At this time, the Fascist movement was growing and Benito Mussolini came into power as dictator. Roncalli's temperament was judged not to find favor in this climate. He was made a bishop and dispatched as apostolic visitor (later upgraded to apostolic delegate) to Bulgaria, where there were not many Catholics. He stayed there ten years, until he was shifted to Turkey, where he served another ten years. This was a total of twenty years virtually in the wilderness in the affairs of the church. However, during World War II, his presence in Turkey put him in one of the few neutral spots in the Western world, where his great love for, and acceptance of, all people flowered. He was friendly with diplomats on both sides and is credited with negotiating the saving of many Jewish lives. During a good portion of these twenty years in exile, he was at odds with his "bosses" in the Curia, but he was obedient. He had learned obedience in his ten years as secretary to Bishop Radini Tedeschi, who also was in trouble with the Curia and was obedient. His friendliness and his love for everybody earned him a reputation among the conservatives in the Curia as being naïve.

When France began to be liberated near the close of the war, Charles de Gaulle returned and immediately drew a bead on the nuncio, whom he regarded as a collaborator with the Nazis. Rome at first demurred but finally acceded; it was not accustomed to having nuncios thrown out of Catholic countries. This was quite a problem for Rome. Whom should they send to France, the church's top diplomatic post, who would get along with this crazy man de Gaulle? Over the unanimous objection of the Curia, Pope Pius XII picked Bishop Roncalli, whose loving, accepting ways were very influential in that troubled period. He continued to be at odds with the conservative Curia and had trouble living with some of the pope's actions. But he was obedient; on one occasion when he knew that a ukase with which he disagreed was coming his way, he disappeared on a trip, leaving his assistants to carry it out. But the pope apparently appreciated what he did in France during a very difficult period because in 1953 he made Bishop Roncalli a cardinal and installed him as patriarch of Venice, where he fulfilled his longfelt wish to be a pastor, not just an administrator or a diplomat. On October 28, 1958, the assembled cardinals elected him pope on the eleventh ballot.

The procedure of the conclave of cardinals is that they remain in session until two-thirds plus one of them select a pope. There was strong conservative opposition to Roncalli. But he had enough support that the conservatives couldn't elect their man. In the minds of some of the conservatives who ultimately voted for him, at age seventy-seven Roncalli was regarded as one who would be a caretaker pope and therefore not dangerous. They were wrong.

The name of John XXIII was chosen by Roncalli. He explained his choice to the assembled cardinals as a wish to renew the exhortation of the Apostle John: "My children, love one another. Love one another because this is the greatest commandment of the Lord. Venerable brethren, may God in his mercy grant that we, bearing the name of John, may with the help of divine grace have his holiness of life and strength of soul, even unto the shedding of blood, if God so wills." John's biographer comments, "The message was love, the means sacrifice" (Hebblethwaite, 1984, p. 287).

As soon as John was settled into his new role, he announced the convening of an Ecumenical Council, the first in one hundred years. It was called Vatican II because it was regarded as an extension of Vatican I of 1870. Vatican I was largely concerned with dogma; it was there that papal infallibility was proclaimed. Vatican II focused on liturgy and on the relationship of the Roman church to other Christian churches and to the world.

One of John's first official acts, and a momentous one it turned out, was to make a cardinal of his old friend Bishop Giovanni Battista Montini of Milan (who had been banished from the Curia for being too liberal). By doing this, John put him in the running for being the next pope, Paul VI.

Bringing off the Council, of which John only lived to see the first of four sessions, was not easy. The Curia, the powerful and archconservative bureaucracy, was solidly against it and used every tactic they could to prevent or delay it. At one point, when the Curia made a strong case for delaying the start of it, John responded by advancing the date a few months. He knew he didn't have much time. John was truly a conservative; he wanted to save and strengthen the church. But he was not the kind of conservative who believed that nothing should ever change. That, he believed, was the path to sure decline.

The task of preparing the working papers for the Council was assigned to the conservative Curia. That reassured the conservative wing of the church; the "no change in anything" element was numerous and powerful. But then he made what may have been the most significant appointment of his pontificate, naming Cardinal Augustin Bea as head of the Secretariat for Christian Unity, to work independently of the Curia in preparing for the Council. Cardinal Bea, a venerable Jesuit, a few months older than John, had been confessor to John's predecessor, Pope Pius XII, and had drafted some of his encyclicals. He was one of the great respected men of the church; he accepted John's hope that this Council would prepare the way for Christian unity.

John proved to be a master strategist; he first announced, and stoutly defended it during the first session, that the assembled bishops would have the final voice in the conclusions of the Council. Then in his opening charge to the Council he practically assured that they would throw out almost all of the Curia's preparatory papers. And in the course of the intense struggle in that first session he delivered two of the church's greatest encyclicals: *Mater et Magistra* (Christianity and Social Progress) and *Pacem in Terris* (Peace on Earth), the latter addressed to "all men of good will." This was the only papal encyclical ever to be set to music (by Darius Milhaud).

A commentator noted that "the encyclical marked the end of the Catholic ghetto, of that period of history when Catholics had cut themselves off from the world as a besieged fortress. With *Pacem in Terris* and the Vatican Council, Catholicism was finally emerging into full participation in the human community. It was a fitting climax to Pope John's reign, offering a standard of human rights and world peace against which to measure the pastoral effectiveness of the changes initiated by the Council" (O'Brien and Shannon, 1977, p. 123).

Pope John XXIII is, to me, one of the greatest examples of all time of the servant as the nurturer of the human spirit—both his own spirit and the spirits of millions who know about him.

As I read about him, several qualities seemed to support his role as nurturer of the human spirit.

John had great love for people, for all people—no exceptions. This was consistent, from his earliest statements, with what he said to the assembled cardinals when they elected him pope, with his opening address to the Council, and with *Pacem in Terris*. He loved those with whom he strongly disagreed. And these people responded to his love. He accepted the criticism that he was naïve, too idealistic. His nurturing power, sustaining his own spirit and igniting the spirits of millions, was that he radiated this love and talked freely about it. It was too deep in him to be shaken by slights and criticism. He summed it up in addressing seminary students: "It is one thing to say it or believe it, and quite another to be holy." Some of the things he said in the mouths of others might have seemed trite. But with him they simply revealed what he was, deep down inside.

John was humble. Walking in the Vatican gardens with his secretary after he had been pope for one month, he said, "A month has gone by and everything has happened with great naturalness. . . . I feel in my heart the problems of the whole world. But my soul is at peace. If a commission of cardinals came to tell me that, all things considered, I should return to Venice, it would not cost me anything to retire" (Capovilla, 1978, p. 252, as cited in Hebblethwaite, 1984, p. 302).

"I'm not afraid of opposition," he said, "and I do not refuse suffering. I think of myself as the last of all, but I have in mind a program of work and I'm not fussing about it any more. In fact, I am pretty well decided" (p. 302). In another conversation with his secretary he observed, "The Holy Spirit doesn't help the pope. I'm simply his helper. He did everything" (p. 312). John's humility seems rooted in the feeling that he was but a channel for inspiration.

John had a sense of history. He was a historian and taught church history in seminary. And he was a reader and researcher of history all of his life. While he was nuncio in France, he was asked whether he read Camus and Sartre. He said no, he was too busy. But he was not too busy to read French history; he was thoroughly steeped in it. A sense of history is something different from a mere knowledge of it. John was a true conservative, but his sense of history set him apart from other conservatives who were simply anchored in the past.

John was also a master strategist. He had two main aims in what he knew would be a short tenure as pope. The two were contradictory. He wanted to preserve and strengthen the church while keeping all of its disparate parts firmly linked to the whole; and he wanted to reform the church in fundamental ways. His reform goals would have been easy if he had used his authority and promptly replaced the conservative Curia with people who thought as he did. He didn't do that because he needed the conservative Curia to keep the extensive and powerful conservative wing within the church. He didn't even bring his old friend and collaborator, Cardinal Montini, back into the Curia because he wanted him to be his successor. Cardinal Montini probably remained a stronger candidate for being the next pope and a better helper during the first session of the Council by staying in Milan.

John was dying of cancer during that first session; he died before they had agreed to anything. It remained for Paul VI to see the Council through their agreements in the last three sessions and to hold the church together during the confusing years that followed, as it struggled to adjust to its new view of itself.

The other great strategic decision John made was the role he gave Cardinal Bea, a Jesuit who was very old when appointed. His was a powerful voice, and he was solidly behind John's vision. John stayed out of the struggle during that first session, but he followed it closely on TV. He rarely intervened except to restrain the Curia from dominating it, which they tried hard to do. He had given them their say in writing the planning papers. The decisions were in the hands of the bishops; John was firm on that.

John was a pastor, first and foremost, not an administrator or a diplomat. The care and concern of his boyhood parish priest, Don Francesco Rebuzzini, may have set John's pastoral temperament for life. He never had a chance to be a parish priest, but in everything he did he was the consummate pastor right to the end. He dealt with the Council as if he were their pastor, even though he was dying of cancer at the time.

John had faith, first in the Catholic Christian tradition of which he was a creature. He not only believed it, he lived it. In convening the Council and guiding its first session, he put his faith in the collective process of two thousand bishops from around the world, all of whom were rooted in the same tradition he was. He trusted utterly their collective wisdom and committed himself to putting the seal of his office on what they concluded.

Despite his great, loving feeling and gentle, persuasive ways, John was a tough-fibered man of great courage. At a crucial point, when two members of the Curia simply had to go, he dropped unmistakable hints that they should. But they seemed determined to stay, so John quietly announced his acceptance of their resignations.

His poise and assurance under stress may have come from his ten years as secretary to Bishop Radini Tedeschi of Bergamo. Radini Tedeschi was a tough-minded, decisive, and determined man who had held an important post in the Curia and was thrown out. John's presence at the death of both of his early mentors must have had a profound maturing influence. Cardinal Carlo Andrea Ferrari of Milan became a close mentor for seven years after Radini Tedeschi died. So John had a relationship with a strong mentor until he was past forty.

A different kind of influence might be attributed to St. Charles Borromeo, who lived four hundred years earlier as archbishop of Milan, founded the seminary John entered at twelve, and was the moving spirit in the reforms of the Council of Trent. John, somewhat prophetically in his coronation address as pope, noted St. Charles's great role as a reformer. His lifelong involvement as historian of St. Charles culminated in a significant event during the first session of Vatican II, when he dropped his broadest hint about his openness to reform, especially in the liturgy.

On Nov. 4, 1962, he participated in a celebration of the feast of St. Charles that coincided with the fourth anniversary of John's coronation. Cardinal Montini of Milan, John's old friend, celebrated the mass in the ancient Ambrosian liturgy of Milan. John preached the homily and praised the Ambrosian rite as an example of liturgical diversity; he gave a Latin quote that translated: "Though the creative impulse is one, it produces manifold forms" (Hebblethwaite, 1984, p. 452). Then he spoke of St. Charles, who "contributed to the renewal of church life through the celebration of provincial councils and diocesan synods . . . and this, thanks be to God, gives us hope for the future" (p. 452). So without openly challenging the Curia's hard-line position on uniformity of liturgy, he made a strong case for diversity. His biographer notes that even the "most dullwitted Council" father could not have missed the point. Change was in the air, the conservative Curia to the contrary notwithstanding.

I know of no certain answer to the question of what sustained John's remarkable spirit. No one but a person of great courage would, at age seventy-seven, have called the Council in the first place. Only a tough-minded person would have gambled on entrusting the planning to the ultraconservative Curia, with whom he had been at odds for thirty years. He knew they deeply opposed the idea of a Council and would wreck it if they could. John set out to defeat them by the faith he manifested, at every turn, in the total body of the church as represented by the two thousand bishops, plus faith in his ability to inspire them to great things. I see it as a signal triumph of the human spirit in our century, perhaps in many centuries.

As I read about Pope John XXIII and pondered the significance of his life, I wondered what could be learned from this that helps us in the exploration of how a servant can nurture the human spirit, both in oneself and in others. One can only speculate, and enough of the record has been given that the reader's guess is as good as mine. My guess is that John's first two mentors wielded a powerful influence on both John's own spirit and his capacity to inspire others.

Offered here is a sharing with others who will form their own opinions. What nurtured John's extraordinary spirit? Perhaps if we could ask Monsignor Loris Capovilla, John's secretary both in Venice and as pope, he could give us the best answer. I doubt however, that it is a question that John himself could answer, so elusive are all matters of the human spirit. But on his deathbed, as he spoke to those around him, he gives some clues:

> The secret of my ministry is in that crucifix you see opposite my bed. It's there so I can see it in my first waking moment and before going to sleep. It's there, also, so that I can talk to it during the long evening hours. Look at it, see it as I see it. Those open arms have been the programme of my pontificate; they say that Christ died for all, for all. No one is excluded from love, from his forgiveness.
>
> What did Christ leave to his Church? He left us "*et omnes unum sint*" (that all may be one; John 10:16). I had the great grace to be born into a Christian family, modest and poor but with fear of the Lord. I had the grace to be called by God as a child: I never thought of anything else, I never had any other ambition. Along the way I've met holy priests and good superiors. Oh! Don Francesco Rebuzzini, Monsignor Radini, Cardinal Ferrari . . . all helped me and loved me. I had a lot of encouragement.
>
> For my part, I'm not aware of having offended anyone, but if I have I beg their forgiveness; and if you know anyone who has not been edified by my attitudes or actions, ask them to have compassion on me and to forgive me. In this last hour I feel calm and sure that my Lord, in his mercy, will not reject me. Unworthy though I am, I wanted to serve him, and I've done my best to pay homage to truth, justice, charity, and the *cor mitis et humilis* (meek and humble heart) of the Gospel. My time on earth is drawing

to a close. But Christ lives on and the church continues his work. Souls, souls. [compiled from various sources by Hebblethwaite, 1984, pp. 501–502]

Of the three mentors of John's youth and early manhood, I would surmise that Don Rebuzzini was the greatest formative influence on John. His early pastoral care and teaching breathed meaning into that crucifix, to the end that John's religion was not so much what he believed but rather what he was. It powerfully nurtured in him the same nascent charge of spirit that is in all of us so that it grew and flowered with the help of later mentors and was sustained through a long life of much adversity. It came into full bloom as he carried on the reforming spirit of St. Charles Borromeo, from youthful studies to his last years as Pope John XXIII.

John lived in the light of a sense of history all of his adult life: his own personal history, his church's, and his world's. He always knew from youth to old age who and where he was. He had, as he said, "the great grace to be born into a Christian family." But then he was fortunate enough to have three great mentors "who helped me and loved me. I had a lot of encouragement" (Hebblethwaite, 1984, pp. 501–502). What better nurture of spirit could one have in one's youth and early adulthood than three persons of great spirit who help, love, and encourage?

This piece was written in 1985 as one part of the book Greenleaf was drafting on nurturing the human spirit. This essay, which combines two addenda with the main discussion, presents his belief that change is gradual and must come within the institution.

TALKING AND LISTENING

THE FIRST CHRISTMAS after John XXIII was made pope, he visited a prison and talked with the prisoners. In the course of these conversations a prisoner said to him, "I am a condemned murderer. Is there any hope for me?" John did not answer him; he threw his arms around him and embraced him warmly.

John was thoroughly Catholic in his opposition to atheistic communism. But he loved the Russian people and their leaders, all of them. On his eightieth birthday John received a warm congratulatory message from Nikita Khrushchev. When Khrushchev's son-in-law was in Rome he asked for an audience with the pope. John received him warmly, over the vigorous opposition of the Curia. John talked to everybody in the spirit of love for the person, no matter what they believed or what they had done. Every person was seen as sacred, redeemable.

John Woolman, the eighteenth-century Quaker, was such a person. [See the detailed discussion of Woolman in "Religious Leaders as Seekers and Servants."—Eds.] For thirty years, Woolman spent all the time he could spare from earning his living, traveling afoot or on horseback up and down the East coast talking gently and nonjudgmentally to Quaker slaveholders (who were numerous and affluent), with the aim of persuading them to free their slaves. By 1770 no Quakers held slaves. What if there had been more than one John Woolman carrying on this gentle persuasion for the hundred years prior to the outbreak of the Civil War in 1861?

Both John XXIII and John Woolman were dedicated journal keepers. Their journals amply document their pervasive loving attitude toward all people. Both were accepted as friends by those whose views and practices they unequivocally opposed. And both were powerfully persuasive. Both carried a communicable charge of human spirit that will linger long in its influence. Neither of them erected barriers hindering their talking to people, any people.

I believe that the love that Woolman and Pope John XXIII felt for all people is the essence of spirit. They radiated it. It was in what they said, but it had its own independent force. Their presence communicated it.

Woolman's method stands in sharp contrast to that of others who profess nonviolence but whose tactics are coercive. The flaw in nonviolent coercion is that it sometimes breeds violence and does not foster friendship. Woolman's approach, in which he did much listening, builds friendship and does not leave disruption or violence in its wake.

Listening. I have had substantial involvement with listening. About forty years ago, when I was with AT&T, we made studies confirming that much of the disharmony in the organization was due to bosses not listening to their subordinates. We accepted that some of this was built into the role because those who emerge as managers are likely to be more assertive than most and therefore not likely to be natural good listeners. So we put together a three-day course on listening called "Talking with People"; in the end, we gave it to all eighty thousand managers. This would not be an unusual thing today, but then it attracted a bit of notice.

One of the most interesting anecdotes of my work experience came out of this effort to teach managers to listen. One day I received a phone call from a man who introduced himself as the associate dean of one of the medical schools in New York City. He said he had a problem he wanted to talk about and asked to come and see me. When he did, we discussed a study of doctors in practice in medical consultations. One of the findings of the study was that many doctors did not listen to their patients. They were so busy making measurements and recording results that they missed important clues that would have been useful in their diagnosis, if they had done more listening.

This was judged a serious deficiency, warranting a course on listening in the fourth year of the medical curriculum. The teacher who had been selected for this course turned out to be one who never listened to anybody. The course was cancelled. The dean had heard about the management listening course we used at AT&T and wanted to know how we conducted the course. I said that we didn't talk about listening; we talked more about carrying on a good conversation under difficult conditions. The dean took the course material with him, and I never heard from him again!

In my role as director of management research for AT&T, I kept a close watch on what was going on in other large businesses. This led me to visit Delta Airlines in Atlanta. I was aware that whatever the experiences of other airlines, Delta always made money and had a good labor record.

The significant recollection I have from my visit is their way of talking with their employees. Four times a year a representative of the corporate offices visits every location and meets with employees in groups of twenty-five to talk about the business. The corporate officer talks about how the business looks from Atlanta, and the employees talk about how it looks from their perspectives. A remarkable communication process for a company of that size.

With the models of Woolman and Pope John XXIII before me, I agree with Ralph Waldo Emerson's judgment, in his little-known essay "Works and Days," that "the great meliorator in the world is selfish huckstering trade" (Emerson, vol. VII, 1876, p. 159). Why is selfish huckstering trade effective as a meliorative influence? Because, I believe, traders tend not to be assertively judgmental about the people with whom they trade. They are mostly friendly people. They may have their private views about how others ought to behave or think, but with the people they trade with they choose to talk about matters of mutual interest. They don't try to reform people. They will trade with anybody anywhere; some of them will even trade with the enemy in time of war. They are an important glue that holds the world together.

Selfish huckstering trade as the greatest meliorative force in the world is a tenable generalization because it is difficult to think of any other calling that is as numerous and whose practitioners are so universally in contact around the world—friendly, conversational, nonjudgmental. Few businesspeople are saints, but I suspect that the proportion is as great as among lawyers, doctors, teachers, and preachers.

It has been my privilege to have as a close friend Jack Lowe, Sr., a successful Dallas businessman who was a true saint, as close to Pope John XXIII in temperament as one is likely to find anywhere. When the first suit was brought to integrate the Dallas schools, this fellow convened a group of twenty-one people (seven blacks, seven Hispanics, and seven whites) to talk about what solution would be best for Dallas. He told the Federal judge who would hear the case what he was doing, and the judge said the unanimous decision of the group would be his decision. The group worked and worked, but they couldn't get past twenty in agreement. My friend finally went to the judge and told him that they had failed; they had one among them who wasn't ever going to agree to anything. The judge replied that he would settle for twenty.

Another Dallas businessman told me that at any civic meeting the blacks and the Hispanics always gathered around Jack Lowe, Sr.. because they knew he loved them and understood them.

I am by temperament a gradualist (confirmed by long experience) when it comes to changing institutions. They can be changed by coercion, sometimes quickly, but the long-term result may not be so good when that is done. It works better when institutions heal themselves, rather than having change forced on them. Part of my conviction about the efficacy of trade as a meliorator is that it is gradual; it is a healing from within.

I can imagine my friend Jack as an American businessman in South Africa. He would live and work with the whites as if he were one of them. And he would get to know and be accepted by the blacks as their friend. It would be just as natural for him as was his work in Dallas. And because of his radiant love for all people, the whites would be assured by this. He could become a meliorative force that only a white businessperson is likely to become.

The Jack Lowes of this world are rare. But those with the potential to become what Jack became do exist. The key is what John XXIII acknowledged on his deathbed about the three great mentors that guided his early development: "Don Francesco Rebuzzini, Monsignor Radini, Cardinal Ferrari . . . all helped me and loved me. I had a lot of encouragement" (Hebblethwaite, 1984, p. 502).

To find those with the potential, and to love, help, and encourage them, will take a lot of talking with people. And those whose spirits are so nurtured will need to learn to talk with people, because that is how their meliorative influence will be made potent.

It pleases me to think that when the human spirit is well-nurtured, the nurturer listens . . . and talks only when appropriate.

Greenleaf apparently wrote this short piece to advise young people about the importance of learning early in life to be more humane in relationships with others and to be true to oneself.

BEING WHO YOU ARE

YOU NEED TO BE who you are. Let me give you an example out of my own experience.

A few years ago an acquaintance, from the middle management of another business that I knew intimately, came to my office in an obviously disturbed frame of mind. He was puffing violently on his cigarette as he started an outpouring of pent-up feelings which began with, "I am leading a life of quiet desperation." He went on for an uninterrupted hour of bitter complaint about his situation in his company: unappreciated, unrecognized, little freedom to manage, the victim of other people's mistakes. You are no doubt familiar with his story. As I listened I recalled what I knew of his situation, and I was sure that if I could get the honest views of this man's subordinates, they would say the same for their lot.

So when he finally finished his sad story, I said to him as gently as I could, "Did it ever occur to you that if you were to make a greater effort to create a climate for your subordinates where they would experience less frustration than you do, you might feel better about your own lot? Remember that great line from the prayer of St. Francis, 'For it is in giving that we receive'?"

The choice any of us can make, no matter how intolerable our own lot, is to use what little freedom and resources we possess to make the lives of those around us more significant and rewarding. The choice to make life more tolerable for others, in all of our relationships, is open to all of us. Too often, by reacting to the treatment we receive, rather than choosing how we will act when the initiative is ours, we compound someone else's error rather than creating our own good.

Why is it that human beings have such difficulty being human in terms of taking the initiative to make life more tolerable for others in all relationships? Having had some difficulty with this myself, I have a theory to suggest: we do not accept our lives early enough, and we do not enter the responsibilities of early adulthood with a firm enough grasp of what is really important to us. I am leery of conversions, of people who make radical changes in middle life. Youth is the time for conversions.

One of my early bosses in business was a rough, uncut-diamond sort of fellow with limited education but a lot of native wisdom. I forget the occasion, but one day he delivered this opinion. "If a fellow is an S.O.B.," he said, "if that's what he really is, deep down inside, then he had better go ahead and be one. Because if he tries to be something else, he will wind up as both a hypocrite and an S.O.B., and that's worse." I guess the reason I remember this is that along the way I worked for such a fellow, a real S.O.B. with a nice, smooth, human-relations veneer. And it was worse. The human-relations veneer just confused the signals and made life harder. He was what he was and those of us who worked for him had to deal with him as he was. But life would have been simpler, and no less pleasant, if the veneer had not been there.

I am not arguing that if a person has a nasty disposition and lacks ordinary human decency, he or she ought not to adopt a more meliorative front in most human relationships. It might just keep him or her out of jail. Neither am I holding that there are no ways for middle-aged people to change their basic outlooks. But in the fast pace of the business world such a converted person may not be as effective. It might be better to be unsuccessful and pleasant. But if success is sought, a successful person had better not change style in midlife. Get the right style while you are young. Don't assume you can be an S.O.B. until you make your first million and then convert yourself into a saint.

PART THREE

SEMINARIES, CHURCHES, AND FOUNDATIONS

PARTNERS IN SPIRIT

My primary interest now . . . is in the quality of our society, which I judge now to be far below what it could be. I believe that the shortfall could be corrected if churches and seminaries would reach for the best they can achieve.

Robert K. Greenleaf
"My Work with Churches"

Greenleaf refers to this fable at the conclusion of *The Servant as Religious Leader.* Familiar themes focusing on the roles seminaries and foundations should play in developing a theology of institutions appear in this "fictional" piece, which was written in 1983.

FABLE

THE YEAR IS 2000 A.D. A group of men and women ranging in age from forty-five to sixty-five who have shared a unique, intensive experience for the past fifteen years have met to review and evaluate that experience.

It all began with a meeting in the early 1980s of six representatives of foundations that shared an interest in work in the field of religion. They concluded that, with the exception of the evangelical churches, all the rest of the churches were declining in influence, and some were declining in members as well. Most of them seemed not to have in them, or have available from denominational bodies or seminaries, the self-regenerating capacity to rebuild their influence or sustain their members. These foundation representatives concluded that while some of these churches and church-related institutions eagerly sought grants of money, just giving them money really would not help them. Most of them seemed to want for ideas and religious leaders who would put power behind those ideas.

The basic deficiency seemed to be that churches were not adequately serving contemporary society. They were not healing or immunizing society from widespread alienation; and they were not preparing and supporting people as they build and maintain serving institutions in business, government, education, health, and social service. The question discussed at length was whether there was anything foundations could do that would help churches become more serving.

In the course of this discussion they noted that the machinery to rebuild ours into a healthier and more caring society was in place: seminaries, churches, individuals, operating institutions. But this machinery was not functioning well.

Why is this machinery not functioning, they asked? The answer was obvious, they concluded quickly. Neither the needed ideas nor the impetus to develop religious leaders was forthcoming from seminaries, the chief intellectual and prophetic resource for churches. Unless seminaries undertook this leadership, not much more than they were then doing could be expected from churches. Further, the foundation representatives accepted that the influence of foundation money, the major resource that foundations have, was not sufficient to induce seminaries to provide the intellectual and prophetic support that churches needed. There was some discussion of the possibility of building new institutions with a new mission to give leadership to churches, but it was agreed that for various reasons this was neither feasible nor desirable. The conclusion that finally emerged as the only viable initiative was to mount a new, sustained, long-range program of persuasion directed at existing seminaries of all faiths, with the hope that over time some of them would produce programs of greater service to churches and to society.

It was agreed that a new entity would be set up, supported by interested foundations and other donors, to oversee this new program of persuasion. The inspiration for this venture in persuasion was taken from the example of John Woolman, the eighteenth-century American Quaker whose persistent persuasion of Quaker slaveholders to free their slaves was an important influence in making the Society of Friends to become the first religious body in the United States to condemn slavery and forbid its practice among its members. [See "Religious Leaders as Seekers and Servants."—Eds.] In his journal, Woolman records his efforts of thirty years, while earning a modest living and supporting a small family, to free slaves—work done without any compensation. By prudent management of his life he was able to sustain himself in this work both economically and spiritually. He had the dedication and self-assurance to press forward with his mission over a long period, and he had the inventiveness and resilience to absorb rebuffs and keep coming back to his mission with new confidence. He was a strong person.

The new entity that the foundation representatives set up was called the John Woolman Institute of Persuasion.

The first work of the new institute was to publish a brochure bearing the imprimatur of the six foundations and three major church groups. It described briefly Woolman's life and work, and then it stated that there was a critical problem in the church world that offered an unusual opportunity for a few strong, assured, resourceful people between the ages of thirty and fifty. They should be well-enough established in their careers that they could commit their free time without compensation (expenses to be reimbursed) for several years for an important and difficult mission of persuasion. The problem to be dealt with was not described, in order not to undermine any church institution. The brochure was given wide circulation—an estimated one million adults saw it—and responses were invited from those who might be interested.

About one thousand responses were received. Each respondent was sent a comprehensive questionnaire; eight hundred were returned. From the data supplied, the active list was reduced to six hundred. Qualified persons then visited the six hundred and conducted depth interviews. In these visits, the project was described as persuading and assisting seminaries, in addition to their usual programs, to become powerful centers for religious leadership that would support churches seeking to become greater influences on the quality of society. Those eliminated on the basis of interview findings reduced the list to three hundred. These people were invited to a one-week assessment center conducted by the institute, which paid for the assessment, hospitality, and transportation.

Two hundred seventy-five people came in groups of twelve to a series of regional assessment centers. A professional staff of six met each group in turn and spent the week in a program of individual and group tests, work projects involving some stress, closely watched social events, and individual and group interviews. The staff of six then conferred and pooled their judgments to make final decisions that reduced the number to sixty (hereafter called "members"). By the end of the assessment and the first meeting of the members, they were a solidly committed group, evenly divided between men and women, with an average age of forty-one. All religious faiths were represented. They were doctors, lawyers, businesspeople, mechanics, housewives, teachers, and writers—but no religious professionals.

There was much reading and corresponding over the next year, with an occasional seminar for people from the church and seminary field. In sessions they planned their strategy for work with seminaries, generally from denominations other than their own. Each member was assigned four seminaries.

All received group training and individual coaching in interviewing. Each carried out a project requiring persuasion in their home communities. In the course of the year, three members either developed health problems or found the work too demanding and dropped out. The other fifty-seven agreed that they would work anonymously. Also, they agreed that there would be no reporting or publication outside of the group, nor would they be interviewed for publication. They accepted the principle of Alcoholics Anonymous that no one would be paid. At the end of the first year of preparation, each made contact with his or her four assigned seminaries.

The reactions reported on the first contacts were that they were almost all rebuffed, sometimes politely, sometimes rudely. If after several visits a member felt that he or she was not likely ever to be well received, the member traded assignments with another. Soon the word got around in the seminary world (it had a pretty good grapevine) that the resources of this group were virtually inexhaustible and that seminaries would do well to make their peace with the idea that this work was going to move forward.

Then there was an unanticipated development. A ferment began in the seminary field. Articles appeared in scholarly journals, questioning some of the defenses being expressed by seminary staff in contacts with members: "We are an academic institution." "Our mission is God-given and not amenable to modification." "What you are suggesting is the province of denominational bodies." "We have no competence in the field of leadership." "Our work is theology, not service to churches."

About the time this project started, there was an awakening interest in seminary trusteeship. A literature emerged on that subject, and seminars were held on the question of "Whom and what purpose does the seminary serve?" This produced the view that seminaries were more accountable to both churches and society at large than they were accustomed to being. Members began encountering some hostility as a result of the new pressure that seminaries were experiencing. However, the expression of this hostility by seminaries helped to get the issues out on the table and really facilitated the discussions. Members were scrupulously careful not to advocate a specific program or institutional design for a seminary. They stood firm on the ground that churches were not effective in healing and preventing alienation, nor were they supporting those who could build serving institutions of all sorts. They held that seminaries were not providing the ideas or the leadership that would encourage churches to do this work. They urged each seminary to examine its opportunities, within the framework of its own history and myth, and to work to maximize its impact as a servant of society.

Members insistently raised several questions:

Is your view of your opportunities broad enough?

Do you accept that you have an obligation to serve this society and that others may be competent to judge whether you have fulfilled that obligation?

Are you staffed with people who can produce the ideas
and give the leadership that will move churches into a
much more influential role?

When you speak, are you heard by the churches?

We hear a figure quoted that seminaries are accepting, on
the average, 95 percent of their applicants. Are you en-
rolling people who are strong enough, assured enough,
and resourceful enough to staff and lead strong, influential
churches? Does your program give your students the substance and skills that will prepare them to do this?

Members told the seminaries, "Never mind where the money
will come from to do these things. Conceptualize what your
seminary should be, articulate it forcefully, and financing it may
not be as much of a problem as you now think it to be."

Group members remained anonymous throughout and gave
no interviews. But others did write about their work, and by the
year 2000 it was widely known. Perhaps its greatest influence
was supporting a general shift among thinking people regarding
priorities. Coming into dominance just then was the idea that
one of the most important things to accomplish in the United
States was to improve the serving quality of all institutions. It
was accepted that the massive influence of government probably could not be improved as long as so many of its autonomous parts did so poorly. New currency came to a reply
that Laurens van der Post, the South African writer, gave to a
question after a talk he made in New York on conditions in his
native land. The questioner asked what people in America could
do to help. Van der Post replied, "Cultivate your own gardens,
and their fragrance will be wafted across the ocean to us!"

By the year 2000 many seemed to have accepted that advice.
Several seminaries, representing Catholic, Jewish, and Protestant faiths, had collaborated to produce a contemporary theology of institutions which forcefully described the quality of
society we could create in the United States if churches would

minister to people, not only as individuals but as persons occupying positions of influence, large and small, in the complex structure of institutions that serve us. There had evolved an understanding of these involvements that made it possible for churches to support these institution builders in specific and sustained ways. Churches had become pivotal institutions in sustaining a "good society."

Looking back from the year 2000, people saw that one of the significant results of this work with seminaries was on the thinking of foundations. Foundations were essentially a product of the twentieth century. Early in that century the Rockefeller Foundation sponsored a study of medical education by Dr. Abraham Flexner, who wrote a notable report that had the effect of closing some "diploma mills" and radically advancing the quality of medical education in the United States. For the next sixty years, that work stood as a landmark in foundation sponsorship that was not approached until the seminary project began to mature. This stirred some creative thinking in the foundation field. Could some foundation funds be used to better effect to produce people who could persuade those with power and influence in institutions to solve their own problems, rather than simply grant money to try to solve problems?

The members who convened in the year 2000 to review their experience as persuaders concluded that on the whole they had been successful with their seminary mission. In the fifteen years since they began their active work in 1985, many influential churches were noted to have become loving, caring, serving communities; alienation had declined; large numbers of institutions were conspicuously more serving than before. Seminaries, whose initiatives had fostered these developments, were becoming recognized as important, culture-shaping institutions, in sharp contrast to the marginal status that some had been judged to occupy in 1985.

Perhaps most significant was that the forty-five members who stayed with the work for fifteen years had grown remarkably as individuals, and they were firmly established as persons of consequence in the world of churches and seminaries. They had accomplished this in their free time, while maintaining themselves in their careers, their families, and the communities where they lived. But there had been no dull moments.

This short piece prefaces Greenleaf's later work on ministry to the strong, theology of institutions, and the prospects for a servant-led society.

RELIGIOUS LEADERSHIP
FOR THESE TIMES

IN EARLIER WORK, I made three assertions that form the premise of this essay:

- I have a special concern for two pervasive social problems: widespread alienation in the population and far too many low-serving institutions, including churches and church institutions. Each of these problems may be a contributing cause to the other, and neither is likely to be healed without coming to terms with the other.

- A good society has widespread *faith as trust* that encourages large numbers to be society-building influences in the world as it is—violent, striving, and unjust, as well as beautiful, caring, and supportive.

- The root problem of our times, one that underlies all other social problems, is a failure of religious leadership. The source of that failure may be the marginal role of seminaries, whose theological reflection and the educational programs that flow out of it do not deal with the realities of institution-bound society.

Seminaries are seen as marginal partly because they have not produced a persuasive contemporary theology of institutions. Consequently, pastors of churches have not been prepared who will mediate that theology, through churches, to those who are in a position to lead or influence the character of our many institutions. It is not enough for churches to minister directly to the hurt and the needy, important as this service is to the recipients, or to those who minister as a means of finding wholeness in their own lives. It is a losing struggle for churches and other succoring institutions to do *only* that. Too many of our institutions are grinding people down faster than the most valiant rescue effort can recover them. And alienated people are wreaking violence on themselves and others on an unprecedented scale. Hope for the future rests on more institutions becoming constructive healing influences on all persons they touch.

What is urgently needed in our times (and seminaries are in the best position to originate it) is a new, formative influence for the strong, successful people who are within the reach of churches, who have their hands on levers of power and influence within some institution. A more caring, meliorative society will come not so much from large global movements as from incremental acts of leading and serving by individual people using their influence within the structures of our many institutions.

The opportunity for seminaries is to offer a program that will attract and prepare ministerial candidates who are potentially capable of wielding a significant formative influence with the successful and the strong.

One cannot fault present-day pastors for not being effective in this role. In their seminary days, as now, seminaries were not preparing students for this work. Therefore, seminaries were not attracting those who would want the role, or who would be effective in it.

We should not fault seminary faculty or administrators for failing to offer programs that attract and prepare students for religious leadership of the strong and the successful. It is the role of trustees, as public theologians, to give leadership in formulating a mission for the seminary that embraces this opportunity, and then support the achievement of that mission. Public trust (a necessary condition for the existence of the seminary) requires that seminary trustees be alert to opportunities to sustain the seminary as an optimal servant of society. This is religious leadership by trustees.

Religious leadership, in my view, is not a constant thing. Ours is a fast-changing world and will probably continue to change at an accelerating pace. The test of religious leadership, now and always, has been a practical one. Religious leadership rests with those who take the initiatives, sometimes at considerable risk, that have the effect of nurturing the servant motive in others. Especially in our institution-bound society, religious leadership is nurturing the servant motive in those who have the opportunity and the strength to influence the serving quality of some institution. That serving quality is judged by whether those who are served grow as persons. Do they, while being served, become healthier, wiser, freer, more autonomous, more likely themselves to become servants? And, what is the effect on the least privileged in society? Will she or he benefit, or, at least, not be further deprived? No one should knowingly be hurt.

The opportunity for seminaries to prepare students for religious leadership may be the same as what colleges and universities have for leadership in general. Both neglect their opportunity. One common flaw in the assumptions of both seminaries and universities may be their insistence that everything be scholarly. Preparation of students for leadership is not a scholarly process. It is something to be modeled. The teacher who models it may be a scholar, but there is no necessary connection. One may learn *about* leadership in an academic program. But one does not learn *to be* a leader that way.

A seminary student should be informed by a theology of institutions that is scholarly in origin. But the student will learn to be a religious leader by being inspired by someone in a seminary who is a model of that leadership, who renders the theology of institutions into a prophetic vision that has *spirit,* and who coaches the student in supervised practice. It is the *spirit* in the prophetic vision that will move the strong and the successful to become builders of serving institutions.

There are other things to be done by churches and other institutions to build a better society. But unless a new, larger, prophetic vision and inspired new religious leadership emerge to support those who have the opportunity to shape the courses of trustee- and director-governed institutions and small units of government, it is not realistic to hope that the now-limping national and world institutions will do much better than they are doing. The cornerstones for a good society are not in place. Inspired new religious leadership could, in time, cause these stones to be put in place.

Greenleaf wrote this short piece sometime in the 1980s. It was intended to be part of a book on his reflections on institutions, the human spirit, and theology. The themes, especially those concerning the human spirit, have been pervasive since his earliest writings. This piece serves as an introduction to Greenleaf's idea about the need for a theology of institutions, a theme repeated in many of the essays in this volume.

THEOLOGY: A CONCERN FOR
THE CONDITIONS UNDER WHICH
THE HUMAN SPIRIT FLOWERS

HUMAN SPIRIT IS not seen here as mere liveliness. That might be simply animal spirit. A great human spirit may or may not be superficially lively. Human spirit, as I see it, is the "bottom line" of all human endeavor; yet a precise definition of spirit, as that term is used here, is not within the compass of human reason.

I am aware that those who call themselves theologians, as well as some who may be theologians but use some other label, are not agreed on a meaning for the word *theology*, and when they are "doing theology" they may be involved in many different things. From my perspective as a student of organization—how things get done—I am concerned here with the reflections of theologians on the conditions under which the human spirit flowers, and the knowledge generated by reflection that can be communicated to those servants who are dedicated to nurturing the human spirit, especially in the young.

In our complex society, much of the care and nurture of persons is mediated through institutions: governments, businesses, schools, churches, social agencies, philanthropies. These institutions range from small to very large. Sometimes they are incompetent or muddle-headed; occasionally they are corrupt. But whatever their condition, they are the resources through which we must work if we are to be a constructive force in this society.

The effectiveness of servants in nurturing the human spirit will be determined by how well they manage their lives and their serving under the constraints and opportunities of life in institutions as they are—all kinds and qualities of institutions. In order to serve, most of us will need to contend with bureaucratic inertia, as I did all of my active life. Yet on balance, I believe I was able to serve more effectively, working through institutions as they are, than if I had functioned alone and without such support as I had from the institutions through which I worked.

Part of the inadequacy of our many institutions seems to me to result from the failure of theologians to give persuasively the guidance they are best positioned to give by reflecting on, and communicating about, the conditions under which the human spirit flowers in contemporary institutions. The fruits of such reflection may be called "a theology of institutions." To be persuasive, such a theology would need to focus on one category of institution at a time, and the first object of such scrutiny might be the seminaries with which the theologians are affiliated. "Physician, heal thyself."

Seminary theologians are crucial to this process because they are in the best strategic position to support churches. If any theology of institutions is to help favor the flowering of the human spirit, the churches need to mediate that theology and teach, which is to say, *lead,* people to govern their lives by it. As I see it, we have no other resource that is equal to the opportunity.

I try to deal with the nurture of the human spirit in a way that might be listened to by those who embrace any religious tradition. There is, of course, a problem of language. Buddhists, who do not postulate a deity, bridle at the term *theology.* And humanists, good people who seem to be mostly at war with doctrines and churches, are bugged by the word *religion.* But both *theology* and *religion* have roots that are amenable to contemporary meanings that would not offend either Buddhists or humanists. Thus it seems to me that the nurture of the human spirit could become a unifying idea congenial with the traditions and doctrines of any religion, or any system of thought that may be a religion in its effect even though its adherents do not use the term.

The nurture of the human spirit has been a matter of concern for thoughtful people for a long time, especially in societies that once had an abundance of human spirit, then lost it, and would like to recover that favored state. Ancient Greece comes to mind as a society that once had it for a short time, and then lost it, and was never able to recover it despite the valiant efforts of some of the greatest minds the world has ever known. Can we learn anything from their experience that would be useful to us now? I believe we can.

I have not closely studied ancient Greece, but I am aware that Solon (ca. 630–560 B.C.E.) gave the people of Athens the idea of a free society. He was a great military leader as well as a statesman. He must have communicated a charge of spirit along with his design for a free society because for a short time the individual responsibility and participation that were needed to achieve and maintain freedom were widespread. But when Solon's initial inspiriting influence was not maintained and spirit waned, self-interest came to predominate, and freedom was jeopardized.

Socrates spoke about these conditions but did not write, and his message was sufficiently disturbing that he was put death. His followers, Isocrates and Plato, wrote and taught, leaving a literature that has excited intellectuals for two thousand years. But the literary effort of these thinkers seemed to make little imprint on Greek politics. Plato's academy for an elite apparently did not produce, in practice, even one philosopher-king. Demosthenes' oratory was able to arouse sufficient spirit that there was an unsuccessful attempt to repel the Macedonian invaders. But three hundred years after Solon left his legacy, the spirit that free men needed to maintain their freedom was lost and never recovered.

Let us compare the Greek experience with Nikolai Grundtvig's effort to inspirit the young peasants of nineteenth-century

Denmark. [See "Religious Leaders as Seekers and Servants."— Eds.] Grundtvig was a scholar, historian, and poet whose theological treatises were little read. His long and successful advocacy of schools of the spirit for young peasants, the folk high schools, was done largely orally. The initial effect of his advocacy was to inspirit older people to build and operate the schools, in which Grundtvig lectured extensively after they were established. His work ultimately had a great effect on the politics, economy, and social order of Denmark. And one hundred years later, it is being sustained.

From these sketches of two widely separated periods of history in which dedicated and able leaders made a valiant effort to restore health to an ailing society, the following conclusions are suggested:

○ In ancient Greece, the inspiriting leaders, particularly Isocrates and Plato, put their faith in the power of great ideas communicated to mature people, an elite; but they failed to bring health to an ailing society.

○ In nineteenth-century Denmark, Grundtvig and his followers who built the folk high schools put their faith in nurturing the human spirit in the young peasants, and they succeeded in bringing health to an ailing society and maintaining it.

○ I believe the Danes succeeded where the Greeks failed because they were guided by an adequate theology. They understood, and put high priority on, the conditions under which the human spirit flowers. The Greek thinkers, great as was their contribution to our intellectual heritage, seem not to have been guided by an adequate theology of the human spirit, and as a consequence they wielded little influence on the quality of the culture of their times.

From these brief historical references, I conclude that if we are to make a constructive contribution in our time to strengthening and maintaining our precious democracy, we should undergird our effort with an adequate theology. And I suggest that a major element in that theology should be concern for the conditions under which the human spirit flowers in our institution-bound society. Since this kind of society is brand new in the world, a quality and intensity of creative theological reflection will be required for which there are few models in our received experience.

This essay combines the piece "Note on the Need for a Theology of Institutions" with a supplement Greenleaf wrote on the same day, April 9, 1979.

THE NEED FOR A THEOLOGY
OF INSTITUTIONS

I BELIEVE THAT CARING for persons, the more able and the less able serving each other, is what makes a good society. Most caring was once person-to-person. Now much of it is mediated through institutions that are often impersonal, incompetent, even corrupt. If a better society is to be built, one more just and loving and providing opportunity for people to grow, then the most effective and economical way, while being supportive of the social order, is to raise the performance-as-servant of all institutions by voluntary and regenerative forces initiated within the institutions by committed individuals.

It is realistic to expect that enough of these committed people exist, potentially, to raise the quality of the common life substantially. But if this potential is to be realized, positive steps must be taken to favor the emergence and preparation of these people, followed by sustaining support for action they may initiate within institutional structures.

I speak with some feeling on this point because I realize now, in retirement, that in my career I had the opportunity and the motive to take such an initiating, institution-building role; but the preparation and sustaining support were lacking. To remedy this lack in the future, one step the churches may take is to evolve a contemporary "theology of institutions." With the guidance of that theology, the churches may become a vital new society-building influence.

I do not believe that the urgently needed fundamental recon-
struction of our vast and pervasive structure of institutions can
take place, prudently and effectively, without a strong supporting influence from the churches. And I doubt that churches as
they now stand, with only a theology of persons to guide them,
can wield the needed influence. I deem it imperative that a new
and compelling theology of institutions come into being. It is
my hope that contemporary churches will take the lead to produce it. Our times are crying out for such leadership.

In the back of my mind is the notion that when Karl Marx
sat alone in the British Museum composing the doctrines that
would shape much of the twentieth-century world, he was fill-
ing the void that resulted from the failure of the theologians of
his day to deal with the consequences of the Industrial
Revolution. But while Marx wrote, another revolution was in
the making that he did not take note of: the shift from a society
of individuals to one in which people became deeply involved in
institutions.

Institutions, as we know them, are relatively new, a product
of the past two hundred years. The U.S. Constitution was written before there was even a shadow of the present dominance
of institutions. That document, too, is concerned only with persons. The prevailing corporate form of organization is not mentioned in our Constitution. Corporations get their legal status
from the willingness of the courts to construe them as persons.
As a nation, through our legislative, policy-making process, we
have not yet explicitly faced the question of what kind of institution-bound society will serve us best. We have simply impro-
vised from our two hundred-year-old seminal thinking about a
nation of persons. And one of the results, at this point, is a society that does not have a hopeful outlook.

Likewise, those who draw their spiritual sustenance from
churches and are concerned for preparing people who will care
and serve in our complex, tension-torn world have largely ex-
trapolated from the available theology of persons and seem not
to have explicitly faced the question of what a committed

person does—one who is capable of being a strong quality-building force within our institutions. As a consequence, too much of the effort to care and serve is directed to easing the hurt of the "system" that is grinding people down faster than the most valiant rescue effort can help them; and too little caring effort is going into building a "system" (institutions) that will have a positive growing effect on people.

Much of the concern for the quality of society in our times has been directed toward actions by government, with the hope of providing money to alleviate suffering, correct injustice, or use the coercive power of government to compel both people and institutions to behave in socially constructive ways. In an imperfect world, some of these measures will always be needed. But compulsion is mainly useful to restrain destructive behavior, and money is mostly helpful to cushion suffering and injustice. Neither compulsion nor money has much value as a quality-building force that will cause our institutions to be more caring or serving. How can a contemporary theology of institutions be brought into being, one that will encourage, prepare, and support committed people to make careers inside institutions as initiators of regenerative quality-building action?

In the absence of experience that marks a clear path (which, if we had it, would suggest that the work had already been done), the following steps are suggested:

1. Within a given church or church organization, identify a strong leader-type person who has had substantial experience as an operating executive of a major institution and has served as trustee or consultant to several institutions, through which experience this person (hereafter called the *leader*) has acquired a comprehensive grasp of modern institutions large and small.

2. Give the leader support and coaching, with the hope that he or she will make a major investment in leading a process that may in time bring a new theology of institutions.

3. Start conversations among professional theologians and other related professionals to identify those who have the interest to contribute to a search for the new theology.

4. Identify at least one person, possibly an articulate theologian, who has good conceptual and writing ability and wants to write for this mission.

5. Through the leader, start the search for perceptive people who have experience in various institutional settings, and try to find a few who will make a major time investment in the mission.

6. Convene, through the leader, a task force in the setting of a religious retreat. Of all the resources currently available, the retreat environment is the one most likely to encourage the richness of insight and clarity of direction that this mission will require.

7. Successive retreat sessions may be interspersed with writing and sharing ventures that may contribute to an evolving theology of institutions. There may never emerge a "conference document" to which all subscribe. Rather, there may be several documents, individually authored, that get into circulation. The influential document that eventually has widespread impact may not be immediately identified, and it may not be written by any of the retreat participants. Wide ferment and testing by time and experience may be required, and in the process much may be discovered in earlier writing that is relevant. The hope is that there will be continuity of tradition from the existing theology of persons to a new contemporary theology of institutions.

Some questions are raised about these suggested steps. Why, it is asked, is the existing theology of persons inadequate? It is inadequate because it deals only with *persons* relating to *persons*. To be sure, there is some of this within institutions. But within institutions people are hemmed in by intricate technologies; they are involved in elaborate hierarchies; they contend with social, political, and economic pressures; and they must deal with the many power vectors that give institutions their strength as well as make them a threat to individuals. An institution at its best is not just a housekeeping arrangement for an assortment of functions. It has the potential for synergy, for the whole to be greater than the sum of its parts, and for individuals to perform to a higher ethical standard than if they were operating wholly on their own. An institution's justification for being is the realization of these potentials. The all-too-frequent shortfall is one measure of the need for a new theology of institutions.

Further, there is the question of whether the resources of the social sciences are adequate to point the way for humane and socially constructive institutions. The social sciences make their contribution by illuminating problems and suggesting procedures, but they do not supply the faith one must have to risk and venture, which is what institution building requires. Science helps calculate the odds on a decision, but belief sustains one in the inevitable uncertainties and anxieties which the initiator of regenerative action must bear. Science deals with what is experimentally demonstrable. Theology arises from experience, meditation, and inspiration and is made practical by ventures of faith. We have much *science* of institutions, but little *theology* of institutions.

Then there is the question of leadership: going out ahead to show the way. *Lead* is a many faceted word. But in the context of institutions it can be distinguished from *manage* and *administer,* which are more concerned with control and maintenance. Those who manage and administer are usually empowered by authority. But anyone, empowered by authority or not, can lead! Followers make the leader, by giving their trust and respect. Thus the leader, if successful, is also empowered—but not by authority. Since institutions are generally authoritarian in structure, and since they depend on authority for some of their essential functions, a theology of institutions will deal with the many issues that arise out of the parallel existence of authority and leadership and the need to have both of them—not only for institutional effectiveness and survival, but to ensure that the impact of institutions on people will be benign and constructive.

If one accepts (as assumed here) that the vast labyrinth of institutions that engulfs us all is now a major factor in determining the quality of our common life, and if one sees (as I do) the churches as an indispensable leaven for good within that labyrinth of institutions, then one of the leadership initiatives open to churches—an initiative that would give hope for greater power to fulfill their missions—would be a sustained and carefully considered effort to produce a new contemporary theology of institutions. Such a theology, and the process of producing it, will give any church that makes the effort a new window on the world—the world of institutions—that may enable it to re-form its mission toward new ends.

As I see it, the adequacy of any theology is tested ultimately by examining what it produces in the lives of people who have its implications interpreted for them through the mediation of churches. From my vantage point as a student of organization, and within my view of what church-guided people do (or fail to do) with their many opportunities to render our vast array of institutions more serving, I conclude that the available theology of institutions is far from adequate.

Anyone can make a contribution to theology. But established theologians are best positioned to originate and to advocate the much needed theology of institutions—and to be heard in so doing. However, non-theologians who are keeping a close watch on our institutions will make the ultimate judgment on the adequacy of that theology. The test these non-theologians will make is this: does that theology of institutions generate a sufficient moral imperative as a moving force in the persons of trustees and directors of institutions of all sorts—large or small, for profit or not for profit—that induces them to take, and sustain, initiatives that result in the institutions they hold in trust becoming substantially more serving than they now are to all they touch? My experience with institutions suggests that this urgently needed moral imperative is not likely to emerge among trustees and directors until a compelling logic for it has been made quite specific, and advocated persuasively and with a note of urgency, in a new theology of institutions.

In making these assertions I am not judging the adequacy of theology in general; nor am I suggesting a priority among the many facets of life with which theology deals. But I do believe that it will not be possible to raise significantly the caring quality of contemporary society unless and until our many institutions (including seminaries, churches, and church-related institutions) move much closer to the reasonable and the possible as *servants of society*. Further, it seems to me that we ought not to expect governments at any level to do much better than they are now doing until conspicuously clear examples of excellence are set by trustee-or director-governed institutions that have a measure of resources and autonomy to be what they choose to be.

There is no magic "they" who will transform our many institutions on command so as to render them more serving. From the outside, these institutions can be persuaded, cajoled, pressured, and threatened. But nothing constructive happens until individual persons who are strategically placed inside choose to initiate the transforming actions.

So far humankind has evolved in two basic ways (with a third being a combination of the two) to encourage these initiatives: through the political process of control, or through the governance of trustees who manage voluntary institutions. Both governments and trustees hold coercive power; but coercion, which is effective in stopping or destroying something, is of little value in inducing the actions that create truly serving institutions. Fortunately for the healing of world society, only persuasion will do that in a durable way. It is the opportunity of the churches to understand, advocate, and implement persuasion.

The first step in spreading a new theology of institutions for these times may be to learn how to communicate through the churches to all they can reach who hold governmental power or who are trustees or directors of any kind of institution, so as to:

- Instill in them a moral imperative to persuade their colleagues of the need to raise the service quality of the institution they control or hold in trust so that the reasonable and possible are achieved in service to all who are touched by its actions.

- Give support and encouragement with preparatory facilities to help them find prudent ways to accomplish institutional transformation through persuasion.

- Help them sustain openness and strength to persevere. It may be a long struggle, requiring patience, insight, fortitude, and faith.

There are many paths to a more serving society, and the regeneration of our many institutions is but one of them. But without a theology of institutions that is clear and compelling, the contribution of churches to the quality of the common life will be limited. The movement I hope to see is when all institutions will become more serving of all persons they touch, to the end that those being served will grow as persons: while being served they will become healthier, wiser, freer, more autonomous, more likely themselves to become servants.

An essay by a similar name as this one appears in *Seminary as Servant*. Beyond the names, however, there are very few similarities between the two pieces. This version, which is dated July 24, 1979, captures succinctly much of Greenleaf's thinking about the place of seminaries in society. Readers are by this point attuned to his thinking about the importance of seminaries helping churches to be more serving.

In an incomplete draft essay entitled "Church as Servant," Greenleaf presents his vision of a serving church: "Some contemporary people do not choose to be identified with or directly responsive to the service of a church. But if churches are true servants of those who do respond directly, they will provide a leaven in society as a whole that gives some support to those who choose not to be identified with a church. This is part of a church's role as servant . . . church exists for the service of those who are not in it."

The following essay outlines how Greenleaf thinks seminaries should bring that vision to fruition.

THE SEMINARY AS INSTITUTION

I BELIEVE THAT WE make a good society by caring for persons, with the more able and the less able serving each other. Although that caring used to be person-to-person, it is now largely mediated through institutions. As I have written elsewhere, a better, more just and loving society depends on our raising the performance-as-servant of our institutions by way of committed individuals—*servants*—initiating forces of change from within them.

The idea of servant is deep in our Judeo-Christian heritage. *Servant* (along with *serve* and *service*) appears in the Bible more than thirteen hundred times (in the concordance to the Standard Revised Version), beginning with the book of Genesis. Part of the human dilemma is that the meaning of *serve*, in practical behavioral terms for both persons and institutions, is never completely clear. Thus one who would be servant is a lifelong seeker, groping for light but never finding ultimate clarity. One constantly probes and listens, both to the promptings from one's own inner resources and to the communications of those who are also seeking. Then one cautiously experiments, questions, and listens again. Thus the servant-seeker is constantly growing in self-assurance through experience, but never having the solace of certainty. No matter what stature a person reaches as servant, there is always room for more growth. And no matter how notable an institution, it can always do better *if* some of the people who inhabit it constantly probe and listen for inspiration. If they are inspired, they venture and risk by initiating regenerative actions, actions that do not just renew but reconstruct in a truly conservative sense. It seems in the nature of things that both people and institutions must constantly reach for growth as servants, or they retrogress. Neither people nor institutions ever have it made. This is one of the important dimensions of what life is about.

The quality of a society is basically the quality of its people and the level of their caring for each other and for the common good. There is evidence about that ours is a low-caring society, and concern for the low quality of the contemporary social order has resulted in government actions with the intent of providing money to alleviate suffering, to correct injustice, or to compel both people and institutions to behave in more socially constructive ways. In an imperfect world some of this will always be needed. But compulsion is useful mainly to restrain destructive behavior, and money is mostly helpful to cushion suffering and injustice. Neither compulsion nor money has much utility in causing institutions to be reconstructed as more caring and more serving. Only the voluntary actions of people serving institutions can accomplish that.

I believe that there are sufficient women and men, in both the minority and majority populations, rich and poor, young and old, bold and cautious, who have the ability, stamina, and will to serve. This belief justifies a realistic hope that a quantum leap in the quality of our major institutions (and therefore in the quality of our total society) can be taken within the next generation, and that those who take the manifold initiatives to bring this about will lead much more fulfilled lives. But for those who have the ability, the stamina, and the will to serve to take the many initiatives required, a powerful new guiding vision will need to emerge, one that is not now evident.

Where will this powerful guiding vision come from? Where in our vast structure of institutions are those with the potential to keep this prophetic guidance best sheltered and nurtured? This premise holds that seminaries, as institutions, are best positioned to perform this vital service to society.

A Suggested Hierarchy of Institutions

As a frame for the discussion that follows, the hierarchy of institutions that serve us may be seen at three levels.

In the base group are the legions of "operating" institutions, such as schools, governments, labor unions, businesses, hospitals, social agencies, communities, and families.

At the next level one might put churches and universities. They stand somewhat apart because of their role as the "glue" of society, shaping and transmitting the culture and clarifying values.

At the top level are two institutions that are distinguished from the others because of their unique opportunity to harbor prophetic voices that give vision and hope, and that have perhaps the widest scope of all to be and do as they think they should. These are theological seminaries and uncommitted, trusteed resources such as foundations.

The utility of such a hierarchical view of institutions may be that, when there is faltering at the lower levels, one is reminded to ask where the higher-level institutions failed in serving those at the lower levels.

If one views all institutions as intricate webs of fallible humans groping for meaning, order, and light, then the essential problem of all institutions is (and has always been) *theological*. This assumption places seminaries at the top of the hierarchy, even though others may not readily accept or understand this position. It is not a position that is formally designated or authorized. Rather this position is earned by leadership: leadership of vision and inspiration; leadership that gives meaning, order, and light to those less able to generate these precious qualities for themselves. Therefore I see the role of seminaries as pivotal and crucial to the quality of the total society.

The Role of Trustees

In ascending the hierarchy of institutions from level one, a particular element in the structure of institutions changes and becomes more refined and exacting. That is *the role of trustees.* The need is obvious. At level three, particularly, there is no other sheltering institution, no one to whom to turn for wider perspective on the opportunity than can be seen within the constituencies of the seminary. A seminary needs to be supported from somewhere; but it must generate, within its own resources, the vision that elicits and sustains that support. In concept and vision, seminaries need to be wholly self-regenerating. And since seminaries, like all other institutions, are peopled by fallible humans who are groping for meaning, order, and light, those who staff seminaries need a level of caring support from dedicated trustees that is extraordinary. While, in this view, the role of the seminary trustee is the most demanding, it may also be the most rewarding.

If a seminary, in order to work toward its highest potential as a servant of society, needs a level of support from trustees that is extraordinary by usual standards, how can it bring itself the benefit of this kind of leadership? The answer to this question will need to be discovered by each seminary, for itself, within the context of its own personnel, history, doctrines, and available resources. And it will evolve its new trustee leadership by prudent steps over a period of time. One generalization is risked: the faculty and administration of the seminary must fully understand the implications of, and strongly want, this extraordinary leadership from trustees. They must welcome the adaptation to the requirements of a wholly new institution that ultimately may result from this kind of leadership. Achieving these understandings and acceptances is likely to be a challenge of major proportions for most seminaries. In order for trustees to emerge who will give support that only trustees can give, new transforming leadership will also need to emerge among administration and faculty. The recognition of the need for extraordinary trusteeship may be the catalytic agent that brings this about.

This suggestion is made with faith that trustees who can and will rise to this level of service are available to seminaries. While the role envisioned is more demanding than some otherwise good trustees will accept, the potential for creative achievement in such a trustee role will elicit the effort of some to prepare themselves for what could be the crowning achievement of their lives.

Roots

I have my own theological roots as the source of my caring for persons. But the dimensions of this proposal come out of a long experience as a student of organization and hence of how things get done.

Until my retirement in 1964, most of my thinking about organization was directed toward American Telephone and Telegraph. In my later years there, as director of management research, with the help of a professional staff and within a broad charter, I had an unusual opportunity to study the functioning of this vast institution with its involvement in technology, government, and public service. I was concerned for its values, its history, and, intimately, its leadership. This was a good perspective from which to venture, in my retirement years, into a close involvement with a wide range of institutions: churches, church-related institutions, seminaries, businesses, universities, and foundations, around the world. This led me, in time, to a realization of the primacy of trustees and then to a consideration of the hierarchy of institutions, as outlined above. Finally, I came to the view that seminaries occupy a position in which there is great unrealized potential for influence on the quality of the total society.

It is important to realize that our vast structure of institutions has evolved only in the last two hundred years. Prior to that there were governments, armies, churches, and a few universities. But, for most people, it was life in families and simple communities. To the extent that the life of people was guided by a theology, it was a theology of persons.

From my observer's seat, trying to understand the dilemmas of our day, it seems to me that as population grew and as our structure of institutions became more complex, the seminaries did not creatively adapt their roles to become potentially important shaping influences in a society that seems to be growing increasingly frenetic. The opportunity now is not to recover what has been lost. Rather it is to evolve from where the particular seminary now stands to a fully functioning level three in the hierarchy of institutions. How to do this, and to what end?

I have a firm belief that any seminary (faculty, administration, trustees) that has a strong will and a clear vision can move toward that position through a series of prudent steps. The first step, as mentioned above, is acceptance by all constituencies of the seminary that its trustees must take a new leadership role and give an infusion of strength to the seminary that it may not get any other way. The goal would be to build the seminary to a level of competence and stature such that the prophetic vision emanating from it will become one of the important sustaining influences from level three that our tension-torn society so sorely needs.

How to Do It

If a seminary is to move toward its full potential as a harborer and nurturer of prophetic voices that give vision and hope, what is needed first is leadership that wants to take the risk of such a larger dream, from among the faculty, administration, or trustees of the seminary (to be hoped, someone from each.) If such movement is to be taken in prudent steps, this leadership will be wholly by persuasion. If there were a "way," a clearly marked path, tested and tried, the word *administration* might more aptly describe the role of guiding the institution along that path.

Being persuaded by the rightness of a belief or action, I have written elsewhere, follows from an intuitive step that may take time to reach. The leader and the follower encourage one another to find intuitive confirmation of that right belief or action. Seen in this context, the root of all *leadership* is faith (the choice of the nobler hypothesis, as Dean William Ralph Inge put it). Leadership, then, is a risk on a vision, a great dream.

If persuasion is ever to rise over coercion and manipulation as the clearly prevailing modus operandi in our violence-prone society, then the model of an institution governed by persuasion needs to stand at the top of the hierarchy of institutions. "I believe that some seminaries have the potential to occupy that spot—to be influential models for other institutions, *to be the civilizing models!*" (Greenleaf, 1983, p. 19).

Greenleaf wrote this short note during the period when he was doing a lot of thinking about institutions. In this particular essay, he offers a new suggestion. He believes that major foundations could play pivotal roles in transforming institutions by working with seminaries and theologians.

A NEW ROLE FOR SEMINARIES

THE BIG QUESTION might be, why be concerned with seminaries at all? They seem not to be valued highly by society as a whole, not even by many of the clergy who were trained by them. They are a checkpoint in the credentialing process, and that's about all. Harsh, but that's how they're seen.

I begin with the question, is our society adequate—are we satisfied with the state of our civilization? If the answer is yes, then we have nothing to discuss. If it is no, then the next question is, how do we go about raising the quality of our society? It doesn't go up, or down, without somebody taking some action that shapes its direction. It doesn't just change itself. And if its quality is to be raised, then somebody takes an action that starts it to move. Where is the handle, and how can one get one's hands on it? The answer to this question depends on what one believes about the structure of our society and the dynamic forces available in it.

I believe that the most available and useful change agent is the churches, all of them in their great diversity and in the range of their quality as institutions. There are other change agents—schools, for instance—but they seem less available, they somehow seem secondary for this purpose. Churches seem to me to be primary, feeble as they sometimes are. But how to energize and focus the churches so that they become more influential in shaping the quality of the society? This seems to me to be the role of seminaries. Seminaries are best positioned in the structure of our society to inspirit the churches and equip them with the prophetic vision to become a forceful, society-building influence.

But some people may protest that seminaries seem even feebler than churches. My answer is that they are there and they have great unrealized potential. Either we somehow get the seminaries into the leadership role they are best positioned to take, or we have to build new institutions, if the churches are to be led to do what they can best do. And where are the resources to do that? I say if we want to raise the quality of our civilization in time to save it, we have no feasible alternative but to refocus seminaries so that they can and will do what only they can do to lead churches.

I am no prophet of doom, but I am aware that civilizations have risen and fallen before and there is no built-in guarantee that ours will survive indefinitely unless new, necessary, vitalizing forces are constantly built into it by the efforts of farseeing people. Therefore, I see no feasible alternative to revitalizing seminaries if we want churches to become a new vitalizing force in the society. How can seminaries be helped to become the sources of new prophetic vision when they seem not to be asking for that opportunity?

I see this as an opportunity for foundations to take a new vitalizing idea to seminaries, one that would put them on a new constructive tack, one that they might not initially be comfortable with but which a little money might induce them to try. Then, if it proves to be an idea that puts them into a stronger position, they might incorporate it permanently. I see no other feasible alternative. Seminaries are too comfortable in their present role, even though it keeps them poor (but they don't see it that way).

The hitch in this suggestion is that foundations are comfortable in their role of responding to grant requests, and initiating ideas makes them uncomfortable. If foundations looked at their own history, they would know that when they have done seminal work they have produced the idea, not the grantee. Two examples: (1) the much talked about work of Carnegie and Rockefeller many years ago that supported the Flexner Report [see "Fable."—Eds.], which revolutionized medical education, and (2) the more recent work of Rockefeller and Ford in supporting the Rice Research Institute, which brought the "green revolution" to India. In both cases the idea originated in the foundations, not with the beneficiaries.

So it gets down to this question: is there a foundation that is interested in fostering a seminal idea, such as persuading a seminary to set up an Institute of Chairing? I believe the consequences of that action could be just as profound as the two where foundations took the initiative. There are many ways that our ailing society could be helped toward a more durable, humane condition. But we are an institution-bound society, something new in the history of this planet. And it is difficult for me to see how any of these efforts could have good effect if we do not have a way to raise the quality of the performance of our many institutions, both large and small. The best handle on that problem, one that is feasible and for which we have the resources, is for some seminaries—just one at first—to start Institutes of Chairing and encourage strong churches to start them. One foundation, not necessarily a big one, could give that chain reaction its initial push. It is manageable.

This essay combines an early version of "Critical Thought in the Seminary and the Trustee Chairperson's Role" with a piece by the same title appearing in *Seminary as Servant,* published in 1983. The important roles for seminaries and lay chairpersons in helping churches serve society are clearly emphasized in this essay.

CRITICAL THOUGHT
AND SEMINARY LEADERSHIP

WHAT KIND OF CHALLENGE does chairing the trustees of a seminary present? A chairperson's answer would depend on how one sees opportunities and obligations in that position, what one believes about the place of seminaries in society and their unrealized potential for service, and what one's personal feelings are concerning the assumption of leadership. Depending on where one stands on these issues, one chooses a chairperson's role from a range of possibilities. At the low end of the scale is the view of this role as expressed by a seminary executive: ". . . the chairperson serves no more than two years and is, for all practical purposes, the presiding officer only." Near the other end of the spectrum is the view that the seminary can be led by prudent steps toward the achievement of a much greater vision of service to society than most now aspire to, by someone who is disposed to take the risks of leadership to move it there.

What can be said to one who accepts the latter view and leadership role? How can such a leader be helped?

The one who undertakes to give this leadership will need to be prepared to contend with a negative mind-set that predisposes too many concerned and thoughtful people to write off seminaries as having little force in contemporary society. As matters now stand in some seminaries, this may be a valid judgment. But one who chooses to give new creative leadership to seminary trustees needs to believe firmly that we cannot afford to dismiss them since there is urgent need for an effective instrument in the place that seminaries now occupy. We have neither the time nor the resources to replace existing seminaries with more serving institutions that will give needed support to churches. Unless one wants to abandon the idea of building a better society through greatly strengthened churches, there is no feasible alternative to rebuilding seminaries that will give powerful new support to churches. The word *rebuilding* is used advisedly. No mere revision of the curriculum will do it. The acceptance of such a premise may be part of the armory of one who would lead the trustees as they in turn collectively lead the seminary toward a future of greatness as servant.

A further premise concerns *critical thought in the seminary.* Is critical thought a high priority in the seminary? This question may be the key to all the other questions because if critical thought is not adequate, not much else matters. Assuring the adequacy of critical thought is a central concern.

Critical thought is not necessarily identical with scholarship and the writing of books and papers that establish a scholar's reputation with peers. Scholarship is a necessary condition for critical reflection, but scholarship does not automatically produce it. Critical thought is a fulfillment of the root meaning of seminary: *seminalis,* or seed. It is reflective thought that produces seminal ideas—ideas that become new visions in both ministers as persons and churches as institutions, ideas that support both ministers and churches as they nurture servants who may shape the institutions that dominate the lives of all of us.

The adequacy of critical thought in seminaries is tested ultimately by ordinary folk who have its significance in their lives made real by participation in churches. The incremental actions that build the serving quality of society, or maintain such as it has, are taken by legions of people who get inspiration and guidance from somewhere, mostly from churches, directly or indirectly.

I believe that the critical thought now emerging from seminaries generally is far from adequate for the urgent needs of these times. Too many churches are languishing for want of intellectual stimulus from seminaries. And seminaries are therefore not giving the vital leadership to churches that supports them as they undertake to wield their constructive influence on society—leadership of ideas that give hope expressed in language that lifts the spirit. The premise here is that the need for more influential critical thought from seminaries is great.

Where Is the Relevant Experience?

If the trustee chairperson of a seminary resolves to give leadership that will help the seminary become a greater force in strengthening churches in our times, how does one proceed? What experience is there to draw upon to help one devise a strategy of leadership that will bring the seminary to become a great new source of critical thought—both about itself as an institution and about the theology that it provides for churches?

Such a move in many seminaries would call for a substantial regeneration of the seminary as an institution. It would be a major undertaking that would not likely take place without astute, sustained leadership from the trustees, especially the chairperson.

All institutions can be roughly grouped in two classes: those designed so that they fail easily and live under the constant threat of failure, and those that are designed so that failure is difficult and rare. Businesses are generally in the first category, and nonprofit agencies and governmental units are in the second. Because of this sharp disparity, most of the experience with the process of regenerating moribund or low-serving institutions is in business. And the seminary trustee chairperson who is searching for ideas on how to give leadership to the school so as to bring it to greatness-as-servant with an abundance of critical thought will be well advised to look to business experience as one source of ideas. I do not suggest that either seminary faculty or administrators should be concerned with the experience of business regeneration, but that their trustee chairperson take a close look at that experience.

My AT&T Experience as an Example

I had the good fortune to spend my active career in American Telephone and Telegraph, which had experienced a major regeneration shortly before I arrived in 1926 and some of the people who brought it through that great change were still around. From these people I learned much about the accomplishment of that transformation which may never get into written history.

The telephone was invented in Boston in 1876. The company was started in 1878 by Bostonians, but by people who lacked both vision and an adventurous spirit. It remained in their hands until 1907, when J. P. Morgan the elder wrested control from them, installed a great builder, Theodore N. Vail (who earlier had been the company's first general manager) as president, moved the headquarters to New York, and gave it a vision and started it on an adventurous course. Morgan, who earlier had been instrumental in launching both General Electric and U.S. Steel, gave a powerful push to move AT&T from being an ordinary institution into being exceptional.

In 1907 the company was a going concern, but it was burdened by four serious problems. First, there was an acute employee morale problem. Second, the public reputation of the company was very bad. Third, there was a question about its financial soundness. Fourth, the available technology was insufficient to permit the development of the scope and quality of telephone service that we know today and that Vail and Morgan were determined to bring about. By 1920, when Vail died in the harness, all four of these deficiencies were corrected, some seminal ideas about the institution and its technology emerged, and the company was a "blue chip."

I entered the company in 1926 and immediately became interested in its history. The top question on my mind for a number of years was, How did this remarkable transformation come about? The answer was slow in coming, partly because it was so difficult to judge what Morgan's role was. As I see it now, Morgan, as he was then, would not only be out of style today but would be legally restrained. In the context of his time, however, he was a great trustee. He had and used great power, sometimes ruthlessly; but *he cared intensely about the quality of the businesses he controlled,* an extraordinary attribute for a person of great wealth early in this century. We cannot know now how much of Vail's genius as an institution builder should be attributed to Morgan. A safe assumption is to view them as a joint personality.

How did the transformation of AT&T come about? It was very simple in concept, but awfully difficult to do. It required three basic strategies that I believe are universally applicable to the regeneration of any kind of institution at any time.

Strategies for Change
Mission

In his early period as the first general manager, Vail stated the mission thus: "We will build a telephone system so that any person, any place in the world, can talk to anybody else, any place else in the world, quickly, cheaply, satisfactorily." We aren't there yet, nearly one hundred years after that goal was stated. But I believe we are much closer to it now than we would be if the man who piloted the company in those crucial years (1907–1920) had not thought big. In later years the goal was stated more modestly as "universal service"—perhaps because the company had lost a few tail feathers in its first brush with the antitrust enforcers in 1913. When I entered the business in

217

1926 there was still some of the feeling that we were "building a cathedral, not just laying bricks." It would be difficult in any institution to sustain this sense of urgency if the commonly accepted mission does not require it.

The first step toward defining mission for one who chairs seminary trustees is to get an answer to the question, "Whom and what purpose does this seminary serve?" The chair should ask this question and stay with it until all constituencies—trustees, administrators, faculty, students, alumni—are agreed on a concept that the chair is willing to lead. If, after long and patient urging, the constituencies cannot agree, or if what they can agree on seems unacceptable to the one in the chair, perhaps that person should quietly retire and find something better to do. When Vail, the first general manager of AT&T, was unable to move the conservative Bostonians to become builders, he left the company and resisted later importunings to return when the company was in trouble. He did not return for twenty years, until the Bostonians were ousted by Morgan, who was himself a great builder.

If the agreed-upon mission statement for a seminary were one I could accept if I were to undertake to lead the board, these are the answers I would prefer to see to the questions of whom and for what purpose this seminary serves. Whom? Religious leaders, whether in churches or other institutions. What purpose? To provide churches with ideas and leadership, to the end that churches become and be sustained as significant forces that heal and prevent alienation in people, and to nurture the leaders who will build serving institutions everywhere. The seminary might do some other things, but if I were to be the chairperson, this definition of mission, or one close to it, would be primary. Other chairpersons might view it differently. My advice to any such person is not to undertake to lead the board and the seminary in a direction in which you do not firmly believe. Otherwise you will not be able to lead with spirit. Spirit will be needed.

Identifying Obstacles

Obstacles to greatness must be clearly identified and the full ramifications of each described. Then a capable staff person is assigned to each problem, with the clear charge to find the means for turning it around and to persuade all of the people who need to act. For so long as an obstacle to greatness remains as a problem, a capable staff person makes a high priority of finding a way to deal with it. If at any time it appears that the person assigned is either unable or unwilling to press for an answer, that person is replaced.

Sense of Urgency

A sense of urgency is created, and the move toward greatness is widely accepted as an imperative. It was my privilege to work at AT&T under the executive who, as a young man in 1907, was given the assignment of raising the morale and integrity of the women in the business. By the time I entered the company in 1926, the person who brought about this transformation had made an elite corps out of the department where most women worked (switchboard operation). One of the by-products was that in 1926 this department was producing a greatly disproportionate share of the top officers in the company (then all men). The man who piloted this transformation (one of the most perfect gentlemen I ever met) accomplished it from a staff position entirely by persuasion. He was supported by the feeling of urgency that pervaded the business in that crucial period from 1907 to 1920.

From the soundings available about seminaries, I deduce that the principal urgency in some of them these days is the need for money to survive. In a seminary for which this is a valid judgment, could it be that one of the reasons for the primacy of money is that there is not sufficient urgency regarding critical thought, the production of seminal ideas that are sorely needed in a faltering society?

When someone says to me, "You can't cause seminal ideas to emerge where they don't exist," my response is, "Oh, yes you can! If, first, you have a widely accepted mission for the institution that embodies a great dream of what it might become. Second, if you carefully identify all of the obstacles that stand in the way of realizing that dream and see to it that a competent person sets to work to remove or find a way around each obstacle. And if you sustain a sense of urgency about the whole process of regenerating the institution."

Do these three things, and do them well, and the chance that seminal ideas will emerge in the process is very good—no matter how limited the institution may have been at the start. This is what the experiences of businesses in general, and the one I know best, AT&T, have to suggest to the chairperson of seminary trustees who would give leadership to a development that would favor the growth of critical thought, as marked by the emergence of seminal ideas. It may require more acumen from the one in the chair to sustain this urgency in a seminary than it does in the usual business. But there are only two hundred seminaries in the United States, and the nature of the opportunity to serve is such that every seminary should have an exceptional leader to chair its trustees, or the equivalent of that person in seminaries that do not have their own trustees. That urgency will need to be felt at all times if the typical seminary is to move in influence from where it now is to the society-shaping role that it is correctly positioned to carry. Only the chairperson, using tactics that are appropriate for a seminary in these times, is likely to be successful in creating that urgency. If the executive tries to create it, his or her tenure may be short. Trustees (including the chairperson) are expendable; administrators are not.

The chairperson need not be able to design the creative steps that will be taken within the seminary to produce the seminal ideas that will inspire and support pastors, nor need he or she be conversant with the curriculum designs that will prepare pastors as significant religious leaders. Both of these are appropriately the professional concern of administrators and faculty.

Trustees will want to review and comment on these matters, but they will not be the prime movers in these areas.

Trustees, especially the one in the chair, will need to be clear about the ultimate results of the seminary's work: more strong religious leaders everywhere; influential, ably led churches; and whether the seminary's ultimate influence on and support of churches is adequate.

Trustees should be aware of and interested in the effort of administrators and faculty to move the program of the seminary from mission to accomplishment. It is more appropriate for a layperson to maintain this detached position than it is for a credentialed professional. The seminary clearly needs professional strength, although what constitutes optimum professional strength in a seminary may bear fresh examination, one that needs what only wise lay judgment is likely to bring.

Strength in the Lay Status of the Chairperson

The issue of strength in lay judgments is a debatable one, but the case for the importance of trustees, particularly the chairperson, in any institution rests upon acceptance of the possibility of that strength being realized. The best example I have of this is drawn from my AT&T experience, an example of the strength in lay judgments in a situation in which that was where wisdom resided.

The original National Labor Relations Act (Wagner Act) was enacted in 1935. Shortly thereafter fifty great corporation lawyers met and agreed that this law would be held unconstitutional and that they would all advise their client companies to disregard it. When this conclusion was brought back and advocated by our AT&T lawyer, who had been present at that meeting, he was promptly and forcefully challenged by my boss, an able and persuasive older man with but a fifth-grade education. He was not in the upper levels of management, but he was in a position in which he could be heard. Although his grammar was not impeccable, he was a powerful debater, a strong, honest, intelligent man, though with no legal training or experience. The gist of his argument was that this was 1935, not 1905. This was the second time in as many years that the principle in the Wagner Act had been legislated (the first was a section of the National Industrial Recovery Act of 1933 that was declared unconstitutional). It clearly represented a firm social policy that would prevail. If this present law was not upheld, new laws would keep coming until one was sustained. Therefore, my boss argued, we should start immediately to bring ourselves into conformity with it (a condition that AT&T, with largely "company" unions, missed by quite a margin). There was a great verbal battle, but this boss of mine was a tough, formidable man. After much grumbling, he prevailed and the company started with too-deliberate speed toward compliance. If his position had not prevailed, and if AT&T had held to the position that all of those lawyers advocated, AT&T might have been dismembered then. And if this man's kind of thinking could have been more influential in top management councils in the years that followed, the breakup much later on might not have taken place.

Part of the strength of this untutored layman's position was that he was not a lawyer. He was a very conservative man (in the best sense) and he was able to look at the crisis that confronted the company as a social policy question, not a legal issue. And he believed that even the Supreme Court, given a little time, read the election returns. Sure enough, the Wagner Act was affirmed by the nation's top court in 1937.

The strength of my boss in this encounter was not just that he was not a lawyer, although that freed him from the mind-set that seems inherent in all credentialed professionals, or that he lacked formal education. Most important, I believe, was that he possessed the priceless gift of seeing things whole and, because of this, his advice was frequently sought by "better educated" people who lacked that gift. [See the discussion in "Seeing Things Whole."—Eds.] Is this not the quality, above all others, that should be sought in the trustee chairperson of a seminary?

It is not a common ability, yet it does exist. In the two hundred seminaries in the United States, a person could be found to chair their trustees if they were clear that that is what they need and want. Suitable people are more likely to be found among uncredentialed laypersons.

Such a person in the chair, if otherwise qualified by motives, temperament, and skills, would likely be accepted by fellow trustees and other constituencies of the seminary and could supply the essential ingredient of wisdom regarding the adequacy of the critical thinking that is the heart of the seminary's work. This would be accomplished by watchfulness over the three steps suggested earlier as being essential for any institution that achieves greatness-as-servant.

The Idea of the Seminary

If the seminary answers the question "Whom and what purpose should this seminary serve?" the one who chairs the trustees (assuming that that person has the gift of seeing things whole) may then ask, "Is this seminary, as it now stands—people, structure, and assumptions—best designed to accomplish that mission? If not, what kind of institution ought it to be, and how do we move it prudently from here to there?"

Such questions may lead the constituencies of the seminary to search for a creative design for the seminary of the future that, in addition to the present scholarly structure, may accommodate some whose principal qualifications are that they have the twin gifts of seeing things whole and prophetic communication. They may or may not be scholars.

The Problem of Language

Part of my thinking about language in the field of religion comes from the opportunity I had as a young man in New York to attend services at Riverside Church when Harry Emerson Fosdick preached. These sermons were remarkable for their clarity and simplicity. I received some insight into his gift many years later when I was privileged to be in his company along with a mutual friend. In the course of an afternoon's conversation, the elderly preacher told us that as a young man he had had a mental disturbance and had to have help to get himself reoriented. As a consequence, in the years of his ministry Fosdick had reason to believe that he was a good preacher and writer but that the most rewarding satisfactions in his career were in one-to-one consultations with disturbed people. He felt that he was at his greatest effectiveness here because he could say to his counselee that he understood how that person felt because he had been there himself. The clarity and simplicity of his preaching must have been profoundly influenced by the centrality of personal counseling in his ministry.

However gifted they may be, pastors trained in seminaries need to communicate ideas that give hope in language that is powerful and beautiful, words that lift the spirit. The chairperson of seminary trustees needs to be concerned that his school wields an influence on its students that favors this result.

The Seminary Chairperson as a Personal Role Model

By giving oversight to the pivotal part of the seminary's mission, critical thought, one has the opportunity to be a role model for those who carry equally important leadership in a local church, the lay leaders of its congregation.

Prominent in the concerns of many in this lay leadership is the fact that involuntary separations of pastors of Protestant churches are currently reported as disturbingly high. The main reason is inadequate leadership. Could it be that some of this failure is attributable to the pastor's attempting to lead in ways that are only appropriate for a layperson to lead? Also, is some of this failure due to teaching that insufficiently prepares the pastor for leading?

There has crept into the thinking about congregations the notion that there is a "group mind" governed by "a process" that is best manipulated by an outside "expert." But I believe inspired leadership is what moves a congregation toward being a loving, caring, serving community; inspiration is a gift only to individuals. Several may receive the same inspiration, or some who are inspired may influence others who are not, but inspiration is an uniquely individual phenomenon.

What a pastor will bring to a church, supported by seminary preparation, is a vision of a loving, caring, serving community that the congregation will become. Out of such a community, and nurtured by the inspiration that guides their growth, the members will emerge who have the greatest gift for seeing things whole and who will, because of that quality, be accepted to serve as lay leaders.

Being human, any pastor could fail to deliver this vision to a particular congregation, but it would be a failure of teaching-as-leading, not as an executive. The deeply felt belief with which the pastor is imbued in seminary is that there is no congregation that cannot be led, *by someone,* to become a loving, caring, serving community. If one pastor cannot do it with a particular congregation, another may try and succeed. And if enough pastors try and fail, some of those in the congregation who see things whole may rise to leadership and be accepted by the majority when they declare the importance of trying harder to learn what the next pastor tried to teach. At that point, those who are resolved not to learn from any pastor may depart. Pastors who are strong in their faith will accept failure and support one another in such failures, as they persevere in their mission to bring and sustain all congregations as loving, caring, serving communities.

Before the above sequence of events can take place, the seminary chairperson who sees things whole will need to lead the seminary toward critical thinking that postulates as a bottom line the notion of churches that are *loving, caring, serving communities.* Leading by teaching toward that end will become the prime skill to be learned in seminary. And the seminary chairperson will strive to be the model that guides the lay leaders of congregations.

It was argued earlier that seminary trustees and their chairpersons are expendable, but executives and administrators are not. So, in time, lay leaders in churches will come to accept that they are expendable but pastors are not. Laypersons will take the higher risks of leading.

What Does "Serving the Churches" Mean?

How does a seminary know when it is serving the churches?

A consultant who has worked with several seminaries recently on reviewing their missions reports: "One of the observations that comes out of this experience is the propensity of seminaries to give continuity to the safe kinds of ministry that they perceive the churches (which pay the bills) as willing to subsidize." [Cited in *Seminary as Servant*, 1983, p. 61.—Eds.] This states the common problem of *all* serving institutions: what will the constituency, customer, citizen want and be willing to pay for in the future? Making this judgment is probably most critical in business.

Churches cannot tell seminaries what they will want in the future and what they will be willing to pay for. If, as the consultant's observation quoted above suggests, some seminaries assume that churches will continue to want and be willing to pay for what they now receive—a "safe" ministry—then providing that may make for a comfortable relationship in the present. But what about the future? What about the future when the present, in terms of church influence and membership, is not good?

This is a question meant for a seminary chairperson who is disposed to try to influence his or her trustees to *lead,* to go out ahead and show the way and persuade seminary administrators and staff to act now, in the interest of the future soundness of churches. The seminary's prime concern is always for the future of churches. The future of churches will be determined importantly by the ideas, the critical thought, that seminaries produce *now* and persuade churches to consider—*now.*

Because it deals with the future, all true leadership entails risk. The chairperson who sees things whole will be the first to accept that risk and make the necessary leap of imagination. What supports the seminary chairperson in that risk is an inspired vision of what the seminary, and the churches that depend on it for intellectual and prophetic leadership, might become: greater servants of society.

Postscript

The positions taken here, regarding the urgency of the need to raise seminaries from the present marginal state of some of them to fully serving institutions, rest on beliefs about ours being a low-serving society. Every category of institution I know of, including seminaries and churches, has far too many low-serving elements, when judged by the criterion of what is reasonable and possible with available resources, human and material. Why should anybody in government, business, or education try to do better when seminaries, which should be models of doing better, are not conspicuous for their service to society? If the quality of our total society is to be lifted, seminaries and then churches, one at a time, need to be lifted—substantially—into a position of preeminent service.

As noted earlier, both the initiative and the sustaining push to achieve this movement will come from trustees who are laypersons with a strong, determined chairperson to lead their effort. If the current chairperson does not feel up to giving this leadership, that person might quietly step aside and help find someone who can and will give that leadership. It could be the supreme achievement of a person's life to learn to lead a seminary effectively and with spirit.

Alongside my convictions about lay influence of trustees in seminaries, I am equally firm about the importance of intellectual power in the seminary. This power will enable faculty and other staff to support churches and church institutions at a level of excellence in their performance that, on their own and without the support of the intellectual power of seminaries, might be quite ordinary.

Intellectual power could be said to have two main elements: scholarship and wisdom. What may be needed, first, is a new vision from within seminaries as they now stand, possibly a seminary now regarded as marginal. It is the kind of vision that the King James version of Proverbs suggests is one without which the people perish. Such a vision may simply announce a yearning to be served, to be led by a trustee chairperson who has the gift of seeing things whole.

And what would a seminary be like (as contrasted with what most are today) when it comes to be known as both scholarly and wise?

- Its priorities will be reversed. Whereas seminaries are now mostly academic and only incidentally formative, formation of religious leaders will be primary and academic teaching will be secondary.

- The staff of the seminaries will contain a strong element of those who have a passion for "growing" religious leaders—and are good at it. They may or may not be scholars in the usual sense.

- A major mission of the seminary will be to evolve, and maintain, a theology of institutions that deals realistically with the problem of how to recover moribund institutions as vital, effective, caring, and serving. This will not be a theoretical endeavor because it will be forged on the seminary's own experience as it builds itself into, and maintains itself as, the pivotal institution it is determined to become. Seminary students will be deeply involved in this continuous effort to build and maintain this theology. They will not just read and hear lectures about it.

- The primary mission of the seminary will be leading and serving churches and supporting them as strong and influential institutions. Most of the learning of seminary students will result from involvement in this effort.

o There will be creative thinkers among its faculty who are developing and articulating a contemporary theology of what makes religious leaders, and the institutions they serve, strong. Students in the seminary will be deeply involved in responding to this with their own thinking.

o Such seminaries will become known as effective nurturers of able religious leaders, and they will attract a wide spectrum of strong young people in search of such formative development. Some of these students might find their career opportunities in churches, but the seminary will become a prime source of religious leaders for all segments of society. It will acknowledge that any institution where religious leaders predominate may effectively become a church.

I submit these as achievable goals for a seminary whose constituencies (particularly the faculty that holds the predominant power) accept that new critical thought about both the seminary as an institution and its theology is essential. Further, they will accept the leadership of the layperson who chairs their trustees and who is persuasive in helping them to reach those goals.

This essay, written in 1985, moves from a broad discussion of the theology of institutions, with just a brief mention of the Institute of Chairing, to focus on the important role a trustee chairperson can play in his or her relationship with the institution executive. The essay was written two years prior to the following essay, and the idea of including both the board chairperson and the institution executive in some collaborative training was not expressed here. This piece emphasizes the importance of individual roles in making an institution a caring one.

THE TRUSTEE CHAIRPERSON:
NURTURER OF THE HUMAN SPIRIT

ONE WHO CHAIRS trustees or directors of any institution has three main opportunities to nurture the human spirit:

1. By standing as the visible symbol of trust to all constituencies, internal and external, and by public pronouncements and other manifestations of leadership and concern, all of which have great influence, especially on those who are closely linked as employees, customers (or clients), owners, and regulators.

2. As convener of the trustees, there is the opportunity to sustain their spirit and concern for the institution and lead them to be a major force in its affairs.

3. The primary thrust of this essay is that the chair represents the trustees, as a group, as the chief sustaining influence on the spirit of executives, particularly the chief or primus, with whom there is a close and regular relationship.

The primary source of inspiration for writing this piece resides in my good fortune to have been a trustee of the Russell Sage Foundation in the years that Emerson Andrews, an early historian of foundations, had just retired from the staff and was a frequent attender at board meetings. I had many conversations with him about foundations and what makes them, or deters them from being, good contributors. He had particular insight into the affairs of two large foundations that had achieved distinction. Both of them had, or had once had, unusually effective chairpersons. The staff executive in both cases was, in the public view, a distinguished person regarded as both creative and effective in the philanthropic program he headed. In the public view the chairperson's role was largely unrecognized. But to Andrews, as was later confirmed by my own findings, the way the chairperson related to the executive and sustained that person's spirit was a major factor in the high-quality performance of both of those foundations.

When J. P. Morgan took control of the American Telephone and Telegraph Company in 1907, he installed Theodore N. Vail, a great leader and builder, as president. [See the preceding essay.—Eds.] What I know about that period I learned from the surviving Vail organization, which was still in place when I came to AT&T's corporate office in 1929. From them I learned that Mr. Morgan had a major spirit-nurturing relationship with Vail for the six years that Morgan lived after 1907. This is the only way that I can account for Vail emerging as a statesman in his later years, because it did not seem to be in him in his earlier years. At age sixty-two, Vail brought to the job the leader-manager ability needed to build a great institution, but the statesman disposition and skills that enabled the institution to survive by making appropriate adaptations to public policy came after his relationship with Morgan. When Vail died in 1920 there was not a powerful trustee like Morgan to select a successor with statesman potential, and then to nurture that person to be an effective statesman. As a consequence the chief executives for the next sixty-four years, although they were able managers, did not have an able chairperson who would nurture them to become statesmen. Ultimately (and I believe as a result) the great covenantal company that Morgan and Vail built was lost in 1984.

In the 1960s, when the universities were in ferment, I received a few clues suggesting that in several major universities where the president was forced to resign, those unfortunate men too did not have close nurturing support from the chairperson and trustees. But in at least one university that was just as vulnerable as the others, the president did have that support and came through almost unscathed. I recall one poignant experience, in an off-the-record session with a small group that included two university presidents. In that meeting I made the statement that one factor in the university crisis was the tendency of trustees, while trouble was brewing, to counsel the president to "be firm, hang tough." But then, when the situation boiled over, those trustees were nowhere to be found. On hearing this, the president of a large church-related university with a denominational board said plaintively, with tears in his eyes, "That's exactly what happened to me."

Several years ago, in my writing on institutions and trusteeship I advocated separation of the roles of chief executive and chairperson. (In large publicly held businesses, they had tended to be merged.) My main reason for taking this stand was to better position trustees or directors to oversee the top management organization and to monitor its use of power. More recently, I have come to see the unusual opportunity for the chairperson to become the spirit nurturer of the chief executive, or, as I hope will evolve, of an executive group having a "first among equals." Just as I believe that the pastor of a church should not preside at meetings of the governing body of the church, so I believe that chairpersons in all sorts of institutions—businesses, universities, foundations, churches—need to be separated from administrative executives and work to develop a relationship with the executives that is spirit nurturing.

"What do I do?" the conscientious chairperson may ask. The only unequivocal answer I know to that question is one word: "Care." This is all I know for sure about J. P. Morgan and his relationship to T. N. Vail; Mr. Morgan really cared. He passionately wanted this business he controlled to grow into a distinguished serving institution. To be sure, he wanted it to make money. He had a lot of money and he wanted more because money was the source of his power. But the important part of his caring was for the quality of the institution. This was most unusual for a "money" man of his time—or today.

What the chairperson does to build a distinguished institution is probably tailored to each chairperson-executive relationship. I can imagine a zealous chairperson who would be seen as a nuisance and a drag by the executive, who might wish that the chairperson would stay away.

The best chairperson I ever saw in action presided over the board of a small nonprofit institution that had a single executive. This chairperson was not of high status in the world of affairs, but as the chair of those trustees he was remarkable. When his work took him to another part of the country the sense of loss on the part of the executive was profound.

From the few examples I have seen or know about in which the trustee chairperson effectively nurtured the human spirit of the executive, and through this service greatly strengthened the institution, I suggest the following guides:

- Intensely care for the quality of the institution—and be willing to work hard to help it reach its optimum.
- Seek no recognition or reward for yourself, but get satisfaction from seeing the executive perform well and receive recognition for it.
- Do a lot of listening, and have a basis for knowing whether the nurturing effort is constructive, neutral, or hurtful.
- Watch the institutional performance closely, and be able to counsel the executive constructively on how the institution might do better.
- Be available to talk to the executive about problems that arise; the executive's role can be a lonely one.
- Meditate on one's effort, and be open to inspiration about how best to relate to the executive.
- Have yourself a confidant to whom you can talk about how you are doing, and solicit the judgment of another on

the state of your relationship with the executive; your job as chairperson can also be a lonely one.

○ Be willing to limit other obligations that you will be tempted to take on in order to have the time that this chairperson's role really demands.

○

The above discussion of including in the chairperson's role the nurturing of the human spirit, especially the spirit of the institution's executives, is based on a premise. Most institutional performance I know about is mediocre when compared to what is reasonable and possible with available resources, human and material. In our institution-bound society, any improvement in the quality of that society will have at its base the raising of the quality of performance of its many autonomous institutions, one discrete institution at a time. The prime mover in such improvement in any institution—business, school, church, charity—will likely be the chairperson of its trustees or directors. And an important segment of that chairperson's role will be the sustained nurturing of the human spirit of the institution's executives.

The most open and feasible opportunity I know of for moving toward the better society that is reasonable and possible is the establishment of Institutes of Chairing, which will work to raise and sustain the human spirit of trustee chairpersons of institutions of all sorts and sizes. Such institutes give the chairpersons a vision of, and preparation for, the contribution only they can make, becoming themselves spirit builders of those who do the day-to-day administration of these many institutions.

This, as I see it, is the surest path for moving from where we now are to the better society of the future: inspirited chairpersons nurturing the human spirit of the administrators who will build the more serving institutions of the future. I believe it is within our power to move forward along this path.

Greenleaf wrote this essay in 1987; it was one of his last pieces of work. This revision incorporates some contents from his memo on an Institute of Chairing, which is undated but related to this piece. The idea of the institute set forth in this essay differs from Greenleaf's other writings on such an institute in that he incorporates the idea of including both the trustee chairperson and the institution executive in the seminars. This particular essay served as the basis for seminars created at Bangor Theological Seminary, first offered in 1988 and continuing through the early 1990s. However, the organizers did not realize their hope that these meetings would make a difference in how seminaries viewed the distinctive roles of board chairs.

TOWARD A GENTLE REVOLUTION

INSTITUTIONS, regardless of their missions, perform best when they are governed by a shared vision, rather than by the idiosyncrasies of whoever happens to be in power and presumes to lead.

"The leader leads best," said the ancient Taoist Lao Tzu, "when the people say, 'We did it ourselves.'" [It is uncertain which translation of the famous expression Greenleaf made use of here.—Eds.] In contemporary terms, in our vast complex society, it might be said that the leader leads best when she or he is seen as serving, and subordinate to, a shared vision; when a great idea that is widely shared governs and the leader is clearly seen as helping that idea to be realized in day-to-day practical affairs—and when the leader is not seen as pursuing a private agenda, however noble.

I am at one with those who worry about the spread of dictatorships of any kind. But I differ from some on how best to use our resources to check that trend. My preferred tactic is to concentrate on building greater strength, and serving quality, into our free institutions, into all of them—churches, schools, businesses, philanthropies, governmental units—which, with rare exceptions as they stand today, seem to me to miss widely their potential as servants to society. I believe that the most common cause of such discrepancy is inadequate vision, not living out a great dream of exceptional service; and too little effort to cause such vision as it has to be widely shared, by all those involved in the institution. My soundings on contemporary society suggest that these discrepancies infect the whole gamut of existing institutions, large and small, for-profit and not-for-profit. In a word, I see lack of vision as epidemic in our society. And it is on this score that I believe we are both losing the battle with encroaching dictatorships and failing to achieve the quality of life for all our people that is well within our grasp with available human and material resources. We talk a lot about freedom but we do not use the freedom we have, while we still have it, to build the kinds of institutions that would make our society more impregnable and more serving to all of our people and give us the exportable model of vision-inspired institutions that could give hope to the world.

The strength of our nation today does not reside so much in our Congress, or in the vast apparatus of the executive branch, because all seem to be so lacking in vision, and we seem not to have the resources to rebuild those visions. Our real strength is in our Constitution, the court system that our legal profession has (so far) been watchful to maintain, and the legions of free institutions that flourish under the umbrella of these two powerful protectors. Feeble as so many of these free institutions are, they are the main sinews of strength we have to bind over to our children and grandchildren. And we do not have the resources to quickly rekindle vision in these free institutions. But if that can be done gradually, there is hope that our free institutions may achieve a spiritual force that will ultimately infect our Congress and executive branch. The initiative, as I see it, rests with our legions of free institutions.

To those who are willing to accept even a little of this thesis, the following pages are offered as a basis for moving in prudent steps toward institutions that are more vision-inspired, and therefore stronger and more serving, than most that I now know about.

o

"Where there is no vision, the people perish." (Proverbs 29:18, KJV).

I do not have a precise definition for vision. To me, the full meaning of *vision*, like the meaning of *spirit* that is used here as the driving force behind the urge to serve, lies beyond the barrier that separates mystery from what we call reality. Vision, in these pages, is seen as awareness of what is there in good, able people, in a great potential to be realized in building optimally serving lives for people and optimally serving performance in institutions which these vision-inspired people will lead or influence. The stuff of vision has been there all along, and its emergence in conscious awareness is therefore a revelation. Hope that someday one's vision will be achieved in practice is what sustains a vision and makes one watchful and persevering, while one lives under its guidance.

Far too many of our institutions—and, of course, far too many people—are failing to serve at a level that is reasonable and possible for them. If the main reason for this deficiency in both people and institutions is, as I believe, that they are not inspired by a sufficient vision of greatness, then what is the remedy? The remedy proposed here rests on some assumptions that follow about the reasons why these deficiencies in visions are there.

Institutions as we know them today are a relatively recent event in history. Prior to this century we were a predominantly agricultural nation with limited government and commerce and a few professionals. The change to our present state came rapidly, and we seem not to have come to grips with the problem of why so many of our institutions do not serve us well. Government occasionally makes a pass at the problem when the pain becomes too severe. But government is part of the problem because it tends to be dominated by lawyers and economists—both necessary and valuable groups of people, but they tend to view institutions, particularly businesses, as chattels, pieces of property. There seems to be little in the tradition of either profession that makes them sensitive to what makes an institution effective as *servant*.

The two categories of institutions that should be most sensitive to deficiencies in vision, churches and schools, also appear to be a part of the problem. They seem as deficient in vision about their futures as any others. Therefore they lack the perspective to advise the rest who might look to them for guidance.

A deeper reason for the widespread lack of vision may be that, in the process of industrialization in the last 150 years, we seem to have become a manager-dominated society (managers being the people who get things done). Before the Industrial Revolution there were few managers, but they have now become numerous and are a vital necessity. Able managers are required in large numbers to keep our vast complex of institutions viable. And all of our institutions—churches, schools, businesses, philanthropies, governmental units—need able managers to get the work done and keep the places solvent (if not profitable). As an institution watcher, over the years I have gotten to know well a number of managers in all major categories of institutions. I have come to respect their managerial acumen, which I see as indispensable to the ongoing success and survival of the institutions they head. But I also see a limitation that accrues with years of good performance in these roles. Managers seem incapable of generating the much needed visions, the dreams of future greatness which might be approached in prudent steps over time.

I speculate that it would not be useful to a manager to indulge in very much visionary thinking. Managers are necessarily short range in their thinking, bounded by the recent past and the immediate future. They tend to lack a sense of history; it would not be useful to them. And they tend to lack the imagination to project the long-range future. Years of managerial work tend to be limiting for anything but the managing that requires great concentration on keeping the institution afloat from day to day. Doing this well is enough to ask of a person, and it is unrealistic to expect that most successful managers would be visionary thinkers. This is a judgment I have come to quite late in life.

Some of us need to work to make acceptable the idea that a variety of gifts are required to make a good society. But in the guidance of our institutions we seem to have accepted that management is all that is needed to build and sustain serving institutions. It will profit us to accept that trustees who are not managers are needed to supply a complementary gift of vision that is absolutely essential to the long-run health of any institution. It will take a lot of work.

As I look back on it now, I believe I saved my imagination by my choice of career as a staff person, a thinker and planner. My imagination is still pretty good (in my eighty-fourth year), and I don't believe it would be if an important part of my life had been spent in managing. I was able to make a successful life out of institution watching and dealing with ideas about managing, without carrying the role.

Part of my insight in these matters comes from doing a good deal of ghostwriting for top people in both businesses and universities. I don't recall a single instance in which I was asked to write something, usually a speech, in which I was told, "these are the ideas I would like to use." All I ever got was a description of the occasion. I had to produce the ideas. These were good, intelligent, able people with excellent judgments, and they knew a good idea when they saw one. But they didn't produce ideas themselves.

As I reflect on the above observation, it seems to me that the heavy burdens top managers carry, wherever they are, are such that their capacity to do visionary thinking is limited by their experience. There may be some who can do both. But in my sixty years of institution watching, I have not encountered one. Abraham Lincoln may have been such an exception. But even there, his presidency was his first managerial role. If he had been managing for thirty years before the Gettysburg "occasion" came, he might not have had the imaginative power to write that great address himself.

o

How, the incredulous may ask, will visionary trustees ever become influential when trustee bodies today are generally peopled by managers? The obstacles to taking those steps are formidable:

o Managers, especially chief executives and other high-level officers, are loath to accept that managerial excellence inhibits their capacity to produce visions as well as their appreciation of the importance of visions. As they see it now, management is all.

o There is little understanding, among people who are not managers, of the potentially powerful relationships between managers and trustees in which trustees provide the visions managers are not likely to have.

o The resources do not exist for a frontal challenge to the widespread condition of limited vision throughout our society.

If the problem of limited vision is crucial and epidemic in all our institutions, what then can be done even gradually and in a small way to begin to raise the acceptance of the importance of visions, and to cause visions to emerge in the top leadership of more of our institutions?

I believe that the people most likely to begin to think about the need for greater visions in the leadership of all institutions are the chairpersons of trustees of theological seminaries of all faiths, for two reasons.

First, I see seminaries generally as missing their opportunities by the widest margin of any category of institution I know about. While some seminary trustee chairpersons may bridle at so bald a statement, there is an uneasiness that is evident in their awareness of the difficulties most seminaries are having financing themselves. Institutions that are seen as truly serving do not have that level of difficulty.

Second, among the trustee chairpersons of seminaries there are some who will accept at least part of the criticism made above. They would welcome an opportunity to discuss visions for their seminary in order that the seminary could stand as a model for other institutions and better serve churches and church-related institutions that depend on seminaries for both intellectual and prophetic guidance.

The suggestion here is that a start be made by convening a seminar with a group made up of chairpersons and executives, in pairs, from several seminaries. The primary focus of the seminar might be a concept of leadership in the seminary in which the vision-generating role of trustees will be understood and accepted, and, secondly, that a clearly articulated and shared vision, under the leadership of the executive, will become the governing instrument in the seminary. This shared vision will be refined and sustained by theological reflection on trusteeship in the faculty. The stimulus for this faculty participation might be the reports of presentations and discussions at the proposed seminar.

The agenda at the seminar might be partly exploratory: to learn more about leadership in a seminary, both on the part of the executive with the faculty, and the chairperson with the trustees; and about the relationship between the two quite different roles. The seminar could be partly learning from case studies, reading and discussion of reading, presentations by video and live lectures, and creative problem-solving discussions of issues of leadership in a seminary.

Themes to be dealt with in one or more of the above approaches might be:

o The spiritual history of trusteeship

o Consensus finding

- A theology of institutions, including a seminary
- Mentoring of young potential leaders
- Evolving a vision of a seminary, and the seminary as a model for other vision-directed institutions, particularly churches.

There are some acknowledged skills of chairing that could become agenda items in the institute:

- *Listening.* There is an art to being a good listener, and some experience is available in helping people to learn it.
- *Persuasion.* This is an important part of chairing, but how the institute would give help in this area would be one of its important inventions.
- *Foresight.* Seeing it before it hits you is important to any leadership. Again, the institute would invent its own approach.
- *Identifying critical problems.* Chairpersons need to audit priorities. More such items could be listed. Some of these could be dealt with in case materials, but probably most growth will come by alerting participants to the importance of specific aspects of chairing and urging them to observe them in their consultant-observer role with other institutions.

The initial proposal is for a modest seminar for a few pairs of trustee chairpersons and executives of seminaries. The larger view is that this venture would be seen as the start of an Institute of Chairing that would, with experience, slowly expand so as to be attractive to pairs of chairpersons and executives of other institutions. The initial project might, from the outset, be a source of new literature on trustee chairing. That literature would go to potential visionaries now in leadership spots in other institutions and nourish their dreams; it would provide a new and exciting literature of hope in graduate and undergraduate instruction. Not just hope for fine-tuning the status quo, but hope that new institutions, of a quality that today seems a pipe dream, may one day become a common reality. The intent would be to provide a solid basis for hope in young people as they approach entrance into adult society, that is, hope that if they develop their leadership competence and use their lives well so as to sustain their imaginations and their creative powers into their old age, they may emerge into positions of influence and become important forces in shaping stronger and more serving institutions than the ones they have grown up with.

One immediate consequence of Institutes of Chairing might be the explicit preparation of those now in key positions of leadership to mentor the potential young leaders. These key leaders have a chance to help so that stronger and more serving institutions than we are able to achieve in the present may have a better chance to evolve in the future.

Earlier I noted my two primary concerns in writing this piece. First, too many of our institutions are not adequately serving those they touch, and they need to reach for a greater vision of being stronger and more serving. Second, as a nation we are not holding up the model we are reasonably capable of providing for the less-favored people who are tempted toward the easy solution of dictatorship.

I have a vision of a nation, while still far from perfect, that can move steadily and in prudent steps toward a new dream of what it can become, one institution at a time. The prime leaders for this new movement may be chairpersons of trustees, not superpeople but good, solid, ethical folk who have a new vision of their roles and the role of the institutions in their care, and who have the skills and knowledge of processes that enable them effectively to lead their fellow trustees toward achieving stronger and more serving institutions.

What is proposed here is a gentle revolution, but a revolution nevertheless. Nothing that is upsetting or precipitous will be noted by anybody. Yet over a generation, if enough institutions get involved in it, the change could be profound and those institutions that are not caught up in it could in the end be seen as deviant. This, I suspect, is the way cultures evolve best: gradually and peacefully.

The trustee chairpersons who lead this revolution would, at best, be gently persuasive and inconspicuous, a new visionary influence in institutions that are starved for visions. And the ultimate impact of this modest start of an Institute of Chairing by seminaries might be not so much the immediate impact on participants as the long-delayed effect of communicating the findings of this work through colleges and universities. A new expectation could be nurtured among young people, who will get an understanding of the great potential in trustees and evolve a vision of themselves as possible future chairpersons. Some of them might then plan their careers so as to mature the qualities that would prepare them for the kind of leadership envisioned here. The full-circle effect of a modest start for Institutes of Chairing in seminaries might come when well-qualified, ethically grounded candidates become plentiful and are available for all sorts of leadership roles in a needy society.

Central to the consummation of the gentle revolution suggested here is emergence of a new vision of the largely untapped potential in trustees. Trustees have been around for some time, but the view of their role as significant visionaries for the institutions they hold in trust is not now widely accepted. Yet the emergence of trustees as creators of visions for our vision-starved society is well within the grasp of the prophetic resources of seminaries, with their gift of poetry to nurture the human spirit, to the end that institutions of all sorts might be moved toward their highest potential as servants to all they touch. The means are available to seminaries to bring the vision of trustees into a strong complementary relationship with managers and to cause a concept of this new relationship to become a powerful shared vision to all involved. By taking the modest initiative of establishing Institutes of Trustee Chairing, seminaries could become a prime force in the gentle revolution that might, in a generation, raise the serving quality of enough institutions of varied types to make ours a measurably more caring society.

Greenleaf wrote this paper in 1987, just three years before he died. In this piece he continues to examine the roles seminaries and churches could play in making institutions and people more serving. But, he approaches these themes from the angle of making strong trustees who will, in turn, make strong, serving institutions. Greenleaf echoes the theme of churches working with neighborhood institutions to create community, which occurs in his pieces on the center city church.

MINISTRY TO THE STRONG

MUCH OF THE ENERGY of people and institutions of goodwill rightly goes to the care of the weak, the ill, and the disadvantaged who are casualties of our imperfect society. The level of care now given these people falls well below what our present circumstances could reasonably provide. This deficiency could be corrected and our whole society could become more durable and compassionate in the process, if more of the potentially strong among us became more dedicated to the good of our society, including these unfortunate groups. If a significant shift is to be made from indifference and self-service toward such service, then a substantial new effort, one with imagination and force, will be needed. This effort must ensure that as many as possible of those who come to maturity with the potential to become strong and effective people are helped to focus on constructive work and to acquire life patterns of responding with spirit to the abundant opportunities to serve others, either as individuals or through those collectives called institutions. Some of this new effort will go to sustaining the human spirit at all stages of life. This needed new effort, as I see it, is a task for churches.

Some churches of various faiths, as they now stand, are adequately positioned to undertake this new ministry to the strong and the potentially strong. Others might move themselves into such a position when the way is shown. It is not suggested that churches diminish their direct care for the weak, the ill, and the disadvantaged. Rather they might add to their present mission a significant new ministry to the strong. Since this may be a new idea to some churches, they will need some help—help best given by seminaries.

The thesis here is that seminaries might become a much greater force in shaping the quality of contemporary society if, in the theological reflections of their faculties and in their formative influence on students, there were more concern for nurturing the human spirit of the strong. (Human spirit is seen here as the driving force behind the urge to serve.) Following is a sharing from my own experience, study, and reflection on how to help strong people of goodwill be more effective servants of society. My hope is that pastors of churches will become the prime community builders of the future, especially in the inner cities, where the need is great. The pastors could do so by devoting some of their energy to mentoring the strong people they have a chance to help, both in their formative years and in sustaining them as they do their work with community-based institutions. What will these strong people do for institutions that will help to build and maintain a good society? Many will become managers in schools, businesses, hospitals, philanthropies, and governmental units. Able managers are needed in large numbers, but their nurture is not the critical need addressed here. The place of managers in the scheme of things is well understood, and ample resources exist to serve them.

The critical need is for able, alert, dedicated trustees of institutions, who can correct any shrinkage of vision and ensure health to the institution. Trustees are not unnoticed people, but the attention given to their discovery and nurture is woefully inadequate and their vital role is not well understood. Too often they are functionaries who merely give legal cover and only come to life when there is a new chief to be selected or when there is a real catastrophe. The need for able and alert trustees (strong people) in large numbers is not widely accepted as urgent. But it is urgent, because ours is an institution-bound society in which the needs of most people are largely met by institutions—too many of which are not serving well.

I am convinced that one of the surest paths to building a better society than the one we now have, a society that is more just and caring, as well as structurally sound and durable, is to bring a new influence to bear that will produce more able and strong trustees for our vast complex of institutions. The most likely path to accomplish this, as I see it, is for pastors of churches of all faiths to become mentors to ethical people who will evolve as trustees of institutions of all sorts, especially as trustees of small neighborhood institutions. The aggregate of their influence may outweigh the influence of the big ones, because the neighborhood institutions have the opportunity to build community.

What will these pastors be like who can effectively minister to those who have the potential to be influential, ethical people? How might they be described? From my knowledge of a few contemporary pastors who have the strength now to impart vision if they themselves had that vision, I suggest the following description:

- o They are strong, able, well-prepared people.
- o They know who they are and where they stand.
- o They have a clear vision, a sense of direction.
- o They have great sustaining spirit with which to confront adversity.
- o They have unqualified dedication to the mission to which they are committed.

I have had enough contact with the oncoming generation to believe that there are many among them who have the potential to develop into exceptional, strong people in these five dimensions, and to believe that they would be attracted to a seminary program that promises to nurture them in these ways. If seminaries are to be seen as offering this promise, and if they are to attract their fair share of these exceptional people as students, then I believe that they need to add to their current programs competence in two areas.

The first is the important role of trustees in our society. Today we require many strong influential people who will provide the vision that our vast complex of institutions, large and small, so sorely needs and that managers on their own are not likely to possess. Managers are necessary and valuable people, but they are apt to be short-range in their thinking. They must keep their institutions afloat from day to day with much attention to detail. It is important that they do their work well. But years of attention to this demanding work tends to block out the ability of a person to generate visions. The occasional manager may have that gift, but in my experience they are rare. They even have difficulty responding to a vision when one is proposed, unless it is proposed by powerful trustees or directors who hold the ultimate power over the institution. This view suggests that trustees need access to their own staffs, thinkers and dreamers not restrained by managerial thinking.

I found that, in a staff position in a huge bureaucracy, I had to lead two quite separate lives to survive intellectually. In one, I played the managerial game according to the rules. In the other, I led my quite separate intellectual life as a historical researcher and visionary. It required an astute Machiavellian strategy to move anything from the latter role into the former. Clear visions from fully functioning directors would have made that strategy unnecessary. But there were no such directors in my time. These are the kinds of things that need to be thought about in a seminary if it is to attract young people capable of being nurtured in the five ways described above.

The second area is recovery of an awareness of the nurture of the human spirit as a central idea in theological education. I have used the term *human spirit* to name the drive behind the urge to serve. And I see it as the wellspring of the precious quality of vision. I am enough of an optimist to believe that most people approach maturity with some of this quality latent in them. But concentration on an intensive intellectual program like that of a seminary may dull this quality, just at a time when it should grow and flourish. A seminarian needs not only to have her or his spirit nurtured in the course of training, but he or she also needs to get a view of himself or herself as spirit nurturer, both of young people in their formative years and of older people needing sustained nurturance. The latter is important especially for those who carry trustee roles in which (as I know from experience) life can be discouraging. The oppressive weight of managerial thinking that dominates most institutional governance requires a strong charge of spirit to cope with it.

Finally, the seminary needs to become known as a place that holds a powerful, persuasive vision of the church as a vital, contemporary, culture-shaping institution, and that sees itself as a creative, manageable place attractive to those strong people who are capable of being successful pastors of such churches. This is no small goal, but I see it as achievable from the base that most seminaries now occupy.

In short, I suggest that seminaries discover the importance of trustees as a basic theological concern, and that they recover, as a central process in their work, the nurture of the human spirit.

Like so many of my contemporaries, I have opinions about almost everything. But those areas where I have quite settled views on which I would bet my chips are few. Among them are four propositions:

1. If our United States civilization is to move along and if we are to hold up our heads in the world, the institutions that make up our complex society—churches, schools, businesses, philanthropies, governmental units—need to become more effective and more serving to all who are touched by them. Some of them need to aspire to greatness.

2. Great institutions are more likely to emerge when the chairpersons of their trustees or directors are strong, influential people of vision.

3. If more than at present are to emerge who have the ability and the will to lead institutions to greatness, then much more effort needs to be made to nurture the human spirit of those who arrive in their teens or early twenties as persons who have the makings of strong good people: intelligent, stable, with good values and staying power.

4. The culture-shaping influence of churches can be decisive if pastors are effective in nurturing the human spirit of the potentially strong people they have a chance to influence. And if pastors are known to have the ability and the will to make this nurture real, they are apt to gather around them those to whom such nurture would be a rewarding experience.

In making the suggestion that seminaries assume leadership in these matters, I am aware that all of them are likely to be operating under restraints of some sort: financial stringency, staffs of varying strengths and with some rigidities, denominational requirements, traditional expectations, what students demand. Therefore they are likely to project their futures realistically. However, a vision of greatness, one that lifts people's sights, is not bound by such limitations. A vision may ask the impossible, and when people are guided by a compelling vision sometimes the impossible is achieved. When the vision of an institution suggests the aspiration to greatness, some of its people are apt to begin to think in terms of greatness.

This essay is a combination of three unpublished essays from 1984. They present nuts-and-bolts ideas that pull together many of Greenleaf's themes about the roles seminaries and churches could play in fostering caring institutions in communities. These pieces were written in conjunction with conversations he had with some inner city pastors in the early 1980s. The Greenleaf archives contains a great deal of correspondence with these pastors, which elaborates on the themes in this essay.

THE INNER CITY CHURCH
AS SERVANT TO ITS COMMUNITY

MOST OF MY LIFE I have been concerned with big institutions, and I accept that their influence on the quality of society is not always good. But in recent years I have come to see that the infrastructure on which all large institutions rest is the great number of small ones, particularly the legions of neighborhood nonprofit institutions. It is not that "small is (necessarily) beautiful." There are plenty of inferior small institutions and some big ones that are beautiful. It has not been demonstrated that size has anything to do with quality. Quality depends on the ideas, resources, and abilities of those who lead or manage. Nor is it necessarily easier to produce quality in a small institution than in a big one. It is simply that the great number of small institutions are the base upon which the large ones stand. And it may be more important to work first to produce beauty in small ones than in big ones because the quality of the aggregate of small neighborhood nonprofit institutions may be a limiting factor on what can be achieved by large ones. Big institutions alone cannot make a "good" society, no matter how excellent they may be. If enough small institutions are good, the big ones will have to be good to survive, to be tolerated. The test of health of a society, as with a person, is how its innards are working. The question to be discussed here is, what can a church that aspires to be servant to its community do about the state of the innards of its own neighborhood—especially if it is a center city neighborhood?

Peter Berger has given us the idea of mediating structures in society, those institutions that serve (or could serve) as the connective tissue that holds an assortment of disparate institutions together and makes a society viable. Churches could be mediating institutions. The reports I have from observers of center cities suggest that not many of the churches located there do serve as mediating structures. Such churches are but one of the diverse institutions that depend on some other mediating structure to give the community coherence. A church is not accepted as a mediating structure in a center city area simply because it is a church that happens to be there. It moves into that crucial community-building role only where it assumes responsibility for the community and its institutions in some significant way, and takes sustained initiatives to support those institutions.

After reading an early draft of this piece, two observers of center city churches commented that most of them are of two types:

1. They are but the meeting place of a congregation that long before moved out; but instead of rebuilding, the members drive to the center city for worship and the "sacred" portions of their lives.

2. They are true inner city dwellers, and they are struggling for enough money, enough members, and enough program to nourish their "spiritual lives."

The first type is likely to have locks on the doors, a buzzer to push if one calls during the week, and perhaps television monitors and a security guard—all depending on how large the annual budget and the endowment happen to be.

The second type is open to all much of the time, but "break ins" and vandalism and violence are more likely to be part of their ritual life and existence than in the first type.

In the first type, too often no one cares about the community around them, except for Thanksgiving, Christmas, and occasional ventures into gratuitous benevolence.

In the second type, the need to survive and build enough spiritual foundation to cope with life would keep most from an awareness of institutions in the community.

In the first type, a leader/member might be able to define an institution, and community.

In the second, the sophistication needed is wanting.

In the first type, leadership may be trained in theology and in management, but their calling is to serve those who pay their salaries. Can leaders go much farther than their followers?

In the second type, leadership is pitifully underskilled, undertrained, and undernourished in so many ways. [From conversations with Revs. Phil Tom and Philip Amerson.— Eds.]

These are realistic, useful comments. I suspect that there are more than two types of center city churches and that there are varying mixtures of these two elements, but these comments may identify the sources of the limitations that restrain a center city church from being servant to its community. What is important is that, whatever its makeup, the center city church develops an awareness of its neighborhood and its needs and the opportunity—and challenge—that it presents to the church to be servant to its community. Included in this awareness is recognition of the importance of caring, both to the one who cares and to the one who is cared for. From time to time each of us is in both roles; experiencing one of these roles may be essential to appreciating the other.

The Center City as Community

Community is seen here as any gathering of persons in which the incidence of people caring for people is high, in which the more able and the less able effectively serve each other. Community can exist anywhere, but it is seen here as *neighborhood,* people living in a limited geographical area, particularly center city neighborhoods where the need for a servant church is greatest.

The person-to-person caring of earlier times has given way to mediation through institutions, especially in center city neighborhoods. One measure of the center city church as servant to its community is how well it nurtures men and women who will lead, or otherwise influence, the center city neighborhood institutions they are involved in, to the end that those institutions are effective as servants to every person they touch.

Center city neighborhoods are not a standard thing. There are important ethnic differences. Each neighborhood has its own history and myths as well as a unique complex of institutions. Each of these institutions has its own characteristic way of doing business, which may or may not bear a resemblance to Robert's Rules of Order. These center city institutions cover a wide range of organizational forms, from incorporated bodies to informal committees. And they embrace a wide variety of activities and concerns that a caring community will generate. The active leaders of all of them are seen as trustees.

There will be agencies of government that serve the community, and the center city church as servant to its community will work with them to help optimize their service to the community. But the greater opportunity for the serving church is to encourage the neighborhood nonprofit institutions, and help build new ones, when needed, by strengthening their leaders, their trustees. A sign of hope for our society is that there is a lot of unused talent in these center city neighborhoods.

Trustees of Neighborhood Institutions: A Priesthood of All Believers

When Martin Luther advocated a priesthood of all believers he gave us one of the great ideas of this millennium. One of the significant events of our time came last year when, on the five hundredth anniversary of the birth of Martin Luther (1483), the Roman Catholic church formally acknowledged the greatness of Luther's contribution. The recent substantial movement toward larger involvement of laypeople in the churches attests to the impact of Luther's work on contemporary Catholic thinking.

The reformation that Luther started is, however, unfinished, and probably will always be unfinished. He laid the groundwork and gave the great ideas, but it is the task of churches and their leaders of every generation to find the practical applications of those ideas to contemporary situations that people confront. It is the special opportunity of center city churches to serve their communities by helping to empower the leaders of neighborhood nonprofit institutions, their trustees, as a priesthood of all believers.

This empowerment of trustees will be religious, else why would a church be concerned with it? But because of the diversity of most inner city neighborhoods, it cannot be religious in a sectarian or doctrinal sense. *Why* should such empowerment be religious, and *how* will it be religious?

Religion is taken here in its root meaning, *re-ligio,* to bind or rebind. If one is to be empowered, one will be helped to become powerful—not in a coercive sense, but as sustaining strength to create, inspire, persuade, persevere, all within the ethic of servant; in short, to lead as servant. Most effective leaders who serve are religious in this sense.

How will empowerment be religious? It will be religious within my meaning of serving. [See the discussion of the servant-leader in "Religious Leaders as Seekers and Servants."—Eds.] And servant-leaders will achieve this through *faith as trust,* the kind of faith that sustains them as they venture and risk to lead, and gives them a vision of the future, a dream to work toward.

Such empowered trustees of center city institutions may become, in our time, an important achievement of a priesthood of all believers. This is true because the strength of these people will rest on deep inner resources, which these many small neighborhood institutions will nurture in large numbers of trustees and other volunteers who will take on unique caring roles with spirit and resolve.

If a center city church should accept, as a major mission, serving the trustees of neighborhood nonprofit institutions by undertaking to make of them a priesthood of all believers, it will be making itself a different and more vital institution than many of these churches are now. Some suggestions on how to do this follow.

Understanding the Neighborhood and the Church's Place in It

A center city church that undertakes this mission will need to acquire a different view of itself than many churches now have. Someone who sees the vision of an opportunity to make of the church a more serving institution will undertake to lead it to that view. This may be the pastor or influential members. It may require a major venture of faith and persuasion in order to bring the congregation solidly behind it.

The pastor, and others who participate in the effort, will work closely with those from other neighborhood churches and ministries that share the mission. They will make an intensive study of the nonprofit institutions in the neighborhood and their trustees and get to know them personally. This will be undertaken in the spirit of building the neighborhood, not building these churches. The churches will see themselves as instruments of the work, and their compensation will be the same as it is to any other servant: the satisfaction of work well done and gaining strength to serve in other ways. Out of knowing the people who are trustees of neighborhood institutions and talking to them about their work, the pastor and those who may share in this effort will evolve a concept of what the opportunities and obligations of trusteeship are, and they will know when the individuals in those positions need help.

A truly servant church that takes seriously the enlargement of the priesthood of all believers to include trustees of center city neighborhood institutions may accomplish this great mission by suggesting a way that a pastor can give leadership that will assist more residents of the neighborhood to become effective servants of the community as trustees. This is not likely to happen without the leadership of a person as strategically placed as the center city church pastor. The belief that supports this hope is that there are many residents in every center city, some of them members of its churches, some not, who have unused talents for trusteeship; these residents would lead fuller, more rewarding lives if they invested more of themselves in leading. Pastors, individually or in concert with others, can materially raise the quality of life in the community by mentoring trustees, finding and assisting potential trustees, and making trusteeship more attractive. This is the belief that underlies this essay.

Mentoring, as that term is used here, differs from what is usually called *teaching* in that mentoring usually takes place in an actual situation dealing with real live problems, with people in their usual (and sometimes tension-torn) relationships. The mentor may impart ideas. But he or she will be more concerned with counseling the understudy about situations being experienced in a way that develops faith as trust, to strengthen the understudy's intuitive resources and armor that person to venture and risk leadership. Critical to this process is the skill and inventiveness of the mentor in challenging the imagination of the understudy, in encouraging the disposition to withdraw and be reflective in the heat of action, fully confident that resolving insights will come (again, faith as trust).

The role of a trustee is essentially that of mentor. The trustee of a neighborhood institution is usually working with volunteers, and the relationship may be quite similar to that of pastor to trustee. Thus the pastor may be demonstrating a relationship that the trustee may find helpful in dealing with volunteers—a useful learning to the trustee.

The first question to be raised in the mentor's discussions with trustees may be, what is the mission of this institution? What are you trying to do? This is one of the easiest questions to ask and one of the hardest to answer. The temptation may be to respond with descriptions of services rather than a statement of what it intends to accomplish. The mentor might press for a statement of broad aims, such as "building a better community" or "improving the quality of life in the community," rather than simply listing narrowly defined services. A mission statement is not a program; rather, it is a charter, a statement of who is to be served and for what purpose.

Mentoring trustees is not coaching in tactics, although there may be some of that. It is partly (maybe chiefly) sustaining the faith of able people to persevere and to be effective in their caring and serving, and giving support when trustees get discouraged or confused. This helps to build faith as trust: confidence in one's own strength and personal resources and one's ability to cope with stress. Implicit is that one cherishes a covenantal feeling for one's neighborhood and a vision for its future which one holds to on both good days and bad days. One accepts that one is dealing with hopes, and that there may be losses and failures to be accepted. A pastor as mentor will be quick to sustain spirit after a loss. In any issue the mentor will be more concerned to save the trustee as a person than to save an institution. A trustee saved can help build another institution. The pastor will understand the significant contribution that trustees make, in contrast to the paid staff that does the work of the institution. The role of the trustee of a small institution is the same as in a big one. Trustees bear the ultimate responsibility for the performance of the institution and its integrity. They take the initiative to state its mission and they watch over and guide its actions. They control its finances, appoint, monitor, and motivate its staff, or deal with volunteers directly if it has no staff, and they stand as the symbol of the institution and the guarantors of its quality. This is a large order; but it can be a rewarding service for any able person who undertakes it responsibly.

Mentoring trustees of neighborhood institutions to the end that a covenantal feeling for the community emerges may be one of the surest practical steps a pastor can take toward leading the congregation to become servants of the community and move toward the achievement of a priesthood of all believers.

Until seminaries accept the opportunity to train pastors as leaders and generate the vision that sustains them, the task falls on local congregations and centers of neighborhood ministries to assume the role of community builders *and* to produce the vision that guides this effort. In the absence of this vision community organizers may emerge whose outlooks are short-range, and who direct the community toward immediate steps that may help a specific condition but which lack—and possibly defeat—the long-range vision of improving the quality of life in the neighborhood.

The sustained nurturing of local leaders who have this vision is at the heart of the needs of center city neighborhoods. Because of the tendency of "helping professionals"—including some pastors—to dominate, it is important for a pastor to strive to make his or her contribution in a way that strengthens, rather than diminishes, the ability of neighborhood people to help themselves and to evolve strong leaders for their institutions.

I want to turn now to my own experience for an example of a neighborhood institution that will make very exacting demands on its trustees to meet a need that is growing more urgent.

Care of the Elderly

In 1977, when my wife and I were seventy-three, we sold our home and moved to a church-sponsored, life-care retirement community. We made that decision because we wanted the assurance of care in our old age we felt we could not find in normal, middle-class community living. Also, we did not want to be a burden to our widely dispersed children. We did not feel it was a good idea to segregate old people in this way—separating them from normal community living and taking from established communities the contributions that sometimes are best made by old people. But we concluded that since the monetary cost was one we could afford, it was the best option available to us. If, with the benefit of intervening experience, we had to choose again, we would make the same decision.

Our experience has been a happy one. The place is operated by dedicated trustees and administrators; the services are of a high order; and the spirit and competence of those who care for us is excellent. Those of us who want to be active find plenty to do in the community. Opportunities and facilities for socializing and entertaining each other are ample. There is a good community spirit and there are many caring people among our residents; but they are all old. Most of the act of "persons caring for persons" is done by the paid staff. There is little feeling of interdependence here; we could get along without each other. And there is little opportunity for being useful to younger people. On balance, I see it as a synthetic community, not as a model for care of the elderly in center cities.

The opportunity to spend one's declining years in a place like the one we live in is not available to most residents of center cities because it is too expensive. Even some now living in the center city who could afford it might not choose to move to a remote life-care community because the residual spirit of interdependence in the center city would be too important to be left behind (a deprivation that we did not feel when we left the highly individualistic community where we lived). Therefore, if those who grow old in the center cities are to have the assurance of care that we have where we now live, it will be provided in the community where they live by neighborhood nonprofit institutions in which much of the service will be rendered by volunteers.

Keeping the elderly in their accustomed community will be better for many of them because they will be among old friends and in a normal spread of ages where the oldsters can be useful; and it will be better for neighborhoods to have the leaven of their presence. But careful observations I have made of what is involved in giving this assurance of care for old people suggests that such service by neighborhood institutions that are staffed to some extent with volunteers will require extraordinary trustees to manage them. I venture to suggest that this is a feasible idea for some center city neighborhoods because I believe there is a sufficient number of people there who have the makings to be exceptional trustees. Further, I believe that capable, young volunteers would welcome this opportunity to serve, and that the cost of good care for the elderly would be manageable *if* center city churches with able pastors and strong lay leaders would give sustained leadership and mentor the trustees of the neighborhood institutions delivering this care. The ultimate test of whether center city churches will be judged adequate servants to their communities may be if they are able to muster the resources to provide their elderly residents with the assurance of good lifetime care in their local neighborhood institutions.

A center city church that is successful in doing this may be holding a beacon for the wider community, where, despite the proliferation of life care communities, care of the elderly is still a critical problem. The center city may be the pilot project for building community everywhere as a remedy for widespread alienation in contemporary society. The center city church that rises to this opportunity will probably become quite a different place than most such churches now are.

How Will a Center City Church Mentor Trustees of Neighborhood Institutions?

The center city church will need to become committed to raising the quality of life in the center city as its central mission. It may be that a pastor, as a venture of faith, will have to take the initiative to help his or her church develop that enduring commitment among its members. This may entail building a covenantal feeling among the center city church members for the community. It will be important that the pastor be sustained by this feeling among the church members in order that, in the course of mentoring the trustees of neighborhood institutions, the pastor will be effective in nurturing that spirit among the many men and women who carry the trustee roles of neighborhood institutions. This will be the sustaining spirit that supports these people as they persevere against indifference and opposition. A trustee of a neighborhood institution will need to feel the certainty of calling that will make a vocation out of his or her endeavor, something to which one devotes a good piece of one's life. This will require that the pastor of a center city church also feel a similar certainty of vocational calling and, ultimately, that the seminary or other institution that prepares pastors for this role will become a prime source of covenantal inspiration, attracting students who will welcome preparation for such a demanding role.

Two historical examples of extraordinary pastors who have had this dedication to building community institutions come to mind. They are not models for pastors of contemporary center city churches, but both achieved spectacular results of the kind that might inspire pastors today. Both lived to their late eighties and invested over fifty years in the task.

John Frederic Oberlin (for whom Oberlin College is named) was born in the mountains of France near Switzerland in 1740. In 1767 he assumed the pastorate of a church there that served several small communities in an area known as Stone Valley. At the start of his pastorate residents were impoverished, demoralized, and uneducated. He left a transformed community when he died in 1826. He was the moving force in building five schools and the first kindergarten. He introduced new farming methods, inspired a savings bank, brought in a cotton goods industry, and saw to it that roads were built. Oberlin accomplished all of this plus personally providing much of the medical care in the communities and carrying out his normal duties as a pastor.

Nikolai Grundtvig (1783–1872) is known as the father of the Danish folk high schools. [See "Religious Leaders as Seekers and Servants."—Eds.] These schools educated the young peasants and inspired them to improve their agriculture, build community cooperatives for both marketing and purchasing, and reclaim a floundering society.

Both Oberlin and Grundtvig contended with vigorous opposition, but they were quite different. Oberlin gave the hands-on leadership that transformed one small community in his lifetime. Grundtvig gave the vision, the conceptual design, and the sustained passionate advocacy that caused many folk high schools to be built by the peasants with their own resources, thereby, laying the groundwork for a large-scale transformation of Danish society through building new community institutions.

Neither offers a model that can be widely adopted today, because what they did was right for their time and place, not necessarily for ours. But what these two great pastors had that is timeless were these things:

1. They were strong, able, well-prepared people.

2. They knew who they were and where they stood.

3. They had a clear vision, a sense of direction.

4. They had great sustaining spirit with which to confront adversity.

5. They had unqualified dedication, a willingness to commit their lives to their chosen work.

The resources of seminaries today are adequate to prepare a few men and women who have these five qualities as pastors, if the message can be given through the churches to reach the young people who might be inspired to prepare themselves for this work and commit themselves to it. I was inspired by one of my teachers to commit myself to a different but equally difficult mission, and I have strong feelings about the possibilities of reaching people with the vision of an opportunity when they are young.

We do not know how Oberlin and Grundtvig received their visions, but it is clear that they received them. What can be learned from Oberlin and Grundtvig is that, if a pastor is armored with these five attributes, it is possible to raise the quality of a society by strengthening its neighborhood institutions. In particular, we can learn from Oberlin what one pastor can accomplish in his lifetime with one neighborhood.

The accomplishment of other goals of center city churches—peace, caring for the poor, improving justice, nurturing people, passing on the religious tradition—will be importantly influenced by how well the churches serve the local institutions that are the connective tissue of the center city neighborhood. Mentoring the trustees of those neighborhood institutions may be one of the best means available for a church to be an effective servant to its community and, in the process, to offer a tangible opportunity for laypersons to achieve a quality of life, as trustees, that is rare in our alienated society. Such mentoring calls for potential pastors for center city churches who have all the resources for this service that can be reasonably marshaled. With the experience gained by a few churches, it may be possible for seminaries to offer preparation for this important work so that, in the future, they may attract more of the strong, inner-spiritually sustained women and men that such demanding center city pastorates require.

In the meantime it is the opportunity for pastors and congregations to identify young people who have the potential for acquiring these attributes and urge them to get into seminaries even though seminaries may not yet be sending the signals that attract them. Local congregations may need to catch this vision before seminaries see it, and send students to the seminary with a clear sense of the preparation they need.

Unfortunately, the theology of institutions that will support this effort seems not to be in the making. Neither Oberlin nor Grundtvig had such support. What they had was great sustaining spirit and a guiding vision of what could be done for and with the poor in community. Each worked out an adequate theology of his work for himself, and each had the ability to communicate his vision: to lead. There are young people among us today who have it in them to do this. What they really need is encouragement—perhaps some help.

This may be the way that the much needed theology of institutions will have to come in our times: an active, inspired pastor of a contemporary center city church will generate his or her own vision of a greater quality of life for the neighborhood. That pastor will demonstrate, as Oberlin and Grundtvig did, that that vision can be carried to fruition by indigenous trustees of neighborhood institutions with the help of the mentoring care that the pastor and those who work with this leader will provide.

Postscript

I am aware that what is suggested here is a large order and that to bring it off calls for unusually able and dedicated people, both pastors and the trustees whom they mentor. But I am reminded of a great teacher of the past, Daniel Burnham, who said to his students, "Make no little plans; they have no magic to stir men's blood."

Grundtvig and Oberlin seem extraordinary to us because in retrospect we see that they accomplished so much with their lives. But they did not seem extraordinary to their contemporaries. The "cultured" of Grundtvig's time thought him to be a confused visionary and contemptuously turned their backs on him. But the peasants heard him, and they were the ones that counted. Oberlin, in his time, was hardly known by anyone other than the peasants of Stone Valley. It was some years after his death that Oberlin College was founded and named for him. Both Oberlin and Grundtvig were people who in their times "made no small plans"; they made plans that had the "power to stir men's blood."

A pastor, or a student who chooses to prepare for a pastorate, need not think of himself or herself as extraordinary, as that might be an ego-inflating, destructive self-image. Rather, that is a judgment history will make. Any one of us might be judged by history as one who served by standing and waiting. What is important as a self-image is to be "one who serves," and one who "makes no small plans." The accomplishment will be what it is, and will be judged by others.

The larger plan for a pastor who would be servant and who would lead his or her center city church to be servant to its community, will, I believe, include the aspiration to enlarge the priesthood of all believers in the community. What is discussed here is one way that a center city church might do this.

Earlier I noted that Martin Luther's great idea, the priesthood of all believers, stands as a challenge to each generation. The reformation that Luther started is never finished. It is never finished because the roots of the idea are deep in our heritage. Luther was not proclaiming a new idea; he was simply calling on those who regard themselves Christians to go back to their roots. In his essay in *A Handbook of Christian Theology,* Theodore A. Gill puts it this way: ". . . in the little company of Jesus and His friends, there was no division into clergy and laity. In manner, speech, and mood Jesus identified Himself as what today we would call a layman. And the disciples, who might look from here like laymen, were really the preachers who were sent out" (Gill, 1958, p. 281).

In the spirit of this view of history, the trustees of center city neighborhood institutions are a modern priesthood. And they are not likely to achieve the strong covenantal feeling for their neighborhood unless those who mentor and support them regard them, and deal with them, as a priesthood: those who are set apart from others because of the intensity, the quality, and the durability of their caring for the institutions they hold in trust and for the people who are served by those institutions. Thus the center city church achieves servanthood to its neighborhood by being servant to those who are servants to the neighborhood's institutions, their trustees.

The pastor, then, is not *the* priest but the leader and mentor of many priests, some of whom in retrospect may be judged to have been extraordinary but to their contemporaries will likely be seen to be able, dedicated servants.

Acknowledgments

It is outside my experience to know how this is done. What is said here is based on the experience, as reported to me, of two center city pastors: Rev. Philip Amerson (Methodist) of Evansville, Indiana, and Rev. Philip Tom (Presbyterian) of Indianapolis. I am deeply indebted to both of them, not only for sharing their rich experience but for their helpful critical comments on early drafts of this piece. The inspiration for writing this essay came from Dr. Robert W. Lynn, a parishioner in Rev. Tom's center city church. His counsel and encouragement have been invaluable. [All of these people are now in different places and have different affiliations.—Eds.]

This essay combines the best of two incomplete drafts Greenleaf wrote in the 1980s. Roles for seminaries and foundations as keys in fostering a servant-led society were to be examined in this essay. He did develop his discussion about seminaries, but the piece on foundations was not completed. This essay presents themes echoing those in "Fable" in the beginning of Part Three.

A SERVANT-LED SOCIETY

WHY BE CONCERNED about the prospect for a servant-led society? Because, I believe, our present situation, in which we accept so many nonservants in key spots in our vast complex of institutions, does not result in the quality of life for the people of our country that is reasonable and possible with the human and material resources we have available. We miss our potential as a society by a wide margin. And we cannot continue to live with this deficiency and hold our heads up in the evolving world society. We will do the best for ourselves, and we will make our best contribution to other peoples, by demonstrating the quality of life that can be achieved if, using the precious freedom we enjoy, the majority of the able people who lead our many institutions are servants. This is the premise on which the following discussion rests.

The servant idea is deep in the tradition on which American society rests. Consequently, when one notes that servant-led institutions seem not to be numerous today, one is led to conclude that the prospect for ours being a servant-led society is not great. The idea of servant simply has not penetrated the part of our culture concerned with institutions that dominate so many lives. Are there any signs that the servant idea deep in our tradition might someday come through as a new theology of institutions that would favor a servant-led society? Yes, I see some trends that might ultimately cause that to happen.

First, there seems to be a growing awareness that we fall far short of our potential as a society, and that the quality of life of far too many of our people is well below what could and should be in terms of existing resources. Further, we may continue to lose place in economic terms because of the low productivity of our people. Most discouraging of all is a growing realization among literate people that our chief culture-shaping institutions, churches and schools, seem not to be addressing with sufficient force the opportunities that these several conditions present, and that they are declining in influence because of this failure. But the awareness of our society's deficiencies is substantial and, I believe growing. It will make itself felt in time, if we have the astuteness to employ appropriate resources that are now in place.

The second trend is more tangible, and more hopeful. When Ralph Waldo Emerson proclaimed more than a century ago that "the greatest meliorator of the world is selfish, huckstering trade," he may have been more prophetic than he knew. [For elaboration, see "Talking and Listening" in Part Two.—Eds.] From my worm's-eye view of things, the most significant movement toward servant-led institutions seems to be taking place in businesses, particularly in the high-tech industries. The decline in our vital "smoke-stack" industries and their failure to hold their own in a volatile world economy may be attributed to their remaining in a "people-using" rather than a "people-building" mode. When people-building is done, that company is well managed, and concerns for customers and shareholders are taken care of as a matter of course.

I see a glimmer of hope that a predominantly servant-led society is possible. Perhaps it is in the making now. I see enough of a glimmer of hope to prompt me to speculate that this desirable state might be achieved in the lifetime of the young people now living.

What would the servant-led society I see in prospect be like? As I envision it, the majority of our institutions would be led by servants. Such servant-leadership would be the norm, rather than the exception, and public sentiment would clearly be against all nonservants who evolve into key leadership positions.

And who is a servant? What is the person like who, if in charge, makes an institution servant-led? I prefer to identify a servant in terms of the consequences of her or his influence on people. Will the people served grow as persons? Will they themselves become servants? Will the underprivileged benefit?

If our society is to move from its present state to one in which the majority of its institutions are servant-led, this will require a profound cultural change. That change will not come about easily or quickly. If that radical change is to take place within a lifetime, my guess is that some important and hard initiatives will need to be taken soon by those who lead two potentially powerful, culture-shaping categories of institutions: seminaries of all faiths and philanthropic foundations.

I nominate seminaries because of the strategic position they occupy for giving vision and prophetic leadership to churches and schools. They have the opportunity to infuse their offerings with a charge of spirit that will carry over as churches and schools mediate the seminaries' messages to those who do the work of the world.

Seminaries I know only as an outsider. I have not been a staff member, formal consultant, or trustee of a seminary, although I served on the visiting committee of a university-related one for six years. But I have had close relationships with seminary faculty for many years, particularly with professors of ethics. Most of my insight on seminaries comes from reading studies about them and from conversations with administrators and trustees.

Seminaries

Since my essay *Seminary as Servant* was published in 1983, I have made additional soundings in seminaries and concluded that a serious deficiency in some of them is that they are poor in spirit. This impedes seminaries' being the prime sources of prophetic vision that they are best positioned to provide. Of all the institutions I know about, seminaries should be the richest in spirit. Yet as I see them, far too many of them are poor in this sense. Seminaries are strategically placed to provide to our needy society a theology of institutions, and to invest that theology with a charge of spirit that will carry over to churches and schools. But seminaries seem to have neither the disposition to evolve the much-needed theology of institutions nor the spirit to invest in it that would give that theology vital force if they had it.

Some seminaries are poor in money because they are poor in spirit. But like so many impoverished nonprofit institutions, they tend to see all problems as things that more money will solve. Who wants to give money to a dispirited institution, no matter how noble its mission?

Who in a seminary will hear the above message?

The unabridged dictionary I consulted begins a full page of definitions for *spirit* with "the breath of life." It seems clear to me after reading the full page of definitions that there is no well-accepted meaning for this important word.

The meaning of the word, as I use it, lies somewhere beyond what we call reality. Yet, I have a sharp awareness of spirit when it is present in myself and others. I have a depressed feeling of loss when it is absent in myself and others.

I have come to relate spirit, the kind I would like to see more of, to the concepts of *serve* and *serving* in terms of the consequences on those being served. I repeat what I said earlier about a servant-led society: do those being served grow as persons? I see the quality of a society as being judged by what the least privileged in it achieve.

The best I can say for the word *spirit* is that it is the driving force behind the motive to serve. I come back to the first dictionary definition of spirit, "the breath of life." I would ask seminary leaders whether as a collective in an institution they have this attribute. The premise here is that far too many seminaries would answer, "No!"

There is nothing to be gained in saying this to faculties and administrators of seminaries. A dispirited person is not helped simply by being told that he or she is without spirit. They need loving counsel, not pejorative labeling. The same holds for seminaries. But who will give this loving counsel to a seminary? I suggest that it is best done by their trustees, especially the chairperson.

The chair is familiar enough with the seminary to know its problems and to understand the criticism and be sensitive about how to give constructive help. Also, the chair is detached enough not to be hurt or angered by the criticism. The chair is best positioned to give that counsel and the leadership to bring the seminary from a dispirited state to one of having a large and communicable charge of spirit. The seminary may find that financing itself has become a little easier and that its voice is heard and is persuasive in important places where it has not been heard before.

It is only necessary to find one among the two hundred or so seminaries in the United States whose trustee chairperson will be sensitive to the above reasoning. This chairperson will give leadership to persuade the seminary to take on the thinking-through of a theology for the seminary itself. It would lay out a concept of strength for the seminary as an institution, a theology that points to the seminary as a powerful, influential force with churches and schools that will mediate its message.

Armed with that theology, the pioneering seminary will take the lead by proposing a seminar for seminary trustee chairpersons to train them to be counselors of their seminary in the crucial matter of generating a new vision and spirit that will equip their seminary to be the pivotal institution it has the opportunity to be. This would give the seminary credence as a culture-shaping force to prepare the way for a servant-led society.

Foundations

I nominate philanthropic foundations for an important role in this effort because they are freest from market pressures. Also, they have the greatest latitude of any institutions to be what they choose to be and to use their resources for the public good. Foundations are free-floating repositories of enormous, but largely unrealized, potential.

I have a different perspective about foundations than I do with seminaries. I have served as trustee of a moderate-sized one. I have had formal consulting relationships with several, both large and small. I have done extensive staff work, particularly with the Ford Foundation, and I have read a great deal about them.

I believe quite a few foundations face a dilemma: they are long on money, short on ideas and vision. Money without vision really is not very much, not enough to justify an institution that is just going to hold the money and give it away to deserving charities.

Conclusion

Seminaries need to be strong and influential so that they can deliver prophetic visions with a charge of spirit to churches and schools, both of which seem to be languishing for want of vision and spirit. Foundations need to be strong and influential so that they can justify their existence as useful institutions. They can use their resources wisely, so that they stand as models to which other institutions might aspire.

In addressing these notes to seminaries and foundations I am aware that I am not advancing a "bandwagon" idea. But I am hopeful that a few will join the saving remnant of servant-led institutions that already exists, mostly because good conscience requires it, if for no other reason than life is more rewarding in that company. And they just might be party to advancing the quality of our civilization a notch.

PART FOUR

TOWARD THE CARING COMMUNITY

REFLECTIONS ON SEEKING, GIVING, AND RECEIVING

For several years I have been seeking for deeper significance in my spiritual life. Not finding much support or this in my church (and feeling that it is not likely to be found in any church to the depth and with the freedom from dogmatic concepts that I desire), I have been seeking groups and individuals that seem to be on a similar search. . . .

Insofar as I understand myself (and from what others have told me), I am a reserved, reflective person with more than the usual urge to be of service. Outwardly (to all but my family I fear), I reflect calm, composure, gentleness, and concern. But inwardly there is considerable tension, a realization that my "service" urges are more intellectual than feeling, and that my response to people does not have the warmth that it should. I have an intellectual appreciation of aesthetic things but not a "feeling" response in proportion. I realize that I have severely inhibited my natural creative urges—preferring to use my hands in mechanical pursuits rather than artistically, and restraining the normal gestures and show of feeling when communicating. In other words, I have kept myself under tight reign. I have a temper (generally kept under good control) and I have succeeded in keeping my feeling-tone in a middle range between joy and depression and have avoided the kinds of relationships with people that would take me either to the peaks of happiness or the depths of hurt.

Robert K. Greenleaf
"Report on a Journey"

This and the following essay were written almost ten years apart. In some sense, they represent Greenleaf's shift from focusing on the development of the individual to tying that individual development in with the notion of transforming institutions so they will be more serving.

The first essay was written on April 4, 1966. In this essay, he focuses on the individual search for meaning in life using himself as an example of a lifelong seeker. The important point in this piece is that the search is never completed; rather, the joy comes in the search itself.

THE SEARCH AND THE SEEKER

*30 August 1941   This is my journal. . . . This, I expect to be the
record of a search without end. . . . So my search shall bear fruit—not
in final accomplishments on which I shall rest—but in ever widening
horizons. My satisfaction shall derive from the contemplation of
these horizons and in the satisfactions that accrue from expanding
my powers to explore them. Life then is growth; when growth stops
there is atrophy. The object of the quest, then, is the capacity to grow,
the strength to bear the burden of the search, and the capacity to live
nobly—if not heroically—in the situations that develop.*

Robert K. Greenleaf
Journal entry, August 30, 1941

A DISTINGUISHED rabbi and scholar had just finished a talk on
the prophets in which he had spoken of the false prophets and
the true prophets. "How," a questioner asked him, "does one
tell a false prophet from a true prophet?" His answer was simple (though it left the questioner puzzled): "There is no way!"

For some who call themselves Christians it is the same: there
is no way, no clear, single way, no list of sharply cutting criteria,
no set of gauges. If there were, there would be no human
dilemma; life would have no challenge. Can the seeker accept

there is no well-marked path? If there were such a way, there would be a destination. There would be an assurance of accomplishment, a promise of certainty. There would be something to be wanted, something which when found would end the search. Life at that point would be empty.

There is a story of an old couple, thought to be odd, who lived as recluses and seldom ventured forth. But one day the man did go to the city and returned at the end of the day with an old battered cello. It had only one string, and the bow had only a few hairs. He seated himself in a corner and began to saw away on the single open string, playing only one note, and that rather badly. This went on day after day until one morning his wife left for the city. When she returned she confronted him with what she had found. "See here," she said, "I have gone to the city and found other people playing instruments like yours. Theirs all have four strings. What's more, they move their fingers around and play many notes on each string. Why do you sit here day after day playing that one raspy note?" He gave her a cold look and said, "I would expect that of you. Those people you saw are still trying to find the right note. *I* have found it!" An absurd story, but it makes a point: finding can be pretty sterile.

All of this suggests two kinds of seekers: those who seek to find and those who seek to seek. The first see the search as a path toward finding something they want. When they find it, they hope to settle down and enjoy it. The search will be over. The others are interested in the search. They don't want anything but opening vistas for the search. The *search* gives them joy. They do not expect ever to settle down. Instead, they hope to grow.

These descriptions represent tendencies rather than clear types, tendencies that shape choices, and choices make the seeker. Choice marks off the search from fantasy. It is the choice to find one's way in a direction that has no way, no clear path, to a destination. It is the choice that does not name a goal.

Why is it so important not to name the goal, not to seek to find? Because, one can only name a goal that one can conceptualize with the limited vision one now has. No one knows his or her potentialities, in what direction spontaneity might take him or her, or what she or he might become. But in our narrow, rational world one is supposed to know what one is doing and where one is going. Is there not a problem of survival here? Indeed there is. Most of us meet it by living in two worlds: the outer world of conformity, in which the requirements of polite society and vocational competence are met, and the inner world of freedom, spontaneity, and limitless possibilities. Some such compromise is necessary if one is to make a living or raise a family and take on social concerns. It is not too difficult a compromise, provided one knows who one's real self, one's private free self, is. And also provided that one can view with quiet detachment (sometimes amusement, but always tolerance) the outer world of conformity. But one must always hold the conforming role at a safe distance and never lose one's identity in it. Above all, the free inner person, the seeker, must *not* have a goal; he or she must be consumed only with the search. Otherwise one cannot be free, spontaneous, and limitless.

This I have found for myself, out of my own experience and seeking; but it may mean more to others if I give a brief account of where I have been. I consider myself fortunate that my early religious training, the little that I had, did not take very well. I arrived at my mature years with a sense of religion as something not yet found but, rather, something to be sought. It is something that will grow as I grow. At this way station, where I pause to write this account, I choose to use the word *religion* in its root sense: *re-ligio,* to bind (or rebind). I see religion as that which binds (or rebinds) one to the cosmos. The religious person is one who belongs in this world as it is, and who therefore has the chance to be naturally right. This is not *all* the religious person is; but this is a beginning.

I see belief or faith as a consequence, rather than a source. Such faith as I have is a consequence of my own experience framed in the religious feeling that is the light of my search. I am aware of and interested in what others have experienced and believe. But I prefer to see faith as Dean Inge defined it, the "choice of the nobler hypothesis," the kind of choice that only an experienced person can make. But it is *my* choice, *my* affirmation that makes it significant. Such truth as it has lies in my rational, intuitive sense of rightness that leads me to choose it and affirm it. Old truths come into the contemporary world as hypotheses. They become contemporary truths only as contemporary people choose to affirm them, test their validity in practice, and give them viability through their thoughts, words, and deeds.

My father was an ethical man, with deeply felt concerns on which he acted responsibly; but he was not a churchman. He left a profound influence on me that grows with the years. And I had the good fortune to make a bad first vocational choice. I set out to be an astronomer because my favorite uncle was an astronomer, dedicated to his calling. Not much time was lost in disabusing myself of the notion that I would be an astronomer. But I got to know astronomers, and I came away from this brief encounter with my religious roots strengthened.

I never got theological notions when I looked through a telescope. But one brilliant night, when I saw the fantastic image of one of the great nebulae in the 100-inch mirror on Mount Wilson, I had a deeply religious experience. I shook with awe and wonder at the majesty and the mystery of all creation. This primitive unstructured feeling, the powerful sense of awe and wonder, is to me the source of religious feeling at its greatest depth. Experimentally, I have found that my own sense of ethical sureness follows from an intensity of this feeling. (I submit as the ultimate test of the efficacy of religious feeling whether it nourishes the insight and the resolve that are the root and ground of creative ethics. Does one, because of it, act responsibly and with greater rightness and determination in the outside world?)

Once astronomy was laid behind me, I had the additional good fortune to stake my career on a great business in which I invested thirty-eight good years. It is a business that is great because the man who gave it its character was great and a dreamer; he breathed his dream into its tradition. From this I learned that great dreams are a person's hope, and that nothing much happens without a great dream. As a young man entering business I did not foresee the feeling I have today, that there are as many, perhaps more, people living out their own great dreams in business than in other fields, such as education, philanthropy, religion, social service. I have come to judge a person's ethical stature not so much by the ground one stands on in society at any one time but by how far one has moved one's own ethical practice from that prevailing in one's calling when one entered it. Accomplishment, not status, is what counts. I am glad that I did not choose a vocation that carried more of society's stamp of ethical approval, because then I might have been tempted to settle for advocating the good (historically sanctioned) to other people and I might not have felt the urgency to seek a creative ethic.

Then I married a woman who taught me what love could mean, and that it is, as Paul said, the greatest. And we learned together.

Much has followed upon these and other early experiences, but the search did not automatically open from them. I am also a child of my culture, deeply conditioned by it—both the good and the bad. Chief among the good I treasure the Judeo-Christian tradition. I do not value it above other traditions, but it is the one in which I grew up. The great symbolic wisdom of this tradition grows on me day by day. I regret the dogma that people have built around this tradition, which limits access to it. I cringe when I think of the wars that have been fought and may yet be fought because of the human tendency to forge hard doctrine out of the stories by which the wisdom of people and events, which make our tradition, have been handed on to us. I regret that any of this was ever written down. The natural wonder of it all might have been better preserved in an oral tradition, and the hard, literal-minded people who want to fight about doctrine would have fought over something else. Then these stories might have continued to evolve with humanity's historical development, and we would not think of revelation as having ceased two thousand years ago.

But still it is a great tradition in which I feel naturally at home. I am now resolved to go back to the study of the Old Testament, which I know only sketchily, because I have come to see Jesus as a Jew living in the light of the Jewish law and carrying it forward by adding creatively to it through his own experience. This is my present leading. I must better establish my own bond with the great events of story and history in which the human potential for nobility has been tested and refined so that my search can be more a carrying forward from these events through my own experience. Much as I value the tradition in which I live, I feel a compelling obligation to leave it a mite better than I found it. "Man is an unfinished creature," says Gerald Heard. The human tradition is also unfinished. Cannot everyone aspire to carry its development a little farther?

As I pause in my search, I am also sharply aware of the great evil in my cultural conditioning which defines sanity partly in terms of isolation from one's own vast awareness. It teaches us to demean people because of skin color or the families into which they were born. It holds the marketplace to be unworthy of the finest of human talents; it holds abstract knowledge that is extruded by reason and bounded by words in priority over the promptings of the human spirit. It justifies violence in a way that buries it deep beyond our conscious knowing and leaves us with control as the primary basis for a civilized society. Groping my way through the conflict and confusion of these many influences (with little help from sources I should have been able to trust), I went through a long wilderness period in which I sought resources outside myself and ignored the rich endowment in my own uniqueness, the great inward source of inspiration which everyone can claim as one's own because of his or her own access to it. Only as what is uniquely me emerges do I experience moments of true creativity, moments which, when deeply felt, temper the pain of long periods of frustration that are the common lot of most of us, moments that give me the impulse and the courage to act with force and wisdom in the outside world.

I did not begin to find my way to a knowledge of my own uniqueness until by chance (but there is no chance) I became aware of seekers who were on the path ahead of me. They were not necessarily going in my direction; but they were men and women whom I came to accept as guides who only had at heart my getting lost. Because they were seekers, some of them were lonely and welcomed my interest in them so that they could show their interest in me. *Interest* became the lamp.

The search group, with which I have had considerable experience, has not had the same long-term sustaining influence for me as have the individual guides. For short, intensive work, group sharing has been helpful; but then the divergence of individual interests emerges and limits the group's usefulness. Also, beyond the two or three, there is a compulsion to organize all group effort, and organization (as we conventionally practice it) is death to the spirit of the search. The hierarchical principle of organization has plagued Western society ever since Moses took Jethro's advice about it (Exodus 18). [See "Spirituality as Leadership" in Part One.—Eds.] Saddened as I am about the fate of Moses, I have wondered whether his errors, which displeased the Lord, might not have had their origin in the acceptance of Jethro's advice. Maybe the spirit and order are inherently opposed. But, it could be that we are locked into a way of getting order that kills the spirit, a way with so many thousands of years of sanction behind it that we can see no other ways.

This suggests that the search is a lonely affair. Beyond the few with whom I share individually, I have found it so. No group or movement carries me very far, although I value the "lifts" they have given me. When, as with the early Christians, there are brilliant bursts of group effort, they succumb quickly to the leveling effect of organization. This may be for the best, I do not know. But I do believe that every seeker must face who he or she is alone. That is disturbing, sometimes terrifying, until one learns to love oneself and to see, as Emerson put it, "the good of evil born"—not the evil in people's deeds, but the evil in their hearts. Horrible as it is to contemplate, the total destruction of the world in a nuclear holocaust is not the greatest evil. The greatest evil is in the deeply set attitudes of people now living who would bring this about. I feel the same about the monstrous rejection and demeaning, of one person by another human being, that blankets the world. The greater evil is in the hearts of those who deny their neighbor rather than in the wrong itself. And I share this, too.

I may have more control than some, but I carry as great a burden of potential wrong as the next person. When someone says, "But I do not carry such a burden; I feel only love for others," I can only answer, "Oh?" The realization of this burden is partly what makes me a seeker. I do not expect that by some gift of grace I will be relieved of it, but rather that by learning to love and to accept my own evil impulses, the way will be opened to growth, growth in natural religious feeling. I feel grateful that I *am* as other people; otherwise, I would not have this opportunity. "Every saint has a past; every sinner has a future," said Oscar Wilde.

One day a friend told of coming upon a scene in which two boys were kneeling in great concern over a grating that protected a sunken window well. In the enclosed space was a beautiful butterfly that had apparently gone there in its earlier state. When it emerged from the chrysalis as a butterfly it could not escape the bars, which were firmly fixed. Behind the two boys stood two women who had been attracted by the boys' concern; they offered counsel as to how the butterfly might be released. The story was told as one of human concern for the hurt of the natural world. But it can be seen another way. Every aspect of it can also be seen symbolically.

This simple scene, then, has the possible interpretation of a great drama upon the inward stage in which these are parts of each of us. The butterfly might be our beautiful loving self (truly a gift of grace). The bars can be the hardened attitudes of the inhuman in us that keep our natural loveliness imprisoned. The boys could represent our creative capacity for awareness: youthful, naïve, trusting, wondering. The adults may be our rational, responsible, perhaps impersonal, self that thinks of its role as good but would not be aware of the imprisoned beauty except as that awareness is mediated by the boys.

Seeing the story this way does not answer the human dilemma; it is not a key or a way out. But it is a message from the environment that could pass unnoticed. It is part of the vast world of symbolic communication, the riches of wisdom in which we are all constantly immersed but which some of us miss altogether. This could be what prompted William Blake to say, "If the doors of perception were cleansed, everything would appear to man as it is—infinite." And it *is* infinite; I have seen it for brief moments.

Seeking is opening oneself to growth in awareness. It is, in part, a cleansing of perception, both inward and outward. It is an uncalculated response to symbols—something in the environment that is trying to speak to us in a figurative, nonliteral way—symbols from our own experience and from the great wisdom sources of the world. Much that makes the confrontation with the symbol meaningful comes from the deep resources of the beholder. Seeking begins, I believe, with a genuine love of self (without which one cannot really love one's neighbor), with a high value on one's own uniqueness, and with a sense of greatness in one's own life experience and purpose. *Nothing is ordinary.*

Within this frame of reference the seeker may want to examine some of the ways that are offered: religious retreats, group dynamics, general semantics, Alcoholics Anonymous, yoga, Zen. Regard them with openness and interest, but do not expect to find a golden path in any of them. Rather, see in them the struggles of people to find themselves and take heart that there are many seekers but no finders, only joy in search. Look then to the great wisdom sources: literature, scripture, allegory, history, science, music, art, poetry, and *the living symbolism of everyday experience.*

The seeker does not ask what these mean or what actions they require. Rather, the seeker works to clear the fog that blurs perceptions and opens the depths of his or her being to that which speaks to him or her, untrammelled by convention or overly rigid logic. The seeker lets it penetrate dreams. *His or her* way evolves from this as a true inward experience.

Having said this much, I should also say that seekers sometimes read too much, get too much involved in *ways* that others submit to them. I regret that in my own search I did not center down earlier on the few things that I would live with intimately. Now, in my sixtieth year, I feel that I should devote no more than a small part of my search time to new exploration, and the remainder to cultivating at great depth those few gleanings that seem truly significant for my own growth.

I agree with the rabbi: there is no *way* to tell the false prophets from the true prophets; yet one must know the difference. I believe, equally firmly, that there is no *way* for the personal search; yet each of us needs a lamp and a direction. And I also believe that there can be no finding, no "now I have it"; yet one should at all times know who one is and where one is. Paradoxes? Certainly! But at-homeness with paradox, along with a benevolent, kindly attitude toward linear rationality, is a good set of mind with which to undertake the search while living as a reasonably normal person in contemporary society.

I do not know what makes a seeker, or why anybody should undertake the search. I do not urge it upon others. I only know that some *are* seekers and that it is important that every seeker should share, "for it is in giving that we receive." So I have tried in these few paragraphs to give my feelings about the search and myself as a seeker: groping, sometimes falling, but still seeking. While I speak, as I have said, as one pausing at a way station, it is my hope that when at any time this journey is cut short I can say it has been worthwhile.

○

I dreamed that I arose from my bed at night and went to the window of my apartment, from which I could see a broad expanse of skyline of great buildings in New York. Every window of every building was brilliantly lighted; each was a jewel of stained glass patterns as in a church. I thought of the commercial life of this vast city, and of the millions in their own ways struggling for personal significance. It all seemed sacred; every man and woman had the potentiality for sainthood. And I stood in awe and wonder.

This essay, first published in the *Friends Journal* of September 15, 1975, presents Greenleaf's changing emphasis from the individual, as in the previous piece, to linking the individual with institutional transformation and service.

ON BEING A SEEKER IN THE
LATE TWENTIETH CENTURY

THERE IS A THEORY of prophecy which holds that prophetic voices of great clarity, and with a quality of insight equal to that of any age, are speaking cogently all of the time. Women and men of a stature equal to the greatest of the past are with us now, addressing the problems of the day and pointing to a better way and to a personeity better able to live fully and serenely in these times.

The variable that marks some periods as barren and some as rich in prophetic vision is in the interest, the level of seeking, the responsiveness of the hearers. The variable is not in the presence or absence or the relative quality and force of the prophetic voices. The prophet grows in stature as people respond to his or her message. If one's early attempts are ignored or spurned, his or her talent may wither away.

It is seekers, then, who make the prophet; and the initiative of any one of us in searching for and responding to the voice of the contemporary prophet may mark the turning point in his or her growth and service.

Some who have difficulty with theory assert that their faith rests on one or more of the prophets of old having given the "word" for all time and that the contemporary ones do not speak to their condition as the older ones do. But if one really believes that the "word" has been given for all time, how can one be a seeker? How can one hear the contemporary voice when one has decided not to live in the present and has turned that voice off?

Neither this hypothesis nor its opposite can be proved. But I submit that the one given here is the more hopeful choice, one that offers a significant role in prophecy to every individual. One cannot interact with and build strength in a dead prophet; but one can do it with a living one. "Faith," Dean Inge has said, "is the choice of the nobler hypothesis."

This thesis seems to be supported by the record of the times of George Fox. For many years before the start of his mission [see "Religious Leaders as Seekers and Servants" in Part One.—Eds.], there had been an unusual stirring of seekers who were expectantly watching for a new vision with new leadership. Without that sustained readiness, Fox might not have found the response to his initiative that was necessary for his mission to become strong.

The times we live in appear in sharp contrast. Many are seeking but there is a confusing bombardment of communications from those who would satisfy the seeking hunger. Within the last twenty-five years the number and variety of offerings from those asking the support of seekers, usually for a fee, has grown enormously. To name only a few of the better known of these in vogue now, there are: transcendental meditation, sensitivity and encounter groups, a resurgence of intentional communities, healing seminars, transactional analysis, biofeedback, a substantial enlargement of services from the field of psychotherapy, reevaluation counseling, and expanded programs of churches plus some new churches. Standing conspicuously apart is a slightly older offering, Alcoholics Anonymous, which, over forty years ago, resolved that they would be poor, they would own no real property, no one but a participating alcoholic could contribute to their modest budget, and the essential work of one recovered or partly recovered alcoholic helping another would not be done for money. Some who are close to the problem hold that AA has helped more to recover from this dreadful illness than all other approaches (mostly for a fee) combined.

The seeker in these times can be bewildered by the scope and attractiveness of what is available and, unfortunately, some have been tempted into a lifelong pursuit of wholeness, in one's personal terms, to the exclusion of coming to grips with what should be (and in Fox's day was) a fruit of seeking: effective involvement with the ethical dilemmas of one's times.

What made George Fox's service to seekers (and their response to him) so exemplary was the significant move to new and more exacting ethical standards, the force of which carries to this day. Fox's major contribution was not his theology, nor even his encouragement to care for suffering—important as these were. Rather, it seems to me, what gave durability to the Quaker tradition was the practical result that so many of those who called themselves Friends behaved more lovingly toward all creatures and assumed an impressive level of responsibility for their society and its institutions. Perhaps the most innovative result was that, by the effort of those whom Fox inspired, the quality of some contemporary institutions, notably commerce, was markedly improved.

We live in a time that is much more dominated by institutions, both public and private, than was true in Fox's day. And these institutions—all of them, including the very best—are crying out for a new mission to them, that would raise their stature as servants of society and drastically reduce their impact as sources of suffering and injustice. I see little disposition toward this outcome in most current offerings to seekers.

Richard B. Gregg, writing in an early Pendle Hill pamphlet forty years ago, observed, "Christianity needs a means of implementing its ideals of human unity into a social program." The need seems even more urgent today, with little evidence of movement to serve it.

What may be needed, and perhaps now it is a possibility, is a new initiative from some seekers in which (1) they take responsibility for finding and responding to the contemporary prophet who will help them find their ways out of their individual and collective wildernesses so that they will become more effective servants of society, and (2) they respond less to the kinds of cafeteria offerings enumerated above which seem not to dispose them to become servants.

How would *Seekers Anonymous* do for a name? And could the model be taken from AA: that no one will be paid and only funds contributed from active seekers will be used? For those who participate, healing, in the sense of being made whole, will come from deep involvement with creative work on the structural flaws in our society, work that has both meliorative and society building consequences.

Seekers Anonymous will be religious in the root meaning of that word, *re ligio,* to rebind: to bridge the separation between persons and the cosmos, to heal the widespread alienation, and to reestablish men and women in the role of servants—healers—of society.

Someone (it could be many) who has the strength, the vision, the integrity, the competence, and the youthful vigor right now is actively testing our responsiveness to her or his leadership and our capacity to be religious in this sense. And what is being said to us may seem as strange and disturbing—and as compelling if we will listen—as Fox's message did in his day. Are enough of us really listening with a readiness to respond? Are we diligently trying to sort the truly prophetic voices of our time, those that would lead us to constructive service, from the veritable babble of communication that engulfs us all? Are enough of us prepared—emotionally, intellectually, and with physical stamina—for the new demands that may be made upon us? Are we adequately reinforcing one another as seekers in order to build, in each of us, the required competence, clarity, and strength to serve?

Albert Camus wrote in the last paragraph of his last public lecture, "Great ideas, it has been said, come into the world as gently as doves. Perhaps, then, if we listen attentively, we shall hear, amid the uproar of empires and nations, a faint flutter of wings, the gentle stirring of life and hope."

Those who see themselves as part of Seekers Anonymous will learn to listen attentively and respond to that faint flutter of wings, that gentle stirring of life and hope. *By their intense and sustained listening they will make the new prophet who will help them find that wholeness that is only achieved by serving.* And out of that wholeness will come the singleness of aim and the capacity to bear suffering that a confrontation with a basic malaise of our time, the failure of our many institutions to serve, may demand.

> *Do not seek to follow the footsteps of men of old.*
> *Seek what they sought!*

Basho

> *Take from the altar of the past the fire, not the ashes!*

Jean Jaures

The next two short, undated essays are closely related. "Lost Knowledge" lays a portion of the foundation for the following piece, "A Lifeline of Ideas." But the overarching themes in these pieces echo those in the other writings in this volume. The key is the importance of the individual to the "reformation" of society into a more caring, serving one. In these essays, Greenleaf suggests important building blocks for individual development: recovering valuable "lost" knowledge and being sensitive to ideas that failed others earlier but may have been passed down as "noble truths."

LOST KNOWLEDGE

THIS IS AN INTERESTING time to be alive. It is also a most difficult time. Part of what makes it interesting is that it is difficult.

In my adult life I have never known times that were what might be called "easy." There was the depression of the 1930s, the war and the post-war adjustment of the 1940s, another war in the early 1950s, and now we have had a gradual build-up from that point to the cold war, hot war state of affairs with no end in sight.

While all of this has been going on in the past forty years, we have had an accelerated rate of growth of knowledge about everything: technology, medicine, people, society, institutions, and the limitless universe. With this knowledge we have been able to outperform some of the most imaginative exploits of the Jules Verne dreamers of the past. And in many ways we have advanced socially.

But in some important ways, as a society, we have lost some ground. How could we lose ground in a period when knowledge and access to knowledge, including knowledge about people and society, were advancing at such a rapid rate? I know of no simple answer, and you have probably heard many opinions. I would like to share my perspective on it and encourage you to think about it.

Francis Bacon gave us the maxim, "Knowledge is power." But power is value-free. It can be used for good or ill. And I am afraid that in the pursuit of knowledge, we have assumed that the result would always be good. Clearly, our experience tells us that this is not necessarily so. Yet we cannot abandon knowledge if we want to; and even if we could, there is no assurance that this would produce a better society. I am afraid that, starting from where we are today, the people who lead us to a better society will have to know some things that we do not know today. And the things we need to know may be things that we have known before, but somehow have lost.

I am indebted to the anthropologist and Arctic explorer, Vilhjalmur Stefansson, for the concept he called "lost knowledge." He used as an example from his own extensive Arctic experience the matter of how best to treat frostbite. He said that the natives in the far north have always known how to deal with frostbite, and he thought that it must also have been in the traditional wisdom of those who live in more temperate climates but who, on occasion, also have to deal with frostbite. The treatment was simple. If you get too cold, you get to where it is warm as fast as you can. It seemed a common sense thing to do, and it worked.

But, in the temperate climates—which was where "knowledge" burgeoned—this bit of common sense got lost. Knowledge was lost. The first codification of the treatment of frostbite in the Red Cross first aid handbook was that, if you get frostbite, you do *not* go where it is warm; you rub on snow.

"Well," said Stefansson, "snow is about the temperature of the air, and if the air is below freezing, the snow is below freezing, and if you rub enough of it on a cheek or a nose or an ear, you will produce a frostbite in an otherwise adequately warm person. Furthermore, if the flesh is frozen and you rub it, you break the capillaries and open the way for gangrene. A lot of arms and legs have had to be amputated because of this treatment."

This recommended treatment for frostbite stayed in the official Red Cross handbook until World War II, when we did some concentrated research on how best to deal with many kinds of health and injury problems in order to recover people in the safest and quickest ways, and the treatment of frostbite was one of them. Quickly the official advice became: get where it is warm, and above all, don't rub it!

Stefansson's point was that simple, unsophisticated people had known this for ages and ages. But somehow, in the course of building up knowledge in the more sophisticated world, we lost this knowledge, and it stayed lost right down into the era of modern medicine. Lost knowledge had to be rediscovered.

As I look out on our present tension-torn society and reflect on this simple illustration, I have to remind myself that there have been periods recorded in history when societies knew how to live in a more human, humane way than we now know. It is our task to *rediscover* this knowledge and *relearn* how to use it.

I have not made a formal research on this subject, but four examples of great societies and leaders of the past come to mind. There was the age of Pericles in Greece in the fifth century B.C.E; then Asoka in the third century B.C.E. in India, and Akbar in the sixteenth century A.D. in India. These three started out as warring men of conquest who assembled empires and then, in their later years, built golden ages of culture. Asoka ultimately espoused nonviolence in India, more than two thousand years before Gandhi.

The fourth example is different, and closer to our times. This was Nikolai Grundtvig, the Danish theologian who lived through the middle of the nineteenth century and provided the conceptual framework for the regeneration of a dying society. Denmark was seriously set back economically when the grain resources of the West came into the world markets. Losing the wealth of their chief export, Denmark faced ruin as a viable society. Grundtvig must have seemed an unlikely prospect to lead his nation out of this dilemma because his early career was marked largely by the writing of ponderous theological tomes. But addressing his good mind to this problem, he saw clearly what to do and advocated it with great passion. New schools must be built for the training of the spirit. Young people must be given a new goal. "Knowledge itself is *not* power. The *spirit* is power," he proclaimed. Grundtvig himself did not build the new schools for the education of the spirit, but he built a fire under those who did build what came to be known as the Danish folk high schools.

The effect of the new schools was a discovery of old knowledge. This old knowledge was not found in history books but was rediscovered as new knowledge which helped young people find the basis for the needed new society. They found it in the context of mid-nineteenth century Denmark and rebuilt a declining society into a prosperous, peaceful, viable society. It is not perfect, but it has had more goodness in it than most of the rest of the world for over one hundred years. And it came about because of a crisis which was not met by revolution or the imposition of a dictatorship or disintegration, but by the rediscovery of how the infinite variety of human beings can best live together in society, and from learning to use that knowledge.

There is a great pair of lines from W. B. Yeats (1968) in his poem "Lapis Lazuli:"

All things fall and are built again
And those that build them again are gay.

Societies fall and are built again. And their builders—Pericles, Asoka, Akbar, Grundtvig—must have been gay.

The moral from this is that if we see a problem in society that we think we should do something about, and if we are not happy in the process of taking it on, maybe we are still a part of the problem rather than a part of the solution.

Robert Frost, in his mature years, wrote a great poem that most critics feel is his own spiritual odyssey. The title of it is "Directive." It is not so well known because it is so loaded with symbolic references that it does not make much sense without a great deal of study. This poem was the record of Frost's struggle to establish meaning in his own life. And it was a voyage of discovery. He offered it to his readers not to explain Robert Frost to them, but to share a vehicle of discovery by means of which the reader would embark on his or her own voyage of discovery to find new knowledge about oneself—really *lost* knowledge, but knowledge to be found by each individual as new knowledge.

After thirty-five lines in this poem, in which Frost seems to set out to lose his reader in a hopeless morass of symbolism, he says:

> And if you're lost enough to find yourself
> By now, pull in your ladder road behind you
> And put a sign up CLOSED to all but me.
> Then make yourself at home.

What this cagey old fellow is saying to us, out of his own experience with his long and somewhat tortured life, is that you and I cannot know ourselves until we know that we are lost enough that only a voyage of discovery will find us. Only then can we say to ourselves, "I am me," pull in our ladder roads behind us, and make ourselves at home.

Can we not also say the same for societies? Unless we live in a static society that repeats its pattern by rote from generation to generation, will we not have to rediscover, *out of our lostness,* how to live humanly and humanely in society *in the context of the times we now live in?* This is the path that Grundtvig established for the very lost Danes one hundred years ago by proclaiming that "the spirit is power."

Frost closes "Directive," having dealt with new knowledge symbolically as water "Cold as a spring as yet so near its source," and "a broken goblet like the Grail," with these two enigmatic lines:

> Here are your waters and your watering place.
> Drink and be whole again beyond confusion.

Be whole again! We were once whole, but lost it. But this time we will be whole beyond confusion.

Beyond confusion is the promise. Our state may be moving, developing, uncertain, even dangerous. But we will not be confused because we will be at one with the circumstance, whatever it is. We will be at home in the world *as it is.*

I started by saying that this is an interesting time to be alive. I also said it is a most difficult time, and that part of what makes it interesting is that it is difficult.

I am quite sure that the times will continue to be difficult. I hope that you will find them interesting.

All things fall and are built again,
And those that build them again are gay.

As was noted in the headnote of the preceding essay, Greenleaf felt that an important building block for individual development was sensitivity to ideas that had failed others earlier but may have been passed down as "noble truths."

Greenleaf wrote in an editor's note that "A Lifeline of Ideas" would be the first of five articles. The themes for the other four would be the legacy of Moses, competition, coercion, and poverty. He said he hoped to raise "questions about assumptions that are made by people who think of themselves as moral." He hoped that others would respond "with suggestions of what they might contribute to A New Lifeline of Ideas."

A LIFELINE OF IDEAS

IT IS REPORTED that a king once asked Confucius what to do about thievery among his subjects. The answer was, "If you, sir, were not covetous, they would not steal—even if you urged them to do it." The idea is very old: if you want to reform something, begin with yourself—*no matter who you are and how moral and correct a person you believe yourself to be.*

A more recent idea is that which guided John Woolman: if one wants to change something, one should love the person in whom change is hoped. Much as Woolman abhorred slavery, he respected the slaveholder as a person deserving his love. I do not know how he came to be as he was. Did he learn, as an adult, to carry that attitude into the confrontation with the slaveholder, or was he born that way? If I were to undertake to persuade a slaveholder that he should free his slaves, I would have to learn that attitude through some conscious process. I have been conditioned too much by the greed and fear that pervades our culture. I would have to change—a deep and difficult change!

The ancient Chinese had much to say to us on the subject of change. One of the oldest books in the world, which antedates Confucius, is of Chinese origin. It is the *I Ching, the Book of Changes.* It is primarily concerned with the philosophy of change, living with change as an organic part of one's nature, rather than thinking of the good as static and change as threatening, as so many of my contemporaries seem to view it.

During World War II, when Peking was occupied by the Japanese, there was a little colony of Germans there. Among them was a scholar of Chinese matters, Hellmut Wilhelm, who had done much to acquaint the world with the *I Ching*. Here are a few lines from Wilhelm's comment on ancient Chinese thought about change.

> Reflection on the simple fundamental facts of our experience brings immediate recognition of constant change.... It is in constant change and growth alone that life can be grasped at all. If it is interrupted, the result is not death, which is really only an aspect of life, but life's reversal, its perversion.... The opposite of change in Chinese thought is growth of what ought to decrease, the downfall of what ought to rule.... Change is natural movement, development that can reverse itself only by going against nature.... The concept of change is not an external, normative principle that imprints itself upon phenomena; it is an inner tendency according to which development takes place naturally and spontaneously.... To stand in the stream of this development is a datum of nature; to recognize it and follow it is responsibility and free choice.... Safety is the clear knowledge of the right stand to be taken, security is the assurance that events are unrolling in the right direction.... In this point of view, which accords the responsible person an influence on the course of things, change ceases to be an insidious, intangible snare and becomes an organic order corresponding to man's nature. No small role is thus assigned to man." [Wilhelm, 1960, pp. 17–22]

If something is hung up for want of willingness to face the implications of change (and our present social order seems to be hung up), a useful idea is to examine the language used to talk about the problem. This may give a clue as to what needs to change.

I came of age in the early 1920s, when "back to normalcy" was the political slogan of the day and the idea of "progress" was widely accepted by informed people. The economic collapse of 1929 was a severe jolt; but the talk of the 1930s was in terms of "recovery"; "pump priming" was the popular metaphor.

The underlying thinking which these words connote was redeemed by the war and massive military spending. Today with a gigantic national debt, an undiminished military budget, and recession always around the corner, "recovery" and "pump priming" are still the commonly used terms. Any clues in that?

The current levels of crime, broken homes, dropouts, delinquency, alienation, child abuse, unemployment, injustice, and poverty suggest a society that is disintegrating and diseased. It may or may not be worse than in the past. But there seems to be a sharper awareness of the gap between what we have and what is reasonable and possible. An increasing number seem unwilling to tolerate that gap. Furthermore, there is a growing belief that conventional education is not the panacea that many once thought it to be: some statistical studies support that view. Is it possible that something is basically wrong with some of the ideas that so-called good people hold, including those who are doing the educating, and that a radical examination of our assumptions is in order? Such an admission would not be cause for despair. Rather it should be an encouraging sign. Everything we believe in, all that we do, may not be wrong. But there could be enough error mixed in with the valid that everyone may have to do some serious sorting of her or his own thinking.

The urgent need is for a new lifeline of ideas, which may contain some of the old ideas (lost knowledge) that are reconfirmed. But I am sure that, if we call our traditional wisdom into question and really scrub it hard, some notions that are cherished now, even some that are supported by law and moral sanctions, will be abandoned as error. The parting will be painful. The goal is a better way of thinking about how a person can best use his or her life by the good people who now feel they "have it made."

As I meet with young people today, I am sharply aware of *my* need for a new lifeline of ideas that will stand up under the scrutiny some of these searching young people give. I sometimes ask them why the ideas that have served me so well won't do for them. The usual answer is that, except in the narrow selfish sense of my own comfort and peace of mind, my ideas have failed *me*. I am handing over to them a society they cannot live in. I should have handed them a torch a little brighter than the one I received.

Our language betrays us. Abandon the word *renewal*. That word connotes a dangerous complacency. A coat of paint may be deceptive if there are termites in the foundation. Let us try the word *transform*. It connotes a new, nobler direction, not just a recovery of the past—which probably is not possible and which we would not like even if we could recover it.

Deep in our past are some great symbolic events that might illuminate our search for a new lifeline of ideas. For instance, let us go back to the story of Moses and read it in the context of our search. Then let us ask, what went wrong there? Could Moses have been wedded to ideas that failed him? Something failed him because, in the end, he died alone in the wilderness. Is it possible that some ideas that failed him have come down into our conventional wisdom as noble truths?

The following three related short pieces on giving and receiving gifts of money were written in different decades, but Greenleaf's concerns about money are the same. The two later reflections are addressed more to the institution that gives or receives gifts of money. In any event, whether the individual or the institution is giving or receiving the money, there must be a deeper understanding of the act—a spiritual understanding.

Greenleaf served as a consultant for the Ford Foundation from 1962 to 1971. During the period 1965–1971, he focused his efforts on management education in India and South Asia. The short message which follows presents Bob and Esther Greenleaf's thoughts about their experiences in India, within the context and spirit of the Christmas season of 1965.

OUR EXPERIENCE IN INDIA:
WHAT IT SUGGESTS ABOUT GIVING

IT IS A YEAR NOW since we returned from our second trip to India. We were there about three and one-half months, all told, in January, February, October, and November of 1964. Bob went as consultant on management education for the Ford Foundation. Esther visited with artists and craftspeople in their homes and studios. Bob's work brought him into close relationships with government, industry, and universities. Esther saw more of the great traditional roots of India, and she got to know the people who live close to those traditions. There was some intermingling of the two strands of interest.... Friends were made which gave us a strong personal tie with India. The hospitality of the Indians is unrivaled.

For a year we read little that was not about India. Altogether, for two who had never before been outside their culture, it was a rich experience. Although ours was an intimate view because we penetrated the culture in depth here and there, we do not feel that we know India. We saw a good deal of the countryside and villages, but mostly we traveled by air (some 18,000 miles within India) and lived in the large cities. When Bob told an old professor at Osmonia University what we were doing he said, "But you will not see the real India." "How will we do that?" asked Bob. "Get in an oxcart and ride 1,000 miles from village to village." "But we would never survive it," Bob protested. "Oh, yes, you would," replied the old professor. "If you went from village to village with nothing, you would be better taken care of than in those expensive city hotels where you stay." He may have been right. The Indian countryside is poor and primitive, but it seems warm and hospitable. Someone observed about India that no matter what you hear about it or how much one bit of information contradicts all the rest, it is probably true somewhere.

We have vivid memories of both the beauty and the misery of India. We have seen it only in the cool, dry weather; the clean air and the bright colors have a dramatic quality. The mind's-eye memories of India are etched deep if one goes to India prepared for the shocking evidence of poverty and disease. And if one stays awhile and makes an effort to penetrate the culture, the richness of a great civilization comes through; one gets a hopeful feeling about India in the long view. In the short view, there are difficult and anxious days and years ahead. We remain hopeful.

But the misery is always there. Everywhere there is evidence of malnutrition and suffering. When a leper shoves the stump of an arm in your car window, or an emaciated beggar literally writhes in the dust at your feet as he groans his plea, one's memory is seared by images that will not go away. Seeing it firsthand sharpens the awareness that we live in a shrinking, interdependent world in which the problems of one become the problems of all. It has always been thus, but heretofore remoteness has permitted more aloofness by the favored than the future will tolerate. We welcome the prospect of a world in which these wide disparities will progressively diminish, and we hope that it will not take too long.

We are glad for the efforts made by governments, foundations, churches, and countless individuals who are trying to help. We were thrilled, for instance, to find Ruth Reeves, a distinguished American textile designer, living in New Delhi on her social security and doing yeoman volunteer work for the government of India in their work to preserve their fine craftspeople. But we are haunted by doubts that the most heroic

efforts of the presumed more-favored to "give" of their substance to the presumed less-favored will contribute in a really
meaningful way. It is important that we continue to give. But
our Christmas message for 1965 is to question the assumption
that giving of their excess by those who have more is really giving within the meaning of the spirit of Christmas.

We found a curious response to giving, especially to giving by
governments. It must seem strange to these developing nations
to have governments competing to give them things. In one of
the smaller countries, where we stayed briefly, Bob got acquainted with the man in the government who is responsible
for receiving aid. To preserve some semblance of order and
make the best of the opportunity, these countries have "organized" to receive aid. "The giving nations want to build status
symbols for themselves," this man said. To illustrate his point
he gave this example. "A community may have all of the
schoolhouses it needs, but it may desperately need a new jail.
Nobody will build a jail; but they will build another school-
house that we don't need!"

This overstates the problem because much that is sound and
useful has been given by government and other aid, from many
nations, and we are glad that ours is a generous nation. In this
regard we hope that aid to the developing nations continues on
a substantial scale by nations, churches, foundations, and individuals.

The first order of giving, the sharing by the more-favored
with the less-favored, is the conventional response to the spirit
of Christmas. This is where giving obviously begins. But, it is
difficult to give in this way and assure a constructive result.

Greenleaf wrote this essay on money at the request of leaders of the Church of the Savior in Washington, D.C. A cover letter with this paper is dated May 4, 1977, so we assume that is the period when this was written.

GIVING AND RECEIVING
GIFTS OF MONEY

MONEY IS POWER.

Money may be seen as that which gives power to one person or institution to enlist the service, secure the property, or influence the action or thinking of another.

Lord Acton has reminded me that power tends to corrupt and that absolute power corrupts absolutely. Sometimes the power of money moves toward the absolute.

In giving and receiving gifts of money, such power is held by individuals as well as by institutions. Within institutions that give money, as well as within those that receive money, some individuals are more influential than others in determining how the power of money will be used. In a large institution, such individuals may wield great power.

The central problem, then, of giving and receiving gifts of money is: how can these two roles of giver and receiver be carried so as to minimize the corrupting influence of the power of money, on both giver and receiver, and maximize the benign influence that is potentially in both roles? This has been a problem for as long as humankind has been aware of and has recorded feelings about ethical dilemmas. The problem is aggravated in our times because, as a result of our great growth in material terms, we have moved from the simple exchange of money between persons that is recorded in scripture to a situation in which large and complex institutions have evolved to hold and give money (foundations) and to receive and use gifts of money (schools, hospitals, social agencies, churches). In addition, units of government have become both givers on a large scale, and in some cases they are receivers. And of course, we still have the simpler transaction of one person giving to another and of individuals giving to institutions and institutions giving to individuals. Even businesses have become important givers, and sometimes they are seen as receivers. The power of the government to tax has been used both to encourage and discourage giving by individuals and institutions. It is a very complex problem, and almost everybody, to some degree, is involved in it. The central problem, again, is: how in all of this can the corrupting power of money be minimized and the benign aspects be favored?

Let us consider first the problem of an individual or institution that has money to give. What can they do to minimize the corrupting influence in their role and favor its benign aspects?

First, they can be aware of the risks inherent in their positions. We are reminded of Dr. Merrimon Cuninggim's (1972) writing on this topic when he says that "giving is potentially an immoral act." [See the discussion in the next essay, "Is It More Blessed to Give than to Receive?"—Eds.] While Cuninggim's words are addressed to large-scale giving by a foundation, they apply to any giving on any scale by individuals or institutions. There is a moral risk in being a giver. And being aware of the danger is only the first step in protection against it.

Power in receiving gifts of money is most likely to be a problem for those individuals and institutions who are more adept than others in securing gifts. Since all institutions that receive gifts (churches, schools, hospitals, social agencies, even foundations) tend to be competitive, those that are more successful in securing gifts are more powerful, and the individuals in those institutions who are the ablest negotiators in arranging gifts acquire a disproportionate power within their own institutions. Thus a university president who is a good "money raiser" is generally more secure in his position, and wields more influence within it, than is a president who is relatively unsuccessful in raising money even though the latter may be a better administrator and a greater leader. In a situation where the good money raiser is a volunteer, that person is likely to be more influential than a volunteer who is equally or even more valued in other ways.

Fund-raising, seeking and getting gifts, has become a highly refined and substantial concern of large, eleemosynary institutions. They employ staffs of able people who do nothing but research fund sources, calculate strategies, maintain personal relations, write proposals, and personally solicit gifts. Such staff persons, and the administrators who employ them, are obsessed with raising money. Their preoccupation with it rivals the operating function of the institution. Fund-raising has become a great concentration of power within such institutions. Its justification is in the contribution money makes to the serving capacity of the institution. But it is involved, nevertheless, in the moral hazard inherent in all power.

The danger in holding power as either the giver or receiver of gifts of money is similar to the moral risk to the holder of any kind of power. In another context, concerning trusteeship, it has been said, "No one, absolutely no one, is to be entrusted with the operational use of power without the close oversight of fully functioning trustees." Following this dictum, no morally sensitive person will use power over another (parent over child, teacher over student, pastor over parishioner, physician over patient, police officer over offender, judge over the court, manager over subordinate, the strong over the weak) without accepting a discipline that is monitored by a relatively objective person. This monitor understands how power can be used benignly, as well as the possible abuse of money; is vigilant in watching for the consequences of the use of power; and is an able counselor. This may seem an impossible condition to fulfill, but part of the widespread lack of trust may be attributed to the abuses of such a resource. To establish greater trust in both persons and institutions may require that the impossible be achieved.

The conclusion here is that a moral society will be a disciplined order, and a measure of its morality will be the adequacy of the discipline by which the use of power is monitored. Therefore all givers or receivers of gifts of money in appreciable amounts are subject to the judgment: *is the discipline they subject themselves to sufficient to ensure that benignity, not neutrality or corruption, is the result?* One of the several protections against the corruption of power in giving is for the giver to be open to receive gifts from the receiver—gifts of whatever the receiver has to give.

The essential problem of money is that it is a measure of power, both in the giving and the receiving. Whether the power is held solely by an individual or whether it is mediated through an institution, it is essentially a problem for individual persons. As Cuninggim has advised, any person who holds even a small amount of that power should be aware of the moral danger. But unless that awareness prompts one to accept an adequate discipline, with provision for an able person to monitor that discipline, awareness alone may not suffice.

What would an adequate discipline be, and how would an individual who is vulnerable to the corrupting influence of the power of money be assured that one's disciplined approach to its use is adequate? This is a role for a church, to do these things:

o Make of itself a resource for understanding the full ramifications of the corrupting influence of power, including the power of money, to which its communicants are exposed.

o Have an active program to sustain awareness in persons who are exposed to the corrupting influence of power in all of its ramifications.

o Provide regular counseling to exposed individuals so that there is a continuous check on their use of power: the power of money or any other kind of power.

The obligation is on all who hold or use power to seek such a church and submit to its discipline. If such a church is not readily available (and at this time it is quite unavailable), the moral person will take the initiative to build one—even if it means seeking the support of just one other person as confidant and counselor.

If the moral implications in the role of money are to be faced realistically in our times, we will need a new kind of church, and a new kind of theological seminary to prepare people to serve within that church.

This article is reprinted from the May 1, 1976, issue of *Friends Journal: Quaker Thought and Life Today.*

IS IT MORE BLESSED
TO GIVE THAN TO RECEIVE?

LATE IN JANUARY of 1976 I attended an International
Symposium on Leadership Development that was held in
Indianapolis under the auspices of The Center for the
Exploration of Values and Meaning which is based there. In the
course of the conference I had occasion to say some of the fol-
lowing things.

Our African friend has said that we Americans are arrogant.
It hurts; but I accept the charge. Our arrogance stems, I believe,
from the fact of our great power. In the years that the British
were the great power, they were seen as arrogant. When the
next shift comes, the nation that emerges into that unfortunate
spot will quite likely be seen as arrogant. Civilization, it seems,
has not advanced to a point where, as a natural gift of grace, either individuals, institutions, or governments are likely to be
both powerful and humble without some basic changes in public thinking that are not yet evident. Some may make it but the
odds are against it.

In this conference I have learned from Father Benjamin
Tonna of Malta that humility in the more powerful is ultimately
tested by their ability to learn from, and gratefully to receive
the gifts of, the less powerful. It is in my experience to know
this, but sometimes one needs to be taught before one understands one's own experience.

When I retired from my active business career twelve years ago I was asked by an American foundation to take an assignment for them in India. I found the top cut of Indian society with which I dealt, both in and out of government, to be highly sophisticated. Yet I was treated as if I had a level of expertise far beyond what my old colleagues at home who knew me well would concede. This is heady stuff, a fertile breeding ground for arrogance, and the several thousand who participated in aid programs in India, both private and governmental, in the heyday of technical assistance were all exposed to some measure of it.

In 1971, when I signed off on this foundation relationship, I had some things to say in my report that have a bearing here in this conference on the question of how those in a position to lead can best lead, and why Americans who try so hard at it are seen as arrogant by so much of the world.

> Anyone who has spent even as little time as I have in India cannot help having views about the whole aid-giving/aid-receiving relationship.... It does not seem to me to be a sound basis for a relationship for one nation to be aid giver and another aid receiver for a long period of time. A one-way flow of aid is all right for an emergency or a short period of readjustment. But not as a long term thing....
>
> I believe, further, that, on balance, the Indians have as much to give us as we have to give them (different things, perhaps, but just as much). And it seems presumptuous, over a long period of time, for us to assume that because we happen to have a surplus of money, the giving should be one way. Therefore, I believe that if we want to continue to be useful to the Indians, we should use our resources as much to learn from them as to facilitate their learning from us.

Dr. Merrimon Cuninggim, former president of the Danforth Foundation, in his 1972 book *Private Money and Public Service*, takes a more theological view when he suggests that "giving is potentially an immoral act." He continues:

Its danger lies in its assumption of virtue by the agent, of the virtue of agentry, with an accompanying train of unvirtuous assumptions. The relatively innocent desire to help is so thinly distinguished from wanting to be the helper. But the latter is capable of all sorts of distortions: wanting to be widely known as the helper, wanting to dictate, to paternalize, to manipulate. It is not likely that a foundation, any more than a person, will escape these faults by thoughtlessness or accident. Only by being conscious of the danger is there a chance to escape. In other words, a foundation must believe in the potential immorality of giving.

Out of reflection on my own experience, and particularly in the context of this International Symposium on Leadership Development where the arrogance of power has been so sharply highlighted, Dr. Cuninggim's admonition to the giver, to be conscious of the danger and believe in the potential immorality of giving, is not enough. We in the USA, who are placed in a position of power by our (relatively) massive surplus for giving, from both public and private resources, will not escape the opprobrious label of arrogant, nor will we have a chance to achieve that possible wholeness of existence, as individuals and as a nation, simply by being aware—unless that awareness opens the way to a new basis of relationship between aid giver and aid receiver, both among individuals and institutions in our country and between our nation and others, particularly the developing nations.

In this regard I see no middle ground between arrogance and humility. One may not safely give unless one is open and ready to receive the gifts of others—whatever they may be. Scripture holds that it is more blessed to give than to receive. But if one has the great power of affluence in modern terms, a condition which the writers of scripture may not have foreseen, this may be a questionable generalization, because receiving requires a genuine humility that may be uncomfortable and difficult to achieve, whereas giving poses the risk of arrogance which, unfortunately, is easy to come by—and some seem to enjoy it.

An important dimension of leadership within a nation that has the substantial power of affluence, such as we in the USA have, will be the ability to persuade those who are in a position to give, whether an individual, an institution, or the nation, that they should reach out for, gratefully receive, and help pay the cost of the giving to themselves by the less favored.

In the contemporary world it is at least as blessed, especially for the powerful, to receive as to give—and much harder to do.

AFTERWORD

The Greenleaf Testament:
Recollections of the Father of Servant-Leadership

ROBERT K. GREENLEAF, the subject of this conversation, died at his home in Crosslands, a Quaker retirement center in Kennett Square, Pennsylvania, September 29, 1990, at the age of eighty-six. He is best known for his idea of servant-leadership as the route in a more caring society. . . . He was particularly interested in theological schools as potential seedbeds of social change.

Robert Wood Lynn is a retired consultant now affiliated with Bangor Theological Seminary.

Malcolm L. Warford is [past] president of Bangor Seminary. [He is now at Lexington Theological Seminary.—Eds.]

Christa R. Klein is an American church historian and a consultant on trusteeship and seminary governance.

LYNN: I first read one of Bob Greenleaf's essays on trusteeship in the early 1970s. At that time I was still at Auburn Seminary, where I was the dean and working with the board of trustees. We were very much taken with the essay. I was tempted to call him up, but was too shy to do so. Therefore, when I started working for the Lilly Endowment as a consultant I found to my pleasure that Bob Greenleaf was a fellow consultant. I met him first in and through the work of the Lilly Endowment, and he quickly helped me understand that I need not be shy about asking him questions or calling him up. That was the beginning of a long friendship.

He was very much open to those of us who were concerned about theological education. Indeed, in the 1970s he was increasingly curious about seminaries. He hadn't yet arrived at this conviction, which he later wrote about, that the theological school should be foremost among the serving institutions. But he was moving in that direction. So often those conversations were preceded by his questioning us about these institutions. He had served on the visiting committee at Harvard Divinity School in the sixties, but other than that I don't think he had much direct contact with seminaries until the 1970s.

WARFORD: I remember him most as a teacher. I used to visit him at least a couple of times a years at Crosslands. And he was a very energetic correspondent. He would establish a kind of dialogue that would continue over the phone, through the mails, and face-to-face. For me, it was probably the most important experience of continuing education I've ever had. I think anyone who knew him would understand what I mean when I say he was a powerful teacher who taught primarily through questions.

LYNN: I think that is right, Mac. He didn't enjoy making long statements himself. I never had the sense that he was delivering a speech in the form of a portion of a conversation. Occasionally, we do lapse into well-rehearsed speeches. He had the knack of teaching, as Mac says, through questions. Those questions could be very penetrating.

WARFORD: Bob Greenleaf was a loving but tough and unsentimental person who got to the heart of things. He was the closest thing to a teacher in the Buddhist tradition that I know of. If he didn't know an answer or if he thought that you ought to come up with the answer, he just sat there. The quiet time, the silence, would literally go on for minutes.

LYNN: I think I would also say, Mac, that he was Socratic in the way in which he pushed questions. And each question would lead to a deeper circle of conversation that kept spiraling downward. Greenleaf would outwait people, he wouldn't rescue us by covering up our ignorance or our confusion.

WARFORD: Part of the time that I spent with him was a time of thinking about and reflecting upon the institution I was serving. Often I would present those reflections as problems to be resolved, hoping that he might have some solutions to those situations. He would never offer a technical fix—he kept pushing me, and reminding me, that the only thing that significantly renews and calls an institution is a compelling vision.

LYNN: He was deeply suspicious of the various techniques that flourished in the 1970s and into the 1980s. In the 1970s there was lots of talk of "management by objectives." Greenleaf had a keen historical sense of the development of modern business and could quickly set you straight about how "new" and "novel" management by objectives was. He had the same somewhat skeptical response to any undue preoccupation with planning. He was quick to dig beneath that and to ask if you had anything else to say about management processes.

WARFORD: That's right. He always signed his letters by the phrase "In the Spirit"—he really meant that phrase. That phrase is a signal of his whole approach to God, to reality, and to institutions. In one sense, his view of management was that it came out of the way we discern the power of the Spirit in the midst of institutional life.

KLEIN: That toughness didn't always come through in his writings. He didn't always convey what you are describing right now as that searing, intense, and penetrating quest for what is making an institution work, what assumptions are behind its operation.

LYNN: Let me explain why he was in part reluctant to pose as a tough-minded realist in his prose. He was convinced that if you were going to move people you had to offer them some hope and some way beyond the current scene. He liked to describe himself as an institutional watcher. And he was a realist to the core.

But he also knew that people were seldom moved by harsh criticisms of their activity. One time when he was reading one of my essays, he was kind enough to edit it just as I had edited almost all of his essays from about 1977 onward. He asked me to take out all of the critical or analytical material. I asked him why. His response: "You won't get any place by beating people over the head."

So that was a deliberate effort on his part in his prose to invoke and invite people into thinking about new possibilities. But he ran the risk of appearing to be what he was not—another woolly minded idealist.

Greenleaf's realism reached down to the very heart of an institution, which is its vision. He knew that if an institution didn't have a vision, a specific inspiration or "inspiriting," it would die. In that sense his personal conversations were more revealing of the whole man than these essays which we now have.

WARFORD: In that regard, his personal presence very much was a reflection of the Quaker tradition which he owned. There was a modesty and a humility about him that I think lent a very striking depth to the relationship and that remains so.

LYNN: Your comment about his adopted Quaker tradition is appropriate. He was comfortable with silence. He liked straightforward, direct speech. He did not use "thee" and "thou," but he did believe in the movement of the Spirit and in contemplation. I asked him one day what he spent most of his time doing—this was when he was in his late seventies or early eighties—and he said, "meditating." He would often think about his correspondents or his friends, compatriots, across the country and reflect upon their situation and sometimes call us up and ask us pointed questions about how we were doing.

In my own case, he could quickly pinprick any illusions I had about the ease of moving a foundation out of its deeply cultivated ruts. He understood how tough it was for those of us in foundations, for example, ever to hear criticism from beyond our own ranks because nobody would ever voluntarily tell us the truth. He had a profound sense of how corrupting foundation work could be. So one of his rules for those of us who worked for foundations was that we were never supposed to linger for more than ten years. This became known as the "Greenleaf Law." When I was close to breaking it, I asked him if I should quit now or a little bit later and he was very helpful on that. He helped me prepare myself to leave the Endowment a bit earlier than I had to. He was, therefore, acutely conscious of what subtle forms of self-delusion afflict us. He didn't believe, he said, in original sin but I thought he did a very good job of describing its consequences.

WARFORD: Your mention of how Bob helped prepare you for your own future raises another facet of his life. He often spoke about the extent to which he had prepared himself in his business career for pursuing what he took to be his real vocation: involvement in the life of institutions and service as a consultant.

LYNN: When he quit AT&T at the age of sixty, he was a pioneer in corporate programs for educating executives. When he walked in to tell the chairman of AT&T that he was quitting, his boss said, "Why in the world are you quitting, Greenleaf? You've got everything that you want now. We let you do exactly what you want. What could you want that isn't here?"

Bob said that he wanted to explore the world. So that's what he did. He went to India, served the Ford Foundation there, and I think the pivotal point in his life was his time when he was serving as a consultant to the chancellor of MIT in the tumultuous year of 1968–69. He saw the havoc being wrought by the student uprising.

He didn't blame the students. He blamed the institution for its inability, or colleges and universities for their inability, to offer students any vision. At that time he moved back to the notion of the leader as a servant. It was out of the cauldron of the MIT riots that he was prompted to move back to that earlier and deeper theme.

Then as he fell to thinking about the failure of institutions of higher education to meet the demands of the students, he started to ask himself: "Now who are people who are finally responsible for these colleges and universities?" In that setting of crisis, he came back to the very obvious, simple, but still unthought suggestion that it is the trustees who have to assume this responsibility. That was the major turning point in his life as far as his work on trusteeship was concerned.

WARFORD: Don't you think that idea pushed him to questions about the sources of that vision? I will never forget the passion with which he would often tell of his experience with a group of church leaders, talking about the nature of the church and its institutions. At the end of the conference, he observed that for two or three days he had heard these church leaders talking about institutional issues, but not once had they spoken about God, or the Spirit, or the power of the Gospel to change and renew human life. In that sense, part of Bob's presence was his capacity to push those of us related to religious institutions back to the roots of what those institutions are all about.

LYNN: When he pushed you, you had better be prepared to respond or admit your own ignorance. There is a way, Mac, in which he was genuinely Socratic at that point. He would not ever claim knowledge for himself, but he would help us understand our own ignorance.

WARFORD: I guess the most important thing that I learned from him was: If there is to be hope, if there are to be institutions that bring hope to people's lives and have some capacity to move beyond institutional self-preoccupation, you have to look in the places of freedom that permit the spirit to live without being crushed. Bob Greenleaf helped me to look in some not so obvious places. Part of what I learned in talking with him is that, given the kind of culture and society in which we live, the places of hope are probably not going to be the obvious places of establishment that we've taken for granted.

LYNN: Just to confirm Mac's point, let me say that Greenleaf was fully aware that many people considered theological schools as marginal if not irrelevant. Often his friends from the late 1970s onwards would remonstrate with him about his sudden new preoccupation with theological education. They saw it as something of a fall, if not into senility, at least a lapse into sentimentalism. He was so well acquainted with the difficulties of the colleges and the universities and the foundations and all of those major bulwarks of the establishment that he rejoiced in the relative smallness and the apparent marginality of the theological schools. But that made him all the more critical of the theological schools when they failed to take advantage of their freedom and to offer contrast to other institutions.

KLEIN: I think he was also looking for the place where superb thinking about institutions could occur. He would talk about "the theology of institutions."

I think he was on to probably one of the basic flaws in American Protestantism, something that also shows up in Roman Catholicism. That is the focus on the salvation of the individual. In our revivalistic American Protestant culture, the focus is on converting the individual and then, as we know, we have all of these cause-oriented movements that depended on that mindset. He recognized that what is really affecting society is institutions.

WARFORD: I think the experience that he had with the turmoil in higher education and the society in the early 1970s affected everything he thought about. The alienating character of institutions, and the alienation of individuals, were the situations that kept calling him to respond in all sorts of ways.

LYNN: Mac, you've mentioned the word that is one of the keys to his thinking, to his understanding of human nature. That is, he lay great emphasis on *alienation*. I once pointed out to him that what he described as alienation was what the Christian theologian meant by the word *sin*. That made sense to him.

Isn't this ironic? Here's a person who was born in the early part of the twentieth century in Terre Haute, Indiana, but who in his later years could be very well described, if not as a child of the 1960s, as one who was deeply formed by the 1960s. Much that he tried to do in the last twenty years was in response to the inadvertent revelations of the depth of our crisis.

KLEIN: Let me shift the focus and discuss the way he talks about trusteeship. He puts a tremendous emphasis on the role of the chair of the board of trustees. It's an emphasis that is unusual in the literature, and sometimes confusing.

WARFORD: He and I used to go round and round on that, and I think that if he had reworked some of that earlier writing on the role of the chair, he might have reframed it. My feeling about the ways in which he framed the role of the chair, and the chair's relationship to other administrative officers, was that he was overly influenced by a corporation model. In some of the essays, the chair almost emerges as full-time, as an employee of the institution.

KLEIN: Like the chair of a corporate board.

WARFORD: Yes, exactly. I think what's powerful about the image of the role of the chair he portrays is the singular responsibility to be the one most concerned that the vision and the mission of the institutions are cared for and thought about. That is a major contribution that Bob made to the thinking about trusteeship and about institutions.

He was perfectly on target in his criticism that presidents—who ought to be concerned about institutions on that level—get so swept up with day-to-day management that they lose sight of the institution's calling.

One other thing that comes to my mind is that there is a strange kind of point-counterpoint that existed in the things Greenleaf cared about. One was, he was impatient. He wanted things to change. On the other hand, he had a capacity to realize that basic, fundamental change takes place over long periods of time.

LYNN: In that sense he was much closer to the wisdom of the historian than he knew or understood.

WARFORD: I think what he was impatient about was in getting you to begin.

lynn: He was also impatient with leaders, church leaders, seminary presidents, and the rest of us who, though we said we had hope in God, didn't always act as though we had hope that might actually touch and transform these institutions.

KLEIN: I think that's why he made us feel so uncomfortable. Ultimately, sitting in that chair across from him, the question he either framed explicitly or implicitly was, "Well, what difference does it make for you to say that you believe in God?"

LYNN: In that way, he really was a lot closer to being an evangelist. He might have laughed at that comment and turned it aside. But one of his closest friends from an earlier period, a professor at the Episcopal Theological School in Cambridge who was well known for his work on situational ethics, Joe

Fletcher—he was really one of Bob's closest friends—used to mock him and say, "Oh, Robert, Robert, you're nothing but a preacher." Bob heard that, and simply smiled. He wasn't worried about being called a preacher. The question was, Was anybody going to hear him?

REFERENCES

Allott, Kenneth, and Miriam Allott (eds.). *The Complete Poems of Matthew Arnold* (2nd ed.) New York: Longman, 1979.

Capovilla, Loris (ed.). *Giovanni XXIII, Letture, 1958–1963.* [John XXIII, Letters] Rome: Storia e Letteratura, 1978.

Cuninggim, Merrimon. *Private Money and Public Service.* New York: McGraw-Hill, 1972.

Emerson, Ralph Waldo. "The Uses of Great Men." In *The Works of Ralph Waldo Emerson,* Vol. IV (pp. 8–38). Boston: Houghton, Mifflin, 1876.

Emerson, Ralph Waldo. "Works and Days." In *The Works of Ralph Waldo Emerson,* Vol. VII (pp. 151–177). Boston: Houghton, Mifflin, 1876.

Frost, Robert. *Complete Poems of Robert Frost.* New York: Henry Holt, 1947.

Gill, Theodore A. "Priesthood of Believers." In Marvin Halverson and Arthur A. Cohen (eds.), *A Handbook of Christian Theology.* Cleveland: World Publishing, 1958.

Greenleaf, Robert K. "Spirituality as Leadership." *Studies in Formative Spirituality,* Feb. 1982, p. 53.

Greenleaf, Robert K. *Seminary as Servant.* Indianapolis, Ind.: Robert K. Greenleaf Center, 1983.

Greenleaf, Robert K. "The Servant as Leader." Indianapolis, Ind.: Robert K. Greenleaf Center, 1991.

Hebblethwaite, Peter. *John XXIII: Pope of the Council.* London: Geoffrey Chapman, 1984.

Hebblethwaite, Peter. *Pope John XXIII: Shepherd of the Modern World.* Garden City, N.Y.: Doubleday, 1985.

Journal of a Soul, Pope John XXIII. (Dorothy White, trans.; rev. ed.) London: Chapman, 1980.

Lynn, Robert Wood. Correspondence with Anne T. Fraker. Mar. 17, 1995.

O'Brien, David J., and Thomas A. Shannon. *Renewing the Earth: Catholic Documents on Peace, Justice, and Liberation.* New York: Image Books, 1977.

Warford, Malcolm. Correspondence with Anne T. Fraker. Apr. 3, 1995.

White, E. B. "The Second Tree from the Corner." In *The Second Tree from the Corner.* New York: HarperCollins, ([1947] 1984). (Copyright 1947 by E. B. White; copyright renewed. Reprinted by permission of HarperCollins Publishers.)

White, Joseph M. Correspondence with Robert Wood Lynn regarding essay on Pope John XXIII. Dec. 2, 1986.

Wilhelm, Hellmut. *Change: Eight Lectures on the I Ching.* New York: Pantheon Books, 1960.

Whitman, Walt. *Walt Whitman: The Complete Poems.* New York: Penguin USA, 1987.

Yeats, W. B. In Richard J. Finneran (ed.), *The Collected Poems of W. B. Yeats: A New Edition.* New York: Simon & Schuster, 1968. (Copyright 1940 by Macmillan Publishing Company; renewed 1968 by Bertha Georgie Yeats, Michael Butler Yeats, and Anne Yeats. Reprinted with the permission of Simon & Schuster.)

FURTHER READING

Bennis, Warren. *On Becoming a Leader.* Reading, Mass.: Addison-Wesley, 1989.

Block, Peter. *Stewardship.* San Francisco: Berrett-Koehler, 1993.

Bondi, Richard. *Leading God's People.* Nashville, Tenn.: Abingdon Press, 1989.

Broholm, Richard R. *The Power and Purpose of Vision: A Study of the Role of Vision in Exemplary Organizations.* Indianapolis, Ind.: Robert K. Greenleaf Center for Servant-Leadership, 1990.

Broholm, Richard R., and Douglas Johnson. *A Balcony Perspective Clarifying the Trustee Role.* Indianapolis, Ind.: Robert K. Greenleaf Center for Servant-Leadership, 1993.

Chappell, Tom. *The Soul of a Business: Managing for Profit and the Public Good.* New York: Bantam Books, 1993.

Cheshire, Ashley. *A Partnership of the Spirit.* Dallas: TDIndustries, 1987.

Cosby, Gordon. *Handbook for Mission Groups.* Washington, D.C.: The Potter's House, date unknown.

Cueni, R. Robert. *What Ministers Can't Learn in Seminary.* Nashville, Tenn.: Abingdon Press, 1988.

Cuninggim, Merrimon. *Private Money and Public Service.* New York: McGraw-Hill, 1972.

DePree, Max. *Leadership Is an Art.* New York: Doubleday, 1989.

DePree, Max. *Leadership Jazz.* New York: Dell, 1992.

DiStefano, Joseph. *Tracing the Vision and Impact of Robert K. Greenleaf.* Indianapolis, Ind.: Robert K. Greenleaf Center for Servant-Leadership, 1988.

Drucker, Peter. *Managing the Nonprofit Organization.* New York: HarperCollins, 1990.

Foster, Richard J. *Celebration of Discipline: The Path to Spiritual Growth.* San Francisco: HarperCollins, 1988.

Frick, Don M., and Larry C. Spears (eds.). *On Becoming a Servant-Leader: The Private Writings of Robert K. Greenleaf*. San Francisco: Jossey-Bass, 1996.

Gardner, John W. *On Leadership*. New York: Free Press, 1990.

Grayson, L. Tucker. "Enhancing Church Vitality Through Congregational Identity Change." In Milton J. Coalter, John M. Mulder, and Louis B. Weeks (eds.), *The Mainstream Protestant "Decline."* Louisville, Ky.: Westminster/John Knox Press, 1990.

Greenleaf, Robert K. "Abraham Joshua Heschel: Build a Life Like a Work of Art." *Friends Journal*, 1973, *19*(15), 459–460.

Greenleaf, Robert. K. *Advices to Servants*. Indianapolis, Ind.: Robert K. Greenleaf Center for Servant-Leadership, 1991.

Greenleaf, Robert K. "The Art of Knowing." *Friends Journal*, 1974, *20*(17).

Greenleaf, Robert K. "Business Ethics—Everybody's Problem." *New Catholic World*, 1980, *223*, 275–278.

Greenleaf, Robert K. "Choose the Nobler Belief." *AA Grapevine*, 1966, *23*(5), 27–31.

Greenleaf, Robert K. "Choosing Greatness." *AA Grapevine*, 1966, *23*(4), 26–30.

Greenleaf, Robert K. "Choosing to be Aware." *AA Grapevine*, 1966, *23*(1), 26–28.

Greenleaf, Robert K. "Choosing to Grow." *AA Grapevine*, 1966, *23*(2), 11–13.

Greenleaf, Robert K. "Community as Servant and Nurturer of the Human Spirit." *Resources for Community-Based Economic Development*, 1986, *4*, 9–11.

Greenleaf, Robert K. *Education and Maturity*. Indianapolis, Ind.: Robert K. Greenleaf Center for Servant-Leadership, 1988.

Greenleaf, Robert K. *Have You a Dream Deferred?* Indianapolis, Ind.: Robert K. Greenleaf Center for Servant-Leadership, 1988.

Greenleaf, Robert K. *The Institution as Servant*. Indianapolis, Ind.: Robert K. Greenleaf Center for Servant-Leadershipr, 1976.

Greenleaf, Robert K. *The Leadership Crisis*. Indianapolis, Ind.: Robert K. Greenleaf Center for Servant-Leadership, 1978.

Greenleaf, Robert K. *Life's Choices and Markers*. Indianapolis, Ind.: Robert K. Greenleaf Center for Servant-Leadership, 1986.

Greenleaf, Robert K. *Mission in a Seminary: A Prime Trustee*

Concern. Cambridge, Mass.: Center for Applied Studies, Windy Row Press (N.H.), 1981.

Greenleaf, Robert K. *My Debt to E. B. White.* Indianapolis, Ind.: Robert K. Greenleaf Center for Servant-Leadership, 1987.

Greenleaf, Robert K. *Old Age: The Ultimate Test of Spirit.* Indianapolis, Ind.: Robert K. Greenleaf Center, 1987.

Greenleaf, Robert K. "Overcome Evil with Good." *Friends Journal,* 1977, 23(10), 292–302.

Greenleaf, Robert K. *Robert Frost's "Directive" and the Spiritual Journey.* Boston: Nimrod Press, 1963.

Greenleaf, Robert K. *Servant Leadership.* New York: Paulist Press, 1977.

Greenleaf, Robert K. "The Servant as Leader." *Journal of Religion and the Applied Behavioral Sciences,* Winter 1982, 3, 7–10.

Greenleaf, Robert K. *The Servant as Religious Leader.* (rev. ed.) Indianapolis, Ind.: Robert K. Greenleaf Center for Servant-Leadership, 1983.

Greenleaf, Robert K. *Servant: Retrospect and Prospect.* Indianapolis, Ind.: Robert K. Greenleaf Center for Servant-Leadership, 1980.

Greenleaf, Robert K. *Teacher as Servant: A Parable.* Indianapolis, Ind.: Robert K. Greenleaf Center for Servant-Leadership, 1987.

Greenleaf, Robert K. "The Trustee and the Risks of Persuasive Leadership." *Hospital Progress,* 1978, pp. 50–52, 88.

Greenleaf, Robert K. "Trustee Traditions and Expectations." In *The Good Steward: A Guide to Theological School Trusteeship.* Washington, D.C.: Association of Governing Boards of Universities and Colleges, n.d.

Greenleaf, Robert K. *Trustees as Servants.* Indianapolis, Ind.: Robert K. Greenleaf Center for Servant-Leadership, 1990.

Greenleaf, Robert K. "Two More Choices." *AA Grapevine,* 1966, 23(3), 22–23.

Hesse, Hermann. *The Journey to the East.* New York: Noonday Press, 1992.

Holmes, Urban T. *Spirituality for Ministry.* San Francisco: HarperCollins, 1982.

Ingram, Richard T. *Making Trusteeship Work.* Washington, D.C.: Association of Governing Boards of Universities and Colleges, 1988.

Little, Sara. "'Experiments with Truth': Education for Leadership."
In Parker J. Palmer, Barbara G. Wheeler, and James W. Fowler
(eds.), *Caring for the Commonweal: Education for Religious
and Public Life.* Macon, Ga.: Mercer University Press, 1990.

Lombardo, Michael M. *Values in Action.* Greensboro, N.C.: Center
for Creative Leadership, 1986.

Mead, Loren B. *The Once and Future Church.* Washington, D.C.:
Alban Institute, 1991.

Messer, Donald E. *Contemporary Images of Christian Ministry.*
Nashville, Tenn.: Abingdon Press, 1989.

Moore, Thomas. *Care of the Soul: A Guide for Cultivating Depth
and Sacredness in Everyday Life.* New York: HarperCollins,
1992.

Nouwen, Henri J. M. *In the Name of Jesus: Reflections on Christian
Leadership.* New York: Crossroad, 1989.

O'Connor, Elizabeth. *Call to Commitment.* Washington, D.C.:
Servant Leadership Press, 1993.

Palmer, Parker. *Leading from Within.* Washington, D.C.: Servant
Leadership Press, 1990.

Palmer, Parker. *The Promise of Paradox.* Washington, D.C.: Servant
Leadership Press, 1993.

Peck, M. Scott. *The Road Less Traveled.* New York: Simon &
Schuster, 1978.

Peck, M. Scott. *A World Waiting to Be Born: Civility Rediscovered.*
New York: Bantam Books, 1993.

Perry, Lloyd, and Norman Shawchuck. *Revitalizing the Twentieth-
Century Church.* Glendale Heights, Ill.: Spiritual Growth
Resources, 1991.

Rieser, Carl. *Claiming Servant Leadership as Your Heritage.*
Indianapolis, Ind.: Robert K. Greenleaf Center for Servant-
Leadership, 1988.

Russell, Letty M. *The Future of Partnership.* Louisville, Ky.:
Westminster/John Knox Press, 1979.

Sampson, Patsy H. *The Leader as Servant.* Indianapolis, Ind.: Robert
K. Greenleaf Center for Servant-Leadership, 1987.

Sergiovanni, Thomas J. *Moral Leadership: Getting to the Heart of
School Improvement.* San Francisco: Jossey-Bass, 1993.

Shawchuck, Norman, and Robert Heuser. *Leading the Congregation:*

Caring for Yourself While Serving the People. Nashville, Tenn.: Abingdon Press, 1993.

Spears, Larry C. (ed.). *Reflections on Leadership: How Robert K. Greenleaf's Theory of Servant-Leadership Influenced Today's Top Management Thinkers.* New York: Wiley, 1995.

Weems, Lovett H., Jr. *Church Leadership: Vision, Team, Culture, and Integrity.* Nashville, Tenn.: Abingdon Press, 1993.

Wheatley, Margaret J. *Leadership and the New Science: Learning About Organization From an Orderly Universe.* San Francisco: Berrett-Koehler, 1994.

White, E. B. "The Second Tree from the Corner." In *The Second Tree from the Corner.* New York: HarperCollins, 1984.

Whitehead, James D., and Evelyn Eaton. *The Promise of Partnership.* San Francisco: HarperCollins, 1991.

Whyte, David. *The Heart Aroused: Poetry and the Preservation of the Soul in Corporate America.* New York: Doubleday, 1994.

Wind, James P., and others (eds.). *Clergy Ethics in a Changing Society.* Louisville, Ky.: Westminster/John Knox Press, 1991.

Woolman, John. *The Journal and Essays of John Woolman.* Edited from the original manuscripts with a biographical introduction by Amelia Mott Gummere. New York: Macmillan, 1922.

INDEX

A

Acton, Lord (John Emerich Edward
    Dalberg), 58, 59, 321
Akbar (Mughal emperor of India), 305
Alcoholics Anonymous (AA), 34–35,
    172, 293, 298
Alienation, 17, 23, 33, 40, 61–62;
    causes of, 45; churches and, 173,
    218; as contemporary malady, 13,
    15, 169–176, 179, 270, 313; defin-
    ition of, 12; as sin, 338; among
    young people, 44–48
Allott, Kenneth and Miriam (eds.):
    *The Complete Poems of Matthew
    Arnold,* 129
American Protestantism, 337–338
American Telephone & Telegraph
    (AT&T), 3, 31–32, 205; gradual-
    ism at, 66, 68, 77–80; lay persons
    at, 221–223; listening course at,
    158–159; management training at,
    53, 335; power-centered control at,
    78–80, 82–84; seeing things whole
    at, 131; spirit and servant idea at,
    122–125; spirituality as leadership
    at, 52–54; transformation of,
    216–221, 232–234
Amerson, Rev. Philip, 258–259, 273
Anderson, Hans Christian, 119
Andover Newton Theological School:
    Greenleaf archives at, 102, 112, 128
Andrews, Emerson, 231–232
Anti-leader: age of, 95–96
Anti-trust laws, 60

Arnold, Matthew: "To a Friend," 129
Asoka (king of India), 305
Athens, 46–47, 187
Auburn Seminary, 331

B

Bacon, Francis, 303
Bangor Theological Seminary, 236,
    331
Baptists, 120–121
Basho. *See* Matsuo, Munefusa
Bea, Cardinal Augustin, 149, 151
Being who you are, 163–165
Belief: of religious leaders, 15; as
    trust, 62
Benigni, Msgr. Umberto, 145
Bergamo (Italy), 143–144, 146
Berger, Peter, 258
Bible, examples of: coercion, 59; com-
    petition, 61; organizational theory,
    57, 291; servant, 121, 201; spirit,
    142; vision, 228
Blake, William, 36, 38, 293
Borromeo, Saint Charles, 145–146,
    152–153, 155
British Empire, 75–76
Buddha, 13, 332–333
Businesses: competition in, 60–61;
    consulting programs in, 31–32;
    gifts of money by, 321–325; gradu-
    alism and, 77–80; great spirits in,
    138–139; listeners as vital to,
    157–165; melioration in, 160–161,
    163–165; obstacles to visionary

THE EDITORS

ANNE T. FRAKER is a project associate with the Robert K. Greenleaf Archives project, funded by Lilly Endowment, Inc. She has undergraduate and graduate degrees in education from Indiana University and has done additional study at Indiana University and Christian Theological Seminary. She is a member of Pi Lambda Theta honorary society, the American Society of Church History, and various committees and boards within the United Methodist Church. She has been recognized in *Who's Who in the Midwest, Who's Who in the World,* and the *World Who's Who of Women.* She is the author of several reviews and articles and is the editor of *Religion and American Life: Resources,* published by the University of Illinois Press in 1989. Her latest publication is "Robert K. Greenleaf and Business Ethics: There Is No Code," which appears in *Reflections on Leadership,* published by Wiley in 1995.

LARRY C. SPEARS was named executive director of the Robert K. Greenleaf Center for Servant-Leadership in 1990. He grew up in Michigan and Indiana and is a graduate of DePauw University. He lived and worked in Philadelphia for fourteen years prior to returning to Indianapolis to head the Greenleaf Center. He has previously served as director or staff member with the Greater Philadelphia Philosophy Consortium, Great Lakes Colleges Association's Philadelphia Center, and *Friends Journal,* a Quaker magazine. As a writer and editor, he has published over three hundred articles, essays, and book reviews in the past twenty years and has written numerous successful funding proposals. He is the editor of *Reflections on Leadership: How Robert K. Greenleaf's Theory of Servant-Leadership Influenced Today's Top Management Thinkers* (Wiley, 1995), coeditor of *On Becoming a Servant-Leader* (Jossey-Bass, 1996), and a contributing author to *Leadership in a New Era* (New Leaders Press, 1994).

CREDITS

Some of the original titles of essays have been altered for this
volume to make them more readable. The following credits include the original titles of essays in the Andover Newton
Greenleaf archives and/or in miscellaneous materials not in the
archives.

"Afterword," a conversation with Robert W. Lynn, Malcolm L.
Warford, and Christa R. Klein, first appeared in the New Year
1991 issue of *In Trust: The Magazine for Leaders in
Theological Education* as "The Greenleaf Testament:
Recollections of the Father of Servant-Leadership." Reprinted
with permission of *In Trust: The Magazine for Leaders in
Theological Education.*

In "A Lifeline of Ideas" the excerpt by Hellmut Wilhelm appears in *Change: Eight Lectures on the I Ching*, New York:
Pantheon Books, 1960, pp. 17–22. Reprinted with permission.
"A Lifeline of Ideas" is edited from an unpublished manuscript
by Greenleaf as contained in the Robert K. Greenleaf Papers. It
is used with the permission of the Franklin Trask Library,
Andover Newton Theological School.

"An Opportunity for a Powerful New Religious Influence" is
edited from unpublished manuscripts (originally "A New
Religious Mission" and "An Opportunity for a Powerful New
Religious Influence") by Greenleaf as contained in the Robert K.
Greenleaf Papers. They are used with the permission of the
Franklin Trask Library, Andover Newton Theological School.

"The Collapse of Civilization: A Fantasy" is edited from an unpublished manuscript (originally "3200 A.D.: A Phantasy") by
Greenleaf as contained in the Robert K. Greenleaf Papers. It is
used with the permission of the Franklin Trask Library,
Andover Newton Theological School.

"Ministry to the Strong" is edited from an unpublished manuscript (originally "Reflections on Ministry to the Strong") by Greenleaf as contained in the Robert K. Greenleaf Papers. It is used with the permission of the Franklin Trask Library, Andover Newton Theological School.

"Types of Leaders" is edited from an unpublished manuscript (originally "Opening Speech: Person/Team Track of the National Council of Catholic Laity") by Greenleaf as contained in the Robert K. Greenleaf Papers. It is used with the permission of the Franklin Trask Library, Andover Newton Theological School.

"The Inner City Church as Servant to Its Community" is edited from unpublished manuscripts (originally "The Center City Church as Servant to Its Community," "The Inner City Church as Servant to the Community," and "Community as Servant and Nurturer of the Human Spirit") by Greenleaf as contained in the Robert K. Greenleaf Papers. They are used with the permission of the Franklin Trask Library, Andover Newton Theological School.

"A Servant-Led Society" is edited from an unpublished manuscript (originally "The Prospect for a Servant-Led Society") by Greenleaf as contained in the Robert K. Greenleaf Papers. It is used with the permission of the Franklin Trask Library, Andover Newton Theological School.

"Being Who You Are" is edited from an unpublished manuscript (originally "You Need to Be Human") by Greenleaf as contained in the Robert K. Greenleaf Papers. It is used with the permission of the Franklin Trask Library, Andover Newton Theological School.

"Lost Knowledge" is edited from an unpublished manuscript by Greenleaf as contained in the Robert K. Greenleaf Papers. It is used with the permission of the Franklin Trask Library, Andover Newton Theological School.

"Our Experience in India: What It Suggests About Giving" is edited from an unpublished manuscript (originally "Some Reflections on Our Indian Experience: What It Suggests About Giving—A Christmas Message for 1965") by Greenleaf as contained in the Robert K. Greenleaf Papers. It is used with the per-

"Religious Leaders as Seekers and Servants" was originally entitled "Religious Leaders: A Position Paper."

"Seeing Things Whole" was originally entitled "Seeing Things Whole: Builder of and Derivative from the Human Spirit."

"The Seminary as Institution" was originally entitled "The Seminary as Institution: Premise."

"The Trustee Chairperson: Nurturer of the Human Spirit" was originally entitled "The Trustee Chairperson as Nurturer of the Human Spirit."

"Critical Thought and Seminary Leadership" was originally entitled "Critical Thought in the Seminary and the Trustee Chairperson's Role."